AF413223

Rub Some D.I.R.T. on it!

[God's Favorite 4- Letter Words]

Inspired by

The Holy Spirit

Written By

J. M. Bayne

Publisher: WoW! Publishing and Distribution
Printed in the United States of America
Aka...Mr. Wonderful

Front Cover Artwork : J.M. Bayne and Keri Jackson

Back Cover Artwork: Jennisue Jessen

Cover Layout Design: Keri Jackson

My Forever Thanks Ladies!!

CONTENTS

Introduction 1

Ch 1: Rub Some D.I.R.T. On It...................7

CH 2: Working My S.O.I.L........................14

CH 3: Watch Your W.A.V.E........................39

CH 4: When the F.A.S.T. Feels Slow..........50

CH 5: What Now? W.A.I.T.!........................70

CH 6: What's the P.L.A.N., Lord?...............85

CH 7: F.O.R.K. It!..102

CH 8: G.R.O.W. Up and Get to W.O.R.K.....119

CH 9: S.I.N.K. or S.W.I.M. – You Choose.....141

CH 10: I Was M.A.D.E. for It!.......................167

CH 11: Stop Slamming the D.O.O.R.!..........179

CH 12: Am I D.O.N.E. Yet?........................190

CH 13: I L.O.S.T It!....................................208

CH 14: Q.U.I.T. It.......................................236

CH 15: Hey H.O.M.O.! God Loves You!.........269

Final Thoughts..296

RUB SOME D.I.R.T. ON IT.....

Introduction

Do you show up when God invites you on a **D.A.T.E.** with him? A **D**ivine **A**ppointment **T**o **E**ngage with Him? A "date" requires three ingredients: a place, a time, and the parties invited. This **D.A.T.E.** with God was His invitation to me to write this book with Him. God likes morning dates—early morning dates—like 6 a.m. early. He meets me in my office, waiting to share with me the lessons behind His favorite 4-letter words.

Confession: I love 4-letter words. I use them more often than my family would like me to, but they add color and emphasis to my stories, and in my heart, I long ago heard God speak to me about this saying that He doesn't mind a little "cussin" in how I get excited or express myself, but He does mind cursing. A very big difference there. Never curse what God has made, either in yourself or another, because He delights in each of us and has a gift in each situation that we might be inclined to see as a curse.

Still, I was shocked and delighted when He gave me the title of this book; I burst out laughing, covered my mouth, and thought, "Wow, My God is so cool!" He speaks my language and knows that sometimes in life you will need some 4-letter words. The years from 2020 till today have had many moments in which some 4-letter words were needed!

For me, the last three years have felt like the whole world fell apart and came to a crashing halt. As so many friends, family members, and even the random people I have swapped stories with over the last several years have shared with me, this seemed to be the consensus around the world and to just about everyone.

It was a kick in the stomach, a throat punch, a wake-up call, a dark cloud, a sense of confusion, the loss of someone we loved either through death or through division of beliefs. We all lost something: a sense of self and our understanding of this world we now live in. We have all been forever changed.

I struggled with depression during this time stemming from the loss of my vocation in the medical field that I loved, the destruction of my home through flooding, the death of a mentor, the loss of friends, the loss of the feeling of freedom and safety in my country that I had so deeply believed in, the sinking feeling that came with being stuck in a town I never intended to come back to, and it all started with the ending of my intimate relationship on the last day of 2019, December 31 ... my birthday.

The day before 2020 and all that was to come ever kicked off! Through all the overwhelming changes, losses, and sorrow, I still kept God close, or more accurately, He kept me close! I prayed, I begged, I cried, I hoped, I lost hope, I argued and shook my fist, and I'm sure there were some choice 4-letter words used. I studied Scripture, I journaled on every topic and barren area in my life, but through it all, a primary focus was on relationships and more specifically, on dating again.

Should I date? Could I date? When would be a good time to date? How would I know if it was the right person for me to date?

I didn't want to keep attracting the wrong partner into my life and repeat the same patterns that ended in the destruction of two hearts and two lives, followed by a deeper sense of despair that God would never grant me this blessing of a loving, healthy, Godly relationship.

I had never liked the idea of "dating" anyway; I was more of an idealist, a dreamer, a romantic who wanted to skip the awkward dating process and go straight into a committed, loving relationship. I'm sure you can see how this could lead to problems. How do you honestly commit to someone you never took the time to get to know on a deeper level?

So, I put off dating for almost three years; then God began to reveal this book to me, word by word, chapter by chapter, life lesson by life lesson. Even in all the excitement and wonder of these lessons being discovered that were changing my life daily, I continued to ask him about dating. Finally, one morning at 6 a.m., I woke up and God told me that I had a **D.A.T.E.**.

He showed me that a **D.A.T.E.** was profoundly sacred to Him; it was a **D**ivine **A**ppointment **T**o **E**ngage, and I had a **D.A.T.E.** with GOD! I had a **D**ivine **A**ppointment **T**o **E**ngage with Him, to deepen my relationship with Him, to listen to Him, and to get to know Him on the deepest, most intimate level. I had His undivided, all-encompassing attention and love. I was awestruck as these words came through me.

How can you get a better date than a **D.A.T.E**. with God? So, I am finally dating again! Of course, God's ways are weird (and this was not exactly what I thought I was praying for; it's better!), but as weird as His ways may be, they work, and every morning around 6 a.m. He would gently wake me up and whisper, "We have a date, are you coming"?

I would love to say that every single time, I jumped right up and ran to my study, but there were a few mornings when I rolled back over, put a pillow over my head, and went back to sleep only to wake up later agitated and knowing something was off or missing. So now, when that internal invitation wakes me up, I smile and think, I have a **D.AT.E.**!

I believe God will use this book to let you **D.A.T.E.** Him as well. If you are reading these words, it is not by coincidence you have a **D.A.T.E.** with God! He invited you to this place, at this time, for your chance to accept or reject this **D**ivine **A**ppointment **T**o **E**ngage with Him! This book's lessons helped me radically change how I hear and see the world around me. Words that once had no deep meaning to me are now signposts for me to look more carefully at the situations placed in front of me. To be more aware of the words I use when I speak to myself and to others.

I appreciate myself in a whole new way. I see the originality in the gifts God gave me that I once thought had no value. These little 4-letter words helped me to feel God's presence surrounding me, to notice His love and patience as He abundantly pours out His wisdom and humor, as well as His genuine interest in teaching me that He can take even the most mundane, unimportant things, and show me that there is a beautiful lesson He has planted in it.

I was reminded of the story in Scripture where Jesus heals a blind man by mixing His spit in the dirt and creating mud, wiping it on the man's eyes, and then giving him the task of going and washing the mud off of them. When the man went and washed the mud from his eyes, he could see! As I read the story, my 4-letter words started to jump off the page and come to life. Scripture said Jesus **S.P.I.T** in the **D.I.R.T** and with that, his **S**piritual **P**ower **I**mmediately **T**ransformed the dirt into a healing balm, that if the man would do his small but important part, go wash his eyes, he would understand that the **D.I.R.T.** on his eyes gave him **D**eeper **I**nsight **R**enewing his **T**hinking, his faith. He was blind, but now he could see.

How many of us are walking through life, seeing but blind? What if God is offering to rub some **D.I.R.T.** on your eyes to give you the gift of insight that will change your heart, calm your fears, and give you signs to look for along the way that would help you catch yourself whenever you come to a fork in the road and have to decide how you will choose to see a situation?

Maybe you didn't pick up this book to seek a change. In the passage, it never says that the man asked for healing; he was a blind beggar was all it said, so if he was asking for anything, it was probably for money, not realizing the "change" he was about to get would come from spit and dirt. The change you will get will also come from **S.P.I.T.** (**S**piritual **P**ower **I**mmediately **T**ransforms) and **D.I.R.T.** (**D**eeper **I**nsight **R**enews **T**hinking)!

I'm pretty sure if the blind man could have seen what Jesus was doing, he would have pulled away disgusted and confused, not letting some stranger rub spit and dirt on him. I wouldn't blame him, but so many times, this is precisely how God works, and thank God we can't see what He is doing, or we might throw up our hands in disgust and run in the opposite direction. His unseen actions can bring the insight we need back to our lives. We have to let Him rub some **D.I.R.T.** on our hearts, our eyes, and our minds to be able to live out the lyrics of that old gospel song, *Amazing Grace*, that says, "I once was lost, but now I'm found, was blind but now I see."

Be open to your **D.A.T.E.** with God, and the **D.I.R.T.** this book has to offer that could transform your life and the lives of those around you. We need more light in this world, and what God promised Abraham so long ago, He now promises you: you will be blessed to be a blessing!

Embrace the **D.I.R.T.** and save the **D.A.T.E.**!!

Chapter 1
Rub Some D.I.R.T. On It

Deeper - **I**nsight – **R**enews – **T**hinking

Do not be conformed to this world, but be transformed by the renewal of your mind, that by testing you may discern what is the will of God, what is good and acceptable and perfect.
(Romans 12:2)

For as long as I can remember, I have prayed. I prayed for my family, my friends, for an "A" on the test, and for healing the patients I worked with. I prayed that I would get the job, the house, the mate, that I would get 21 at Blackjack in Vegas or win the lottery; (Okay, so they all weren't always the most pious prayers) but in all those prayers, over all those years I am positive I have never ever prayed for DIRT!

I had to laugh because dirt (and bugs) is something I am not fond of at all. I don't often think of myself as a total "girly-girl." I'm strong, independent, and adventurous, but when it comes to dirt, I quickly pull away in disgust and run to wash it off. I don't like the feeling of it, the look of it, and I certainly don't want to submerge myself in it entirely, but now my perspective has changed so radically that I seem obsessed with finding more ways to get God's **D.I.R.T.** into my mind, my heart, and my spirit. I fervently pray, "Lord, continue to show me how your **D**eeper **I**nsight **R**enews **T**hinking". I would catch myself singing that old kindergarten rhyme: *"God made DIRT, and DIRT don't hurt!* So, bring on the **D.I.R.T.** Lord!" And He did!

God spoke to me everywhere I went, renewing my thinking with every new 4-letter word. Here is a little bit of the **D.I.R.T.** to come in each of the upcoming chapters. All will be explained if you are patient and willing to dig deeper. Each chapter in this book is the **D.I.R.T.** I needed to get through each day. I hope you find joy, laughter, and the wisdom you need as you uncover for yourself the lessons in these 4-letter words that God spoke over me.

After reading this book, you will never look at these words the same again. You will increase your arsenal of the 4-letter words you can now use to get your life, and your mind, back on track! Each word has a hidden message that will be a lifeline for you. Each word will offer guidance for the next step you are facing in this journey called life.

My hope in writing this book is to cover you in God's **D.I.R.T.** to help you renew your spirit and brighten your smile. I hope your understanding of each life lesson helps to deepen your connection with our Creator, and that you delight in watching as one light after another turns on in your soul. There is power in words. I pray that as you move through your day, you will begin to listen to the words you say to yourself and the words others are speaking around you.

You will start to notice all the ways these 4-letter words begin to creep into your awareness. Let them be a reminder for you that there is a lesson here to be discovered, a truth to unfold.

Here are the 4-letter words that you will never see the same again, because now you have the lowdown **D.I.R.T.** on them!

S.O.I.L. The lesson from this chapter will give you the question you need to focus your prayers and ask God to show you exactly what He wants you to work on. It will take you through each of the fruits of the spirit and what we often have to go through to get those fruits to manifest in our lives. When God's **D.I.R.T.** is added to your **S.O.I.L.**, stand back and watch out because an abundant, fruitful garden is about to grow in your life. This book is a profound blessing that was born out of my own dedication to discovering and working my **S.O.I.L.**

W.A.V.E. In this chapter, God taught me what a **W.A.V.E.** is, what it often does to me if I don't recognize where it has come from, and the power I have to control it. I share how this happened to me when I was sure I couldn't handle one more **W.A.V.E.** in life. How the Holy Spirit came and rubbed some **D.I.R.T.** on my eyes and I began to see new, life-giving ways to direct my **W.A.V.E.** and how to react to **W.A.V.E.**s that others bring into my life. I will share lessons on the gift of climbing onto your Father's shoulders to see the **W.A.V.E.** from His perspective and hold fast to His strength as your foundation when the waves seem too much for you.

F.A.S.T. I was given the gift of the **F.A.S.T.** and added this spiritual practice to my life to help me work my own **S.O.I.L.**, but when God rubbed some **D.I.R.T.** on my **F.A.S.T.**, I saw why it is so much more than simply not eating.

It is a door to experiencing expectation, frustration, and finally, transformation. It is advice on focusing on what is standing in the way of the life you want and often how the **F.A.S.T.** needs a slow and steady approach.

W.A.I.T. The **D.I.R.T**. on how to **W.A.I.T.** was the wisdom I needed to see how I was hurting, instead of helping, myself. I went through years where I felt stuck in situations or places that I didn't think I should be, and I became bitter. The more bitter I became, the more stuck I felt and the more unwilling I was to see a different way to approach this frustrating time. When God rubbed **D.I.R.T.** on my mind and gave me the secret of what to do while I **W.A.I.T.**, I was given my smile back, and it enabled me to have a lighter, grateful, and more expectant heart, even as I went through the discomfort of waiting.

P.L.A.N. Whenever the topic of waiting comes into my mind, the next question is always about the **P.L.A.N.**. What's the plan? I need a plan. I have no plan. If I just had a plan, and the final pleading to God, "Please tell me your plan, and I will do it"! As I struggled with all of these questions, God finally revealed to me just what the **P.L.A.N.** was for each day. The Holy Spirit took that magic **D.I.R.T.**, that **D**eeper **I**nsight **R**enewing my **T**hinking, and laid out the **P.L.A.N.** It was not exactly the answer I had hoped for, yet it was what I needed. It was the **P.L.A.N**. He calls each of us every morning when we are given a new day. This deeper insight helped me create a physical "Life Garden" that gives me a concrete image of how well I am working the **P.L.A.N.** In this chapter, I will share the **P.L.A.N.** and how to build your Life Garden so you too can see how well you are working the **P.L.A.N.**!

F.O.R.K. There are times in my life that I have wanted to sit down and cry "**F.O.R.K.** it! I don't know where I am going. I don't know the right steps. I don't know how to use the tools I have been given to get me where I think I want to go, and even if I think I do know where I want to go, oftentimes when I get there it looks nothing like what I hoped for and God feels even farther away than when I started. I have been in desperate need of learning how to use a fork for my health and sanity, not realizing God put the advice into the tool I was trying to use this whole time. When lost in this life, God said, "**F.O.R.K.** it!", and that is the best advice He could have ever given me!

G.R.O.W. & **W.O.R.K.**   Sometimes God speaks in such a loving way to me; comforting me, holding me, and letting me know He has got this. At other times, He throws **D.I.R.T.** on me, which seems cruel at first glance, until I realize there is love in the message, and it is leading me to the life He wants for me. I was shocked when I heard "**G.R.O.W.** up and get to **W.O.R.K.**" as His advice. What a rude thing to say to someone! But as I looked closer at the **D.I.R.T.** in the message, I realized His gentle calling to my heart was to join Him as a light in the world. I had to learn to **G.R.O.W.** up and adjust my attitude to be able to **W.O.R.K.** for Him. If anyone other than God told me to "**GROW** up and get to **WORK**," I would be furious and defensive. But the **D.I.R.T.** of the Holy Spirit opened my heart to hear this message and God's more profound meaning behind the words spoken. He wanted to expand my **W.O.R.K.** if I was willing and ready to **G.R.O.W.** up.

S.I.N.K./S.W.I.M.   Some choices seem obvious when presented, such as this one. Who would choose **S.I.N.K.** versus **S.W.I.M.** if given the option? But what if all we know is how to **S.I.N.K.** because no one taught us how to **S.W.I.M.**? The lesson in this chapter makes it clear what we all are doing when we **S.I.N.K.**. I was amazed to realize that, even though I consider myself a "water baby" in life, when God uncovered the **D.I.R.T.** in my mind, He showed me how often I actively choose to **S.I.N.K.**, and what tremendous power there is in choosing to **S.W.I.M.** instead.

Now, whenever I notice that I have started to **S.I.N.K.** into a thought pattern or unhealthy habit, I can recognize what I am doing and change course! We all are created to have the capacity to **S.W.I.M.**

M.A.D.E. This chapter takes the proverbial "He made me do it!" blame game that all of us have probably said at one time or another, and puts a twist on it to show you the incredible power of what God had in mind when He **M.A.D.E.** you in physical form and how He **M.A.D.E.** you to do something that you know you could never have done on your own! In this chapter, I will share personal stories of when the hand of God **M.A.D.E.** me do something I would never have known how to do or to say. This book you are holding is one of those times when He **M.A.D.E.** me do it, and I am so grateful that He did.

D.O.O.R. Every **D.O.O.R.** we come to in life does not compare to the **D.O.O.R.** that we are toward ourselves, toward God, and finally toward the world. Your **D.O.O.R.** not only opens outward, but inward as well. The **D.I.R.T.** on **D.O.O.R.** in this chapter will return the power to your hands and give you hope as your mind is opened to what exactly is behind your **D.O.O.R.**, and who or what you are allowing to control it. Every next step, next opportunity, and next relationship we have in life all hinges on our **D.O.O.R.**

D.O.N.E. I almost started the book with this chapter because the first time I heard about this book from God was when I told him I wanted to be DONE with life! He promptly responded, *"NOPE, We have a book to write,"* when I asked Him the question, "Am I done yet?" This book wasn't even on my radar as I was having this conversation. I knew that nothing I was doing was working, and I was miserable. The **D.I.R.T.** on **D.O.N.E.** is one of the most beautiful and tender messages of love God gave me.

He showed me why and how I get to the point of feeling "done," yet still feel incomplete inside and how I would then turn to the next thing that I would soon enough be done with as well.

After getting rolled around in the **D.I.R.T.** of His deep and ever-abiding love, God showed me why He would never be **D.O.N.E.** with me.

L.O.S.T.   How many of us have been there? **L.O.S.T.**? It feels like a destination, and we have all packed our bags and moved there unintentionally, or so we thought! The **D.I.R.T.** on **L.O.S.T.** is the key to getting found! It was so apparent that I was surprised I had missed it all these years. This chapter will help you see what you are doing in your mind when you have found yourself living in Lostville! When you have moved in and unpacked or pitched a tent while thinking the whole time you don't want to be here, asking yourself, "How on earth did I get here?" and "How the heck do I get myself out of here?" The lesson of **L.O.S.T.** will guide you back home with its powerful truth hidden in a 4-letter word that none of us has found much comfort in. So don't worry, you will never again be able to stay **L.O.S.T** once this truth is found!

Q.U.I.T. When you are ready to quit anything, turn to this chapter. The **D.I.R.T**. on quitting is to **Q.U.I.T.**! It's not what you think...Whether you are trying to stop a habit that is bad for you, or you are contemplating giving up on something that could be life-changing but is also daunting and causing you to doubt your ability to do it... you have to **Q.U.I.T.**!

What kind of advice is that! No motivational speaker ever said the answer is to **Q.U.I.T.**, but God knows most of us are good at quitting; it's much easier to quit, so our mind is willing to accept that word, and when you think you are off the hook, He takes you deeper into a message showing you what is causing you to want to quit, and then how to take back the dreams that He planted in your heart if you would follow His guidance and "**Q.U.I.T.** it!"– God-Style

H.O.M.O. When God spoke this word to me, I burst out laughing and then feared writing it down. I didn't even write it on the official chapter list for days, but God was relentless in sharing the message behind it, and because of the message God spoke over this word and how profound and beautiful it is, I knew I had to include it in the book. This chapter is for everyone, and I mean EVERYONE. Every person you see is a **H.O.M.O.** And do you know why? This chapter will throw some **D.I.R.T.** on how God sees us and how we should see each other.

Those are the 4-letter words that changed my life, and it all started with being open to a word I thought I already knew the meaning of, and then asking the Holy Spirit to come in and change the way I saw the word, and in turn, change the way I saw the world. I hope this book excites you to use more 4-letter words in your life and gives you permission to go ahead and get **D.I.R.T.Y.** !!!

Deeper **I**nsight **R**enews **T**hinking, **YEAH!**

Chapter 2
Working My S.O.I.L.
Soul- Opening-Individualized-Lessons

*But the good soil represents honest, goodhearted
people who hear God's Message, cling to it, and
patiently produce a huge harvest.
(Luke 8:15, NLT)*

Say this with me, "God, what is the **S.O.I.L.** you
have planted me in? What lesson and gift have you been
trying to give me that I have not yet let into my heart?"
Then listen... The answer is all around you. What season
of life have you found yourself in? Oftentimes, your
season will indicate your **S.O.I.L.**: your **S**oul **O**pening
Individualized **L**essons.

Are you angry, fearful, agitated, mean, vengeful, abrasive?
Have you felt betrayed, filled with sorrow, or
overwhelmed?

Are you uncomfortable in your body or not caring for it as you should? Are you finding your health spinning out of control? Is there an area of your life where you feel that something is getting choked or smothered, a deep sense of frustration or pain, and an unwillingness to let it go?

This indicates that "something" is trying to grow, move, and expand in you. You are experiencing the growing pains of your **S.O.I.L.** – The **S**oul **O**pening **I**ndividualized **L**essons God has planted you in. If you are willing to say "Yes" to it, God will bring forth the gifts and fruits He intended for your life. However, if you don't tend to the soil, nothing can grow, or weeds will grow, which are planted beliefs that choke out the truth and rob you of the fruit that would bring abundance to your life.

God won't come barging into our lives, strong-arming us to accept His love, but He will continue reaching for us again and again, hoping, this time, an open hand and an open heart will be reaching back toward Him. This isn't some one-size-fits-all invitation; this is a personal, handcrafted, unique plan for our lives with Him. The fruit of the Holy Spirit mentioned in Scripture are all the same, but the **S.O.I.L.** that we experience to be able to manifest them: the heartache, the hurt, the frustration, the tears, the excitement, the adventures .... the life we live and the people we live it with are all unique and were all chosen to enrich our **S.O.I.L.** so the fruits we need most in our life will be able to grow.

It blew my mind to think that everything I thought was unfair, unnecessary, hurtful, or hard was an invitation to add **D.I.R.T.** to my **S.O.I.L.**. To add **D**eeper **I**nsight **R**enewing my **T**hinking to this **S**oul **O**pening **I**ndividualized **L**esson God was waiting to share with me.

Some **S.O.I.L.**, I seemed to be a natural gardener in. Some gardens flourish early in our lives, and we should be grateful for those gifts that God helped to flourish without much laboring and tilling of our **S.O.I.L.**.

However, what I have found is that the real **S**oul **O**pening **I**ndividualized **L**essons in our lives will be the ones that seem to come around again and again. These are the ones we struggle with, pray about, and often pray to have taken away. It is in these struggles that we often think if we just had more willpower, different life circumstances, different genes, different parents, or more money, then we would be able to handle it better, but God is saying that this is the thing that you won't surrender completely to Him. You won't open this part of your soul to Him and trust that He is the Master Gardener and He can turn your frustration into fruit!

It's not our willpower, our genetics, or our bank account that is limiting us; it's our mindset, and our belief that it cannot change, that it cannot grow, that is causing these barren areas in our lives. These are the difficult and frustrating experiences that seem to repeat themselves over and over. God says if we can give Him a small opening, a whisper of a YES, He can take that **S.O.I.L.** and make something amazing grow. It is a personal invitation. It is a personalized lesson to learn because it is a personal gift He is trying to give to each of us!

As that revelation sunk in for me, I found myself willing and excited to be open to digging a little deeper into what my walls were that I kept running into. What dead ends did I keep finding myself staring at? What weeds had I let grow in the garden of my heart? I was ready to find out what my **S.O.I.L.** was and how to work on it! I would pray: "Lord, I want to understand how to work my **S.O.I.L.**. Don't let me waste this opportunity that the last three years have been trying to teach me".

I didn't want to lose out on these lessons, these deeper insights renewing my thinking that were produced from all the pain and heartbreak, confusion and betrayal, longing, and loneliness, as well as the lessons of strength and courage, faith, and forgiveness, and even Love. My heart's question was " Lord, How do I make sure I am working my **S.O.I.L.**?"

All I had seemed to be doing for the last three years was complaining and whining about the "dirt" or, as I lovingly referred to it as, the "nothing but crap" I saw in my life, not realizing God had allowed me to use this time for more profound insight that would help renew my thinking and restore my life. I wasn't renewing anything. I was bitter, angry, and blaming everyone, everything, and the town I was in for how my life was going.

Then, He gently showed me all He was doing and how He was building my heart up with fertile **S.O.I.L.** so I could produce lasting fruit. I was so grateful for this chance. I long to learn these lessons and not try to cover them up, numb them out, or frantically find someone else's **S.O.I.L.** to try to focus on and work in to escape my own. The garden of my heart is my gift.

My happiness is my habit to form. I had to ask myself some hard questions about these last years. I had to make sure they were not wasted and still needed to be focused on whether I wanted to have any lasting change come forth from the **S.O.I.L** I had been given to work with. What lessons have I had in my life over these past years? I realized I had worked through more lessons than I had given myself credit for such as the lesson of refusing to compromise my values and faith, the lesson of loneliness, the lesson of forgiveness., the lesson of discontentment, the lesson of self-worth and self-care, the lesson of friendship, the lesson of disappointment, the lesson of waiting, the lesson of learning, the lesson of listening, and the lesson of love verses lust and escape.

As I pondered these lessons, the Lord spoke to me and asked me....

"Have you learned anything yet? This has been a season of growth, but do you seem any different? What has changed? What fruits of the Spirit can you now point to that have grown in you? What relationships have improved? What heart habit have you invested in or weeded out? What mindset do you now hold, or what toxic thoughts have you banished from your heart, no longer allowed to taunt you, or lie to you?

What physically have you improved to honor this temple I have given you? Are you doing anything different? To become different, you have to do something different!

These are questions you can ask yourself as you work your own **S.O.I.L.** to see what externally observable facts you can point to and say, "There is the fruit of the **S.O.I.L.** I have been working!"

When God speaks, He is gentle and kind but still straight to the point and pulls no punches when bringing light to the truth of the matter and helping me to correct it. If anyone else spoke to me so directly, I would go on the defense and put my best foot forward, pointing to my "highlight-reel" life to show how great I am doing. But with God, I can't hide or embellish, and I don't even feel like I want to. I feel loved and wanted and like we are onto something extraordinary when He corrects me and tries to show me that the plans He has for me are the same as those He promised Jeremiah in Scripture when Lord explained:

....then I will come and do for you all the good things I have promised, and I will bring you home again. For I know the plans I have for you, says the Lord. They are plans for good and not for disaster, to give you a future and a hope. In those days when you pray, I will listen. If you look for me in earnest, you will find me when you seek me.
(Jeremiah 29: 10-13)

I was chasing down God like He was the last bus leaving the station for the night! Luckily, He was standing there waiting with open arms, ready to share His wisdom with me and answer all my questions. He continued to share where the fruit of the Spirit comes from and the types of **S.O.I.L.** He uses it to produce them.

... the Holy Spirit produces this kind of fruit in our lives: love, joy, peace, patience, kindness, goodness, faithfulness, gentleness, and self-control. There is no law against these things!
(Galatians 5:22-23 NLT)

Each fruit of the Spirit comes from a different **S.O.I.L.** (a **S**oul **O**pening **I**ndividualized **L**esson). While each person's final "fruits" might be the same, whether they are love, joy, peace, patience, kindness, goodness, faithfulness, gentleness, or self-control, the **D.I.R.T.** and **S.O.I.L.** will be personal and unique to each of us. God only makes originals, therefore, every person's **S.O.I.L.** is made of different **D.I.R.T.**!

If you are trying to figure out where He has you planted in this season of your life, just read the description below of the fruit He is trying to grow in you and what kind of **S.O.I.L.** produces that particular fruit. I know for me, God didn't try to hide which gardens in my heart needed more attention to be able to flourish, nor did He hide His love for me or how vital it was that I fully accept that I deserved to have His fruit grow abundantly in my life. It wasn't because I worked hard for it that I now deserved it. It was because it was part of my inheritance that God promised each of us if we would only open our hearts and our hands to accept the abundant gifts He has always been ready to give.

The first gift of the Spirit He offers to us is the fruit of love. God Is LOVE. His heart is the first **S.O.I.L.** He ever planted us in. He birthed each of us out of His Love and created us with the ability to love Him in return.

We are made to love Him and to worship Him. This is the first **S**oul **O**pening **I**ndividualized **L**esson we all come to in life. It is whether to accept His love, to give Him access to our hearts, or to reject Him and try to live this life on our own with an ever-aching feeling like something inside is forever missing.

None of the other gifts of the Spirit can even be planted without His love being accepted first. We are imperfect people, and God knows that, but He is madly and completely in love with us. All He needs is our YES, to come in and flood our hearts with all the other gifts of the Spirit that He has been ready to abundantly pour into us. Say Yes to His love, say Yes to Jesus as the love of your life, your mentor, your guide, and your best friend. Say "Yes" to the Holy Spirit coming into your heart and beginning the greatest adventure this life could ever give, an adventure that begins when you and God get together to light up this world and fulfill your purpose:

To love and be loved in this broken world.

Such love has no fear because perfect love expels all fear. If we are afraid, it is for fear of punishment, and this shows that we have not fully experienced his perfect love. We love each other because he loved us first.
(1 John 4:18-19 NLT)

We are never done working this **S.O.I.L.** of love. Every day, we practice how to better love and serve each other. This **S.O.I.L.** is renewed by remembering how much God loves us and how He blesses us every day.

The more we allow God to pour His love into us, the more we will be a well of love for others. It is the gift that keeps on giving. The more love we give away, the more we will have to give.

Joy comes from the Lord, but the **S.O.I.L.** (**S**oul **O**pening **I**ndividualized **L**esson) is often borne out of sorrow and hopelessness.

It is often said, "Joy comes in the morning," or "It is always darkest before the dawn," and this is true, but would we even recognize the light if we never found ourselves in darkness? Would we even recognize Joy as Joy if it was the only state we existed in? No, of course not. Joy is learned and chosen. When we finally realize that heartache will never be enough to get us up in the morning to face the day and that no dream can gain strength from looking down, we will choose to reach for Joy. Oftentimes, this is done by searching for something, anything, we can be grateful for.

I know that so many times I have had to pull myself out of a pit by praying for God to show me what I should be grateful for, and to remind me of what He has blessed me with. Even if it seems small, each grateful thought still brings a spark of joy as I recall that being able to breathe or walk, when some people struggle and have pain, is something to be joyful about!

I'm grateful that I have a roof over my head that is in a safe neighborhood, and that I have people who love me, are all things to rejoice in. I have listed all the people in my life, near or far, who have ever been there for me, even if they no longer are, and with each prayer of thanks, I usher in the joy God has for me. It is only when I have closed the door of my heart to acknowledge these blessings and chosen instead the door of self-pity and fear, that the flow of Joy ceases. It is never because there is a shortage of Joy that God is sending through us, but instead, a question of how open the door to our heart is to receive that Joy.

We choose Joy by remembering daily who God is and all He has done in our lives. Joy is fought for daily; it is only yours to lose or give away. You can either sink in your fears or swim in your Joy!

The soil of KINDNESS: Kindness is often grown out of the **S.O.I.L.** of witnessing and experiencing harshness, cruelty, abrasiveness, and hatred while having this innate knowing that there has to be a better way to be treated and to treat others. For most of us (sociopaths not included), after we have treated someone else cruelly or harshly, we never truly feel good about it. The endless replaying of the hurt they caused us doesn't seem to stop even after we had our "rightful revenge," and our ego whispers to us, "They deserved it! That's what they get!". If that is what they deserved, and we were the "righteous deliverer" of that judgment, why do we feel no peace in our minds or a settled feeling in our hearts?

It is because the "fruit" we shared with another was not a fruit of the Spirit, it was poisonous, not only to them but more importantly, to ourselves. We will never heal anything by intentionally causing harm to someone else as part of the process. We watch all these "tit for tat" interactions happen in the world, in our city, in our neighborhood, and even in our own family, and we think; There has got to be a better way to treat others! Jesus came to model kindness in the face of the most atrocious acts of hatred and hurt any human could endure and endure unjustly at that.

He was beaten, He was spit on, He was whipped, and His best friends even betrayed Him. He was imprisoned and He was killed, yet in all of those moments, when He had every right to be furious, to get revenge, to curse and call down the powers of Heaven to inflict pain back upon those who hurt Him, He didn't.

He just opened up His heart and His arms even wider and showed kindness to the world as He saved us through His pain. He smiled upon us and blessed us. With His last breath, He chose kindness.

Of all the pain I have gone through, the little hurts or cuts to my ego or my body, nothing even comes close to the **S.O.I.L.** Jesus was planted in.

I know that I too can choose to grow in kindness if the Holy Spirit is willing to continue to rub some **D.I.R.T.** on the cruelty I face and help me respond in the way Paul advises me to in Scripture when He says:

Therefore, as God's chosen people, holy and dearly loved, clothe yourselves with compassion, kindness, humility, gentleness, and patience.
(Colossians 3:12, NIV)

The Soil of PEACE: Peace is that fruit that we all long for, beg for, pay high dollars to look for in the solace of nature, or simply, in a quiet empty house, free from chaos, for an hour... We all long for peace and think that we have to find it, create it, spend money on it, get rid of things to make space for it, or work hard to hold on to it. In truth, it is part of our birthright when we invite the Holy Spirit into our lives! He brings His gifts with Him, and Peace is part of the package! Thank God! But the **S.O.I.L.** that brings about the fruit of Peace is almost always internal or external chaos, and who wants chaos? Who prays for chaos to come into our lives and minds so we can see the fruit of Peace? No one! Unfortunately, in this broken world, chaos is here to stay. But fortunately, as Scripture says, we are in this world but not of this world! As the waves of the world crash all around us, God whispers to us on how to hold on to the peace Christ brings with Him everywhere He goes.

It was the first thing He said to the disciples when He appeared to them in a locked upper room after they had just watched Him be nailed to a cross and die. Can you imagine how freaked out and chaotic their spirit was to have Jesus appear out of nowhere? And what were the words Jesus spoke over them as they looked at Him terrified?

.... "Peace be with you", He said. As he spoke, he held out his hands for them to see, and he showed them his side. .... He spoke to them again and said "Peace be with you.

As the Father has sent me, so I send you." Then He breathed on them and said, "Receive the Holy Spirit".
(John 20:19-22, NLT)

I have struggled with bouts of depression throughout my life, and I have learned many techniques to help control my thoughts that can bring some short-term relief. I value these psychological tools greatly, but nothing helped me as much as these words did after a deeply disturbing couple of days. I was sobbing and not sleeping well. I felt like a zombie, and I was grasping at anything at all to keep me afloat.

I told myself to think of Bible verses, and I was randomly saying whatever verses came to mind, but all of them felt like some fake, cliche, overly used (and not helpful) words that were frustrating me more than helping. Suddenly, in my heart, I felt Jesus enter the room and speak those words to me repeatedly, "Peace be with you. Peace be with you". That verse hijacked my mind; no other thoughts could enter for more than two seconds before being ushered out. For an hour, He spoke those words to me as He instructed me to get out of bed, put on clothes, brush my teeth and hair, get in the car, and go to church, where we were having a day of service.

"Peace be with you"... was the verse that saved me. Simple, short, and yet so powerful were these words. Assuring and confident that what He had to give me, I was made to receive. That day was a blur, and I can't say I didn't cry throughout the day while I was serving. Yet His peace was greater than my fears, and as I lived out that second part of His promise, "Just as the Father has sent me, so I send you," I found a deeper and deeper sense of peace as I brought His peace to others.

Keeping our minds and eyes fixed on Him as we do His work in this chaotic world will continue to increase the peace that He breathed into us the day we opened our hearts to receive him.

With every breath in, hear Him say, "Peace be with you," and with every exhale, feel His love and encouragement as He reminds us, "Just as the Father has sent me, so I send you."

As you take your next step, may His peace be with you! Be excited to work your **S.O.I.L.** to produce the Peace that is not just an option but a promised part of the package deal that God offered when He sent the Holy Spirit to live in each of us.

The soil of PATIENCE: Oh Patience, how I have misunderstood you for so long. I ran from you like the plague, and even thought it was a badge of some kind that I had no patience. How wrong was I, and how grateful am I that I finally understood the gift God is trying to give us when He plants us in the **S.O.I.L.** that offers us Patience. Do you find yourself feeling defiant, insubordinate, resistant, willful, impatient, agitated, irritated, fearful, frustrated, intolerant, exasperated, nervous, or restless? This **S.O.I.L.**, these experiences, hold the seed of Patience perfectly planted in you, ready to grow as soon as you are ready to let them. The question is, will you accept that you deserve the gift of Patience?

We don't often recognize the soil or dirt we are planted in, and I speak from experience on that one. After reading the list of what the exact opposite of patience would look like and what the lessons would feel like, I recognized how many times I refused to accept the gift Patience was trying to give, preferring to choose to suffer through it instead, like this was a noble path of some sort. My pride got in the way of me accepting this gift, and it might be the same for you. My ego refused to accept patience because the gift of patience is given when you finally admit that you are not the center of the universe.

Patience is the humbling of our pride and our ego. Patience is admitting there might be more to a situation than just me and my part, and that is why something is not happening how I want, when I want, where I want, and with whom I want. Patience is about opening your heart to let God, and others, play out their parts in your story too. God's story is one that only time can tell, and you will enjoy it more if you accept this gift of Patience. Patience is the gift of bearing pain or trials CALMLY and without complaint.

The **S.O.I.L.** of patience is anything but calm. The **S.O.I.L.** is often formed out of fear. We don't trust that HE is God, and we are not. We are afraid we will lose what we think we want, not have enough, or not get something we think we need to be happy and content. Impatience is discontentment. It is believing that what God has given you in this moment is not enough. We are running after something that, if it were meant for us to have now, we would already have it. Our impatience has often caused us to miss every reg flag God was sending our way, but we didn't care because the hole in our soul that was causing such discontent was demanding that we chase down something or someone until we got it, grabbed it, and took it for our own.

Yet somehow, after we spent all that time and energy chasing "it" down and demanding that "it" be ours, at some point, we seem to find ourselves with that old familiar feeling of discontent and are back on the hunt again, on the run again, irritated, agitated, restless—"knowing" this time, THIS will be the thing that will stop the hurting, the restlessness, the irritation, and the agitation in our hearts.

We are chasing the wrong things. Whatever we are so impatient to have does not have the power to fill us and bring us peace. At its best, it will be a blessing in your life if it is meant to be, and at its worst, it will be a gut-wrenching pain that comes at a high price.

The price will be time lost and an even greater fear inside that you are not enough, something is wrong, that you are asking for too much, or that nothing will ever satisfy the hunger inside. None of these beliefs are true. You were just running after the wrong thing.

No one and nothing in your life has the life force to be your personal life source. Only God was created to hold that space in your life. He made you; He can sustain you and help life flourish in you. Patience is one of His gifts to your soul to do just that: help you flourish! Patience helps prevent pain more often than not.

Patience is God's gift of calmness and eagerness in your heart. It is a willingness for you to let Him direct your steps. He can see what you can't. He has the map that you don't. He can see the intentions of others and can direct you away from those who intend to hurt you if you only accept this gift of Patience and see it as a gift, not a hindrance or a restriction. Patience protects your dreams. Patience calms your heart and washes you with a sense that each step you take is a chance to check in with God and make sure you have not run too far ahead but have kept Him close so you can hear Him clearly.

Patience lets you smell the roses, watch the grapes grow, and anticipate the harvest of the dreams to come. Patience is the gift that renews your faith and helps conquer your fears daily.

When you no longer fear slowing down, stepping with intention, and discerning each path before you, when your heart no longer screams at you to "run, or you will miss it!" whatever "It" is that you are running after.

When you know God is here, surrounding you and leading you, it brings a sense of confidence that you are no longer TRYING to be patient; you are now simply embracing that you no longer allow fear and restlessness, irritation and intolerance, agitation, or anger, to guide your life and your actions. You have laid down the fear and picked up your faith.

Believing that if God spoke a blessing over you, a calling on your life, a relationship meant for you, a spot on the team or job at the business, a perfect home in a city you resonate with, or even as a spokesperson to the world; if he spoke it, it IS happening!

Hear Him say, "Wait for it, this is going to be so good, watch and see!" We no longer need to join the rat race, where we are forever running over, pushing down, or stepping on someone else to get what is ours!

We can calmly and confidently walk, like the royalty we are, to our rightful place, and there we will find that He did indeed save a seat for us.

Be glad for all God is planning for you. Be patient in trouble and always prayerful.
(Romans 12:12, NLT)
.... know that God causes everything to work together for the good of those who love God and are called according to his purpose for them.
(Romans 8:28, NLT)

That Scripture says we KNOW, but I would have to ask, do you know, in your heart, do you really know and embrace this as a fact? Whose plans do you believe in— Yours or His? If these don't align, you will find yourself in a world of hurt, trying to make things fit into your life that were never intended for your greater good. If you feel like your plans are all dead ends and hopeless, turn around and ask God what plans He has in mind for you. Give the map back to God, the original map maker, because He already knows the plans He has for you, and He already promised you that His plans for you would give you a future and hope!

If your plans and visions for the future aren't getting you excited and leading somewhere you somehow know is good, really good, then trash your plans. Let God back in the driver's seat and embrace His calming presence in your heart that will be seen and felt as the fruit of Patience. Patience is the gift you hold when you can finally take the next step in your life filled with His blessed assurance.

May God, who gives this patience and encouragement, help you live in complete harmony with each other...
(Romans 15:5, NLT)

If I could leave one Scripture to encourage you, I would leave is!

... do not throw away this confident trust in the Lord, no matter what happens. Remember the great reward it brings you! Patient endurance is what you need now, so you will continue to do God's will. Then you will receive all that he has promised.
(Hebrews 10: 35-36, NLT)

The **S.O.I.L.** of FAITHFULNESS: The Fruit of Faithfulness is our opportunity to live out and demonstrate our faith daily. As you demonstrate your faithfulness and willingness to stick by God through your actions toward yourself and others, God expands His opportunity to demonstrate His faithfulness and His devotion to stick by you! The more you trust in Him, the more He can trust in you. The more He can trust you, the greater the opportunities He can bless you with to continue to show your faithfulness in following Him.

It is a relationship that is never-ending, and ever-increasing, with blessings. The depth of this relationship and the capacity to be open to receive these blessing falls squarely on our shoulders because He has already committed to being faithful to each of us in all things; now it is our turn to show if we will be faithful to Him in even the small things! Because

Unless you are faithful in small matters, you won't be faithful in large ones. If you cheat even a little, you won't be honest with greater responsibilities.
(Luke 16:10, NLT)

It is incredibly difficult to stick with things we don't wholeheartedly believe in. It is difficult to be faithful to God, ourselves, our dreams, or one another if we don't have much faith in them. I find in my life I struggle with faithfulness, not in relationships with others, but with my relationship with myself, and oftentimes I only do things when I "feel like it". I am a fair-weathered friend to myself, and I was so ashamed when I realized I was doing the same thing to God. Was I a true and faithful servant? Did I cling to God, bond to him, grip tightly to him, and stick to what He had shown me would help elevate my life to align with His purpose? Did I go to church when I didn't feel like it or join a small group even if I didn't think I would fit in? Did I show up every morning for my **D.A.T.E.** with God to work on this miracle He had for me in the creating of this book?

I wish I could say my answer was always, "Absolutely, you can count on me, God; I'm your good and faithful servant", but that would not be accurate. I thought I was faithful to any commitments I had made, and I am if it is outside of myself. I was humbled and a bit disappointed to see that my punctual, trustworthy, reliable self was not showing up for God the same way He was showing up for me!

The more I work this **S.O.I.L.**, the more I am honest about what faithfulness is and what it looks like when I am growing in it, the more God revealed that faithfulness is a trust issue, a relationship that is lived out in acts and works of faith!

Scripture explained:

...his faith was made complete by what he did .
(James 2:22, NIV)

So, you see, we are made right with
God by what we do, not by faith alone
(James 2:24, NLT)

Faithfulness is your opportunity to open yourself to the life of abundance God is trying to bring forth. God has shown, since the beginning of humanity, His faithfulness to us all. Still, He also tested every one of the great men and women in Scripture to determine their faithfulness to Him before He could bless them with dreams far beyond anything they ever asked for or imagined.

No matter how amazing you think the dreams you have for your life are, God is smiling as He says, "Oh, I can do wayyy better than that for you!!", but He wants to see if you will be faithful in the little things first. Will you follow His lead in the small things? If you won't, how can He lead you into the great things? How can He trust that you will stick with Him when this earthly world doesn't make sense. When your vision is clouded, when your heart and mind are tired and hurting, or the numbers in your bank account don't add up to the budget needed for the dreams that He placed in your heart, will you be faithful then?

Will you still get up early and walk with Him, even when you don't feel like it? God gives people lives beyond anything they could ever want for, hope for, or imagine, so if you can't even imagine it, you will need the fruit of faithfulness to help keep you walking in the direction that God is calling you toward.

God will do this, for he is faithful to do what he says, and he has invited you into partnership with his Son, Jesus Christ our Lord.
(1 Corinthians 1:9 NLT)

But the Lord still waits for you to come to him so he can show you his love and compassion.
For the Lord is a faithful God. Blessed are those who wait for him to help them.
(Isaiah 30:18 NLT)

Don't neglect this **S.O.I.L.**. Every big dream you hope for depends on the continual daily cultivation of the fruit of faithfulness. Hold fast, stick close, and rejoice in every little step you take in life; it is the proof of your trust that God is who He says He is.

The Soil of GENTLENESS: All of us could use more gentleness in our lives, and we can feel the energy change when we are in the presence of someone who puts us at ease, gives grace before judgment, and creates a space for us to reveal our truth and become vulnerable while still feeling valued at the same time. Jesus refers to himself as gentle.

Take my yoke upon you. Let me teach you, because I am humble and gentle at heart, and you will find rest for your souls.
(Matthew 11:29, NLT)

Gentleness is something we all look for in a mate, a friend, a boss, a coworker, or a coach. We hope when things don't go right or when we fall short of expectation, we will be greeted with gentleness, but the **S.O.I.L.** of gentleness that often makes us appreciate it so much often comes from experiencing a much more painful route. Encountering the use of tactics such as harshness, abrasiveness, roughness, heartlessness, spitefulness, malice, unfriendliness, cattiness, hostility, unkindness, and even violence to deal with a person or a situation has caused us all unnecessary pain. As we work this **S.O.I.L.**, we quickly realize this does not seem to get the results desired. Even if we could manhandle and manipulate the situation, we still hurt someone or ourselves by the careless and cruel way the interaction took place.

Jesus is a wonderful example of how to approach people gently and listen with openness and ease. He uses patience and kindness to create gentleness as He speaks to anyone who comes to Him, hurting or lost. We might not realize we are planted in the **S.O.I.L.** that would produce gentleness.

Still, in every situation where we feel a deep desire to blow up, get mad, get even, cut someone off, act cruelly, be dismissive, or demand our own way, this is an opportunity to take a step back and pray for more gentleness in our spirit.

People do not respond well to an abrasive, abrupt, or manhandling style of interaction if you want them to trust you, work with you, respond to you, and create a lasting relationship with you. You might be able to get what you want, and you might be able to wield power and scare someone into submission and into the act you wanted, but you will never have their trust, and they will never have your back.

When you use gentleness, you build a bridge for the person to bring their entire being to you. You are given a chance to get to know who they are, their dreams, and how you can get the best out of them. It may take more time than the demanding, manipulating way of dealing with people, but you will create loyal, faithful, and loving relationships that last a lifetime because everyone loves to be in the presence of someone they can trust.

People want someone in whom they know what to expect in how they will be treated and valued.

> *... the wisdom that comes from*
> *heaven is first of all pure. It is also peace*
> *loving, gentle at all times, and willing to yield to others*
> *(James 3:17, NLT)*

The outcomes we hope for in life will be multiplied a thousand times over if we embrace the **S.O.I.L.** that yields Gentleness and use it in every interaction we have with another. Even tough situations can be handled with humility and gentleness.

The Soil of GOODNESS: "God is good all the time. All the time, God is good". And that is 100% true, but what about us? Are we good all the time, and all the time are we good? I'll help you with that answer... Nope, not even close, but when the Holy Spirit comes into our hearts, we are now holding "the good" all the time, and the Fruit of Goodness is the creative expression of that! You now hold that light within you:

> *For this light within you produces only what*
> *is good and right and true*
> *(Ephesians 5:9, NLT)*

If we find ourselves struggling with evildoing, immorality, wickedness, crookedness, indecency, meanness, viciousness, corruptness, and dishonesty, then let's take this back to the basics and see if we have truly invited God into that part of our lives. Ask Him back in. Ask Him into our friendships, our marriage, our work, our passions, our churches, and any area where we begin to notice that these are the toxic feelings we are experiencing or the toxic fruit of the actions of others we are surrounding ourselves with. Invite good back in; God is good. Goodness will be your compass. Goodness is a gift from the Holy Spirit given as soon as we invite Him in.

It is ready for us now, but we don't always accept the gift. Our nature is selfish, but when the Holy Spirit comes, the gift of Goodness is the change in preference we now hold. He changes our innate moral compass to move toward God, to move toward good. The gift is the fortitude that is developed and expanded that causes those selfish desires to no longer taste good in our mouths and no longer feel at home in our hearts. It is the visceral transformation of how we react inside to the deeds we are doing on the outside. We want to be better in this world because we are now programmed to desire God, to desire good.

It isn't enough to be a good example; that is too vague. We are all a good example of something, but God calls us to be an example of GOOD. The Fruit of Goodness is a verb! We show how filled with God's goodness we are by what overflows from us in what we do. Goodness desires to be a blessing at all times for all people. Is that how we wake up in the morning? Are those the eyes of our hearts? Goodness is the Holy Spirit's favorite way to be creative. Goodness is God's art in action. Working this **S.O.I.L.** will yield the fruit that allows us to align with God's nature daily. As we invite the Holy Spirit deeper into our lives, we shine with goodness. It's not an idea or a metaphor but a physical manifestation that others can feel and see!

God gave us Goodness as our compass to let us know if we are walking toward Him, toward His nature, or walking away from Him. This built-in compass can be felt in our gut and in our chest. We feel good when we do good, even if no one else ever finds out about it.

In the same way, if we do "bad," we feel bad, even if no one knows what we did. God knows and He sends us that indicator to help us notice that now that He lives in us, only goodness will feel good inside of us. With this new compass, all struggles with the flesh and the ego will give us a kick in the gut, and even that gut check is for our own good, to wake us up, to put an alarm in us, that something isn't falling into line with the new creation God has made us to be.

Sometimes as we cultivate this fruit of light, as we work this **S**oul **O**pening **I**ndividualized **L**esson, we will have to let God do some pruning, not only of ourselves, but of our friendships, family dynamics, work life, and intimate partners. We need to shine a new light on all these relationships.

If we notice that we are surrounded by people who enjoy insulting and degrading others, gossiping about others, manipulating people, and finding joy doing so, if we notice excessive alcohol use, indecent conversations, and objectifying people for sexual pleasure, then it is time to ask God to prune these types of people from our life. We are each known by our fruit, and Jesus plainly gives us this advice.

A good tree can't produce bad fruit, and a bad tree can't produce good fruit. A tree is identified by the kind of fruit it produces....
(Luke 6:43-44, NLT)

A good person produces good deeds from a good heart, and an evil person produces evil deeds from an evil heart. Whatever is in your heart determines what you say
(Luke 6:45, NLT)

If this is the **S.O.I.L.** you find yourself in right now, be grateful for the pruning, even if it seems painful. The fruit of "friends" like that will not produce the life of goodness God has planned for you. Pruning produces more growth and more abundance as we move through this process. So don't worry, if you set your heart's compass to God—to goodness—you will never even want to look back at the rotten fruit and so-called "friends" He cleared from your path. Even still, it is always your choice to move toward Him or move toward the world. To move toward His goodness, which He pours over you, or move toward the brokenness this world offers. Ask yourself: How has it been working out so far? Be a light and get your "good" on as you put your God on!

The Soil of SELF-CONTROL… Self-control grows out of the **S.O.I.L.** of the pain and destruction of excess we have inflicted on ourselves. We see the damage we do to our soul, mind, and body when we run full speed into anything the flesh desires.

We find ourselves sick – physically sick, heart sick, spiritually sick, and we wonder, is this really how I'm built to feel, to look, to be loved and to love? HELL NO! Self-control is your way back to freedom.

It looks like restriction, but it is freedom. Freedom from getting your heart hurt, freedom from getting your body fat and slow, freedom from your spirit getting sick and stuck. It is one of the most beautiful and helpful fruits of the Spirit. It is a gift. See it as that.

I have struggled with self-control my whole life because my personality does not like to be restricted or confined or boxed in to conform to the world, which is an awesome trait when it comes to not being affected by peer pressure, but not so great when I tried to put restrictions on myself even if they were for my own good! I wanted freedom!

Freedom to roam, freedom to mingle, freedom to eat, to play, to talk, freedom to do anything I wanted, and I saw self-control as one more way of not letting me be ME! I could not have missed the mark more! I also knew there was not enough willpower in the world to rein me in. If I didn't "feel" like it, I wouldn't do it (diet, exercise, forgiveness, work, studying, praying, socializing... you name it). But God has never stopped lovingly pursuing me, and when He finally rubbed some **D.I.R.T.** on my perspective of what freedom really was and what my "feelings" were doing to my life, I woke up! "Oh my God," I thought, "I have been running headfirst into so many things, and it hurts! I don't want to do that anymore."

How did I not see that all the guidance God gives wasn't to box me in but to keep a lot of unnecessary pain out! Freedom without structure doesn't feel good. It feels like chaos and emptiness instead. I didn't have to experience all the things that I had experienced over and over and over again.... Well apparently, I did. I'm stubborn and a slow learner sometimes, but here I am with **D.I.R.T.** all over me, thanking God as I get out there and work my **S.O.I.L.** so that He can show me all the wonderful seeds He has planted in my life.

And as you discern what **S.O.I.L.** God has planted you in and how to best cultivate the fruit He wants to help you bring forth, I hope you will be as excited as I am to do this work with God as your Master Gardener and experience a deep sense of knowing that even the smallest effort will produce a massive change in your heart and the hearts of the people around you. Your inner soil will produce your outer world. You already have each of these gifts inside you from the moment you gave God a "Yes", so the question is only how much of these fruits are you yielding, are you cultivating? How much are you allowing yourself to flourish, and what areas have you neglected? This is the time to get real and get to work.

Dig deep! Your life depends on it!

Chapter 3
Watch Your W.A.V.E

Worldly - **A**ction - **V**arying – **E**nergy

The Disciples just sat there in awe.
"Who is this", they asked themselves.
"Even the wind and the WAVES obey him!"
(Matthew 8:27, NLT)

Did you know that God created us as a little tiny wave? When He breathed life into us, He sent a shock wave through us, an electrical impulse that started our heartbeat. Because He is our wave-maker, He instilled in us the power of creating our own little **W.A.V.E.** in the world, our **W**orldly **A**ction **V**aries **E**nergy. Just by our existence, we were created to have an effect. The first person to notice this power we have to affect the energy around us and send our little wave out into the world is our mother, and that usually comes in waves of nausea! Sorry Mom!

But it did demonstrate we already had a powerful ability to change the energy around us, even if we didn't know we were doing it yet. It was innate; it was a God-given power that our **W.A.V.E.** works, and that is proof of the power of God if I ever saw one.

As I was contemplating the idea of waves, I was not in the best headspace, and all I saw was the darkness of getting hit with waves of depression and as obstacles that seemed to keep stopping any progress in my life. I believed the waves were all outside of me, crashing into me, but God is so faithful to me and patient with me. He finally explained to me the true value and power of my **W.A.V.E.**. This was the message He shared with me:

*You are meant to be my precious **W.A.V.E.** in this world! When I breathed life into you, I started your unique wave, your worldly action varying energy all around you. Now, you keep asking me to stop the waves in your life, but I don't think you understand what you ask of me, my child. Have you ever seen an EKG of a heartbeat? Have you noticed that it looks like waves going across the screen? That is because you are watching your wave! Those lines you see are called your P-wave, QRS–wave, and T-wave. They are your sign waves of life, so if I were to "stop the waves" as you keep requesting of me, I could only do that if I end your life. Is that what you truly want?*

There is a natural rhythm to your life wave. If it becomes too fast or sporadic, it can wreak havoc on your entire life. Learning to calm your inner waves is vital, and I sent my Son to help you calm those storms. He can calm the waves inside you because without that anchor in Christ, in His peace and ability to maintain a gentle rocking rhythm versus a crashing and thrashing chaotic one, your life and body will quickly be destroyed.

Your physical heart is not built to sustain excessive waves over an extended amount of time; it will wear out, blow out, and stop working if it is kept in that state of stress. Your mind cannot handle excessive waves of worry, or it will make you sick.

Speaking of the brain, what do we call the electrical brain impulses when monitored? Brain waves! And if I stop the waves of your mind, and all you see is a peaceful flat line, you are now brain dead, and a peaceful flat surface on an EKG of your heart means you are Dead-Dead! Even science can see what I am up to, even if they attribute it to an " intrinsic ability of the body". When you see the words "intrinsic ability", that's ME; I Am intrinsic in you! So, you see, I didn't come to stop the waves in your life; I came to help you, either calm them to a rhythm that will allow peace and joy to flow or give you the energy and flow you will need to keep you moving toward my purpose and plan for your life. No pulse means no purpose, and no purpose means no pursuit of my plan. You have to learn to ride the wave to get where you are trying to go, to your destiny, to my vision for your future.

Everyone has a purpose, a precious gift, and an original way in this world. I made each of you able to make a difference and be a wave of light to the world! Each person's wave is unique and has its natural rhythm, but where you go wrong is by looking around at other people's rhythm, other people's "drumbeat", and thinking it is better than yours, but it is not! It is not better, and it is not worse. It is just theirs. So, first acknowledge and embrace that you were:

...fearfully and wonderfully made...
(Psalm 139:14, NIV)

and even the very hairs of your head are all numbered so don't be afraid (and don't compare!) you are more valuable to Me than anything else in the world.
(Luke 2:7, modified)

Embrace and come to understand your inner waves: your brain waves, your heart waves, your emotional waves, and the spiritual wave of power that comes with your openness to the Holy Spirit in your life.

How do I do that, you may ask? By spending time alone with me! Spending time alone is the only way to determine your natural waves and unique rhythms.

If you are too scared to get quiet, unplug, unwind, sit down, and listen to yourself, to the waves of silence, you will have a very difficult time hearing Me! A whisper is hard to hear over the crashing waves; it is impossible. The sound of waves relentlessly crashing is deafening. One has to yell just to be heard over them. I don't yell often, I whisper through the waves, I speak in the spaces of silence, and so my space to be heard is decided by you. Do you make space for me to hear me when I speak? Do you invite me into the waves with you? Do you hear me in the storm or does a part of you want the storm so you can have one more thing to point to and say, "See, it's not my fault; it's out there, out of my control."

*The storm, or the **W.A.V.E.** you see on the outside of you, often mirrors the waves you are creating on the inside of you. The **W**orldly **A**ctions **V**arying **E**nergy comes from you and then out to the world. These waves you create then they crash into the physical and smack right back into your face, and you never realize that you are now the wavemaker in your world. Have you ever been to a wave pool at a theme park, where the waves are set in time intervals, and there is a switch that turns the waves on and off? You are that switch! You are the wave-maker in your life, and your **W.A.V.E.** affects the world. The ripple effect is real, so watch your **W.A.V.E.**, your personal **W**orldly **A**ctions **V**arying **E**nergy! What you put out to the world matters, and how you wave at the world affects how the world waves back at you.*

When you walk into a room, your wave of energy comes rushing over people. What actions are you taking in the world, with others, and with Me? What intensity do you bring? Are you a gently rolling wave so calming that people can breathe a sigh of relief and rest in your presence?

*Do they feel lulled and held in your rhythm of a gentle, loving wave that silences all worries and relaxes the whole body? Do you offer an energy that is an uplifting **W.A.V.E.**? One that raises everyone around you.*

As your tide rises, do the people around you seem to rise up too? As your light shines out over the waters of life, do others seem excited to voyage with you on this shared adventure? Do they want to be an explorer with you, enjoying the winds of excitement at your backs and the exhilaration sweeping across your faces?

*Is that the **W.A.V.E.** you bring, or is it a crashing, thrashing, frantic wave? Does it tear apart everything it touches, a destructive energy that seems to affect others in a threatening or drowning way? Hitting hard as it comes in contact with life and others who find themselves out on the ocean with you. Do people seem to steer their ship away from you when they see you coming like they would if they saw a storm brewing on the horizon? Every good sailor knows if a storm is brewing, you either steer in the opposite direction it is heading or you get out of the open water altogether, find a safe harbor, batten down the hatches, and pray as you wait for the storm to pass, that you and your ship will ride it out in one piece.*

*Are you a **W.A.V.E.** of darkness and thunder? Who is the captain of your ship? Who and what is the anchor in your life? In Scripture, there is a story about Jesus being asleep as the waves pounded and crashed all around the boat He was in. Asleep! He actually found peace in the storm. He WAS the peace in the storm. In another story, He is found playing in the waves that the storm threw at Him.*

He was the original Wave Walker! Is He yours? Yes, the waves were real, and Jesus experienced them; He saw them and felt them but held on to a deeper truth about their ability to have a lasting effect on him.

*Our **W.A.V.E.**, our **W**orldly **A**ctions **V**arying **E**nergy around us, is so powerful that even Jesus wasn't totally immune to our power to connect and affect each other. In John 11:35, it said, "Jesus wept" while mourning the death of his friend, Lazarus. If there is ever an emotion that displays how the world and others can affect us and vary our energy, it is weeping.*

Waves of grief, too much to contain within us, demand to be physically expressed and we weep, often in what looks like waves crashing over us.

Weeping is a body wave of sorrow and a sense of loss due to something that has affected our energy so drastically, and Jesus wept; even Jesus was affected by the waves of the world and by the people in the world. He was affected, and He did experience the variation of emotional energy. Yet, He never lost or forgot what power He had to be able to change the energy around Him. After He experienced their energy in Him, He demonstrated His ability to change the direction of the waves flooding through all the people surrounding Him, grieving the loss of their friend.

He experienced the wave of sorrow that came with the death of his friend, Lazarus, but He never forgot He was the W.A.V.E. of Life and with three words,

Lazarus, come out!
(John 11:43, NLT)

All the waves that had ceased in Lazarus' body began again! The wave of Life washed over Lazarus, all because of the powerful life-giving energy that Jesus held inside of Himself.

*Jesus used His **W.A.V.E.** on thousands of people. He adjusted the waves of life for people, whether He restored their life force completely or gave them access to waves that had been missing for years, decades, and even lifetimes. Sound waves were given to the deaf for them to hear. Light waves gifted back to the blind for them to see. Electrical impulses restored in the legs of a man who had not walked in 38 years. Waves of joy given to grieving mothers and fathers. Waves of peace given to demon possessed souls. Jesus demonstrated over and over that His **Worldly Actions Vary the Energy** around Him and in undeniably powerful ways. He used his powers for the good of all, and He told the world that we all have this **W.A.V.E.** of power living in us because of the goodness of God and the gift of the Holy Spirit. Jesus told his disciples:*

The truth is, anyone who believes in me will do the same works I have done, and even greater works because I am going to be with the Father. You can ask for anything in my name, and I will do it, because the work of the Son brings glory to the Father.
(John 14:12-13, NLT)

*He told the disciples they could use their **W.A.V.E.** just like He used His, and They did! That power, that breath of life that lived and moved in them, lives, and moves in all of you right now!*

*You are all given the **W.A.V.E.** of life. You are all responsible for how your Worldly Actions Vary the Energy around you and in you. You are all known by your fruit, by the energy you produce and create all around you. Do you use your power for good?*

Do you create waves of love and hope, peace, and light? Do you wash people in waves of gentleness and warmth, or are you a storm brewing? Are you a wave of anger and bitterness, of blame and broken hearts, of franticness and fury?

Do people want to swim in your ocean, or do they adjust their route, find a safe harbor, and pray you pass by without causing too much damage to the waters of their world?

I pondered all this, taking a long hard look at what kind of **W.A.V.E.** I was putting myself out into the world and how I was allowing others to determine the rhythm of my wave. I thought about how often I behaved as if I had no power to control it.

I was torn in how I saw myself and my affect on others. At times, I was a wave of comfort and joy, peace, and gentleness, but at other times, I was sending out waves of blame and bitterness while still believing it wasn't my fault because this was simply the affect others were having on me. God continued to speak with me and share how much He wanted to help me with my life waves. This was the second half of my life lesson about the wonder in the **W.A.V.E..**

Now that you understand that, Yes, people do affect you, and that I made you that way, and Yes, your actions and energy affect others. It is also vitally important to recognize the many different perspectives one can have when viewing the waves in ourselves and in others. I offered my Son, The Holy Spirit, and Myself as shoulders to sit on to help you when the waves of life seem too much and too high, when you feel you are getting rolled under by the waves. When you can't get your footing, you can't swim against the tide or when you feel you don't have the strength to remain standing in the storm, in the waves. We want you to remember that you can always look up, with your arms raised high above your head, like every child instinctively does when he or she wants to be held, and cry out, "Abba, Abba, Papa, Papa! Up! Up! Pick me up! Put me on your shoulders! Hold me, keep me safe. I need you."

Jesus had this exact conversation in the Garden of Gethsemane as shown in the gospels of Matthew, Mark, and Luke. You can see that Jesus was getting pounded by waves of grief and telling his closest friends,

My soul is crushed with grief to the point of death. Stay here and keep watch with me
(Mark 14:34, NLT)

He confided in his friends, looking for a safe harbor, but he knew what he needed at that moment, and he called out to his dad, saying Abba,

Papa, Father, you can—can't you?— get me out of this. Take this cup away from me. But please, not what I want— what do you want?
(Mark 14:36, MSG)

He was saying, "Up, Papa, Up! Pick me up and put me on your shoulders; either get me out of this wave crashing over me or show me what you see and what you want. Lift me up H.I.G.H.," because Holy Insight Gives Hope, and then Jesus could face what he needed with greater resolve and confidence.

But there is another important and lifechanging perspective, that only in the Gospel of Luke does it mention how when Jesus cried out , Abba!...

At once an angel from heaven was at his side, strengthening him.
(Luke 22:43, MSG)

At once, as in immediately! And immediately when you cry, We will come swoop you up into our arms and rest you high upon our shoulders. The Father, the Son, and the Holy Spirit will carry you. We will walk through the storm with you, and you will not be afraid, for you are held, you are safe.

You now look at the waves of life from a higher perspective and think, "They aren't even that high; Jeez, I don't know what I was so worried about!" It is such a different perspective high up on your Father's shoulders.

Ask to be put **H.I.G.H.** upon God's shoulders because **H**is **I**nsight **G**ives **H**ope. Things that looked scary.... now look fun.

Waves that seemed over-powering, now seem minor, and a sense of excitement and bravery can come over us as we find ourselves saying, "Papa, go farther, go deeper!" On your Father's shoulders, waves are not problems but playthings! On your Father's shoulders, your energy changes, and you take His energy on as your own. This is the promise Jesus came to give us. He said you can't do this life alone; it will roll you to the bottom of the ocean, destroy you, drown you, and anything you grasp at to help save you will only provide a fleeting hope that sinks below the surface just as quickly as it rose. But He promises if you climb up on His shoulders, you will be changed forever, and all of the life energy, love, and strength the Father placed in Him, you can now stand strong in too. His strength is your strength, His love is your love, and His life was poured out for you. Climb up. That's why He came. His perspective will be your perspective. If you ask to see your wave of life the way God does, He will show you.

If you need Wisdom- If you want to know what God wants you to do – Ask Him, and he will gladly tell you. He will not resent your asking
(James 1:5, NLT)

Ask for wisdom in the waves. Be wise in your worldly actions that vary the energy around you. You are more powerful than you think. Ask for God's guidance to teach you to become a wave-walker in your ocean of life. Grab onto Jesus' hand and ask Him to show you how He was able to connect in every way to the energy all around Him. He could sense and feel everything: every thought wave, sound wave, emotional wave, and even the literal waves on the sea that rose all around Him.

In all that, He was never tossed off course by them; He embraced them, calmed them, and sent His power out into the world to affect them in the way that was right, pure, and good. He controlled his lifegiving **W.A.V.E.**, and everyone who calls upon His name and climbs up on His shoulders will have life abundantly. So, give thanks for the **W.A.V.E.** that lives in you, and give thanks for the Wave-Maker because, without His **W.A.V.E.**, there is no way forward.

Chapter 4

When the F.A.S.T. Feels Slow

Forsake – **A**nything – **S**topping-**T**ransformation

But when you FAST, comb your hair and wash your face. Then no one will suspect you are fasting except your Father, who knows what you do in secret. And your Father, who knows all secrets, will reward you.
(Matthew 6:17, NLT)

You were born to fly; did you know that? Flying so free; free in the body, free in the mind, and free in the spirit more than anything! I gave you the spiritual practice of the **F.A.S.T.** *to help you get there…. Faster.*

*Why then, does the **F.A.S.T.** seem so slow? Why does transformation seem so sluggish, or like you keep stopping and starting, getting some great momentum and then WHAM, you hit a wall?*

This happens because you keeping grabbing at things that you are not meant to hold onto. Like tall telephone poles you are flying by and then all of a sudden you grab onto it and just stay there, holding on tight, stuck now in this one spot, refusing to let go and keep flying toward me, toward your life and your purpose that I am calling you in to. You keep flying from pole to pole, clinging to it for comfort and stability, yet finding none.

*The **P.O.L.E.** will be different things for different people, but they are all a **P**lace **O**ne's **L**eft **E**stranged from me! It could be a place that you really love, but it was only meant to be for a season and yet you still hold on to it. It could be something you hate but have now become obsessed with, festering on it, gripping it in your mind and heart, draining the joy out of your life, but you won't it let go. It could be a **P.O.L.E.** of fear, something you imagine in your future that scares you, so you grabbed onto it, and now are stuck in your fear trying to figure it out on your own. You have chosen to get stuck on a **P.O.L.E.**, a place one's left estranged from me, because you chose to believe the lie that my power and grace are not enough to get you through it.*

*Some of you have completely forgotten about Me, and you find yourself seeking out any **P.O.L.E.** of comfort you can find, whether it was grasping at food, a person, alcohol, drugs, a job you don't even like but at least it is familiar and you know what to expect, or even a relationship that is chaotic but you think is what you deserve. Whatever your **P.O.L.E** is, as long as you are gripping on to it and its false sense of security instead of fastening yourself to Me, you will never be free and truly alive until you let go and Fly!*

*Your hands have to be free to fly. Your heart has to be free to fly and a **F.A.S.T.** is a tool that can get you there.*

***F**orsake **A**nything **S**topping **T**ransformation towards Me. You are always, and in all ways, transforming into something, as all living things are, but what you are transforming into is what matters most.*

*When you fly, you are feeling my highest power coming through you, you are experiencing my **H.I.G.H.**, my **H**oly **I**nsight **G**ives **H**ope, so stay high with Me! Keep flying, keep fasting.*

*When you are stuck on whatever **P.O.L.E.** of this world you have perched yourself on, and you are holding on so tight that you can't focus on anything else, you are now transforming into whatever is in your hands and whatever your heart is now focused on. You are becoming one with that **P.O.L.E.**, that **P**lace **O**ne's **L**eft **E**mpty.*

*What pole are you stuck on? Is it a pole of bitterness, anger, resentment, blame? Are you holding onto sorrow, self-pity, helplessness, or self-doubt? Are you gripped by worldly obsessions for attention whether good or bad, jealousy, greed, lust, pride, or hate? A victim mentality of any kind is a surefire sign you have wrapped yourself around a **P.O.L.E.** in life and are feeling the effects of being in a **P**lace **O**ne's **L**eft **E**stranged from me. You are feeling the toxicity of transforming deeper into that place you have clung to. You will begin to produce the fruit of the place you have planted yourself in.*

A tree is identified by the kind of fruit it produces. A good person produces good deeds from a good heart, and an evil person produces evil deeds from an evil heart. Whatever is in your heart determines what you say
(Luke 6: 44-45).

*What are you feeding yourself? What are you gripping to? What you are feeding your mind is what you will be feeling in your heart and living in your actions. What you keep believing, you will keep becoming. What is your mind and heart set on the most? What **P.O.L.E.** or thought, what goal, what belief do you notice yourself saying over and over.*

*If it's not uplifting, inspiring, or a blessing, let it go. If it's not faith filled, joyful, peace filled, hopeful, loving, patient, kind, self-controlled, or good, it's a **P.O.L.E.**! It's a **P**lace **O**ne's **L**eft **E**mpty, a place one's left estranged from my presence.*

*And as every good earthly father tries to do for his earthly daughter, I am trying to do for all my children: KEEP YOU OFF THE **P.O.L.E.**! You don't belong there, you don't need to stay there, and you are definitely not becoming what you were meant for by hanging onto your **P.O.L.E.**, so Let Go.*

*Let go and keep flying, open your hands, stretch them forward and be free to receive my goodness lifting you to greater and greater heights. Come and see everything I have for you. See a new perspective and receive your full inheritance. You are royalty, but you keep behaving like you are a peasant in your Father's house. Clinging to some earthly thing as if that could ever be your savoir, your comforter, your sustainer, or at the very least, hoping it will be something that you can use as a numbing distraction so you don't have to admit that you are choosing this **P.O.L.E.** you now cling to. You are choosing your empty place.*

Fasting is used in Scripture on many occasions and you will notice that when Jesus gave advice on fasting, He said "When you fast" (Matthew 6:16), not "if you fast". He spoke as if fasting would already be in your life, like it was a given, as much as prayer and praise, breaking bread with friends, and helping others would be in your life. As all those things can benefit you greatly, so too will you benefit from fasting in your life.

This is a gift to help you check in with yourself regularly to see if you have gotten hung-up on anything while trying to fly through this thing called life.

*During this period of time in the world, it seems that a majority of people are clinging to food more than ever as their source of comfort, and a **F.A.S.T.** can help your mind to understand and to retrain your brain to understand that your Spirt must lead and not the body.*

Food is not your comforter, it is not your daily life source either, I AM. Food has taken My place in many people's lives, The amount of time you spend thinking about it, talking about it, planning for it, waiting for the next chance to experience it, this is how you should be looking at ME. I am not to be replaced in your life by food.

You are filling your minds and your bodies with junk, with trash, and then you are shocked that your body and life reflect these choices back to you.

*Fasting frees your mind from its undying belief that you need food constantly, that you are a slave to it. You are not. When you **F.A.S.T.**, you will notice you feel stronger, lighter, your mind begins to calm down, your heart begins to be flooded with a quietness as healing begins when you finally let all the things you have been filling yourself with pass through you and cleanse you, so that you literally become an open channel with no "crap"(pardon the pun), clogging you up.*

You are a clear channel once again, with nothing blocking the energy of the Holy Spirit from coming through you and into the world. As this detoxing begins, the inflammation in your body, that happens due to the bloated food worship you have put into your life, will immediately reduce. You may feel like you are "starving" at first, but I tell you this, You are not experiencing "starvation," not even close, you are experiencing literal withdrawal symptoms from the toxins you have put into your body.

Your body has become addicted to the junk you give it, the sugar, the excess, the over-processed fake food that you have been feeding yourself. You are also going through the withdrawal from the addiction to the experience of eating, the ritual you have made it in your life.

Feel this feeling, embrace it, because this is exactly what your soul experiences when you don't feed it and care for it properly. The hunger pangs of a soul desperately wanting to be nourished and now only surviving instead of thriving as it was intended to do. Finding itself withering instead of flourishing.

Take this time to feed your soul, to take the bread of this world out of your hands and put the Bread of Life into them. Even Jesus spoke this truth as Satan tried to tempt Him during His own 40 day fast saying:

Man shall not live by bread alone, but by every word that comes from the mouth of God
(Matthew 4:4, NIV)

*When you **F.A.S.T.**, start your morning in prayer, set your intention to give up control of how the day will go, what your needs will be, and how I will provide.*

Open Scripture and a verse will speak to you, or research for yourself all the mighty souls in history who used the fast to get closer to Me, to hear from Me alone, and use them on as a mentor and a model.

Jesus is always the epitome of how to live this life and how to walk through a physical fast. There is much written on fasting and the miracles that happened because of the use of prayer and fasting. Select a verse that speaks to you, one that you will "feed" on all day, write it on a piece of paper, a notecard, a sticky note, write it on your hand if that's all you have, but keep it on you one way or another.

In your pocket, your wallet, your purse, your sock, somewhere that you can touch it all day and remember, "My strength comes from the Lord alone." At your usual time for breakfast, take out a large glass of water, bless the water with your intentions for the fast and ask, "Holy Spirit come and fill me today," and thank Him for all the strength you will be given. Read your scripture aloud over and over as you enjoy the water.

Do this at each meal of your day, and all through the day when you experience those feelings of withdrawal as your body detoxes itself. Read your scripture and remind yourself...

For the Lord has not given us a spirit of fear and timidity,
but of power, love, and self-control
(2nd Timothy 1:7, NLT)

You control your body, what goes in and what does not. It will give you an enormous sense of empowerment to be able to say, "I eat when I say so, and not when the flesh demands it!". Have your desires of the flesh, your appetite for things of this world, or your unsatiable cravings, led you toward the life you wanted?

*It's Okay, I already know the answer, because I made you and I created you so that you will never be satisfied by anything, any person, any food item, any amount of attention or fame, or money, or house size, or business network, or anything else of this world. I made you to only be truly satisfied by letting Me fill your soul. So let go and **F.A.S.T.***

The Lord quieted and this thought came to my mind. Did you know that the word "forsake" and the word "forgive" both mean "to set free, to let go, to loosen, and to give completely." I was doing research to fully understand these words, their origin, and meanings, how they came to be.

I realized that while I thought that forsake was the word to focus on, the Spirit spoke through a friend and pointed out that oftentimes forgiveness is the key to getting down off a **P.O.L.E.** we have found ourselves wrapped around that **P**lace **O**ne's **L**eft **E**mpty and estranged from God, from ourselves, and from others. As I continued to look up different ways they were used and formed from Latin, Greek, German, and old English, God began to speak again:

You get where I am going with this, you see the pattern, forsaking and forgiving are for YOU, not the other person. It is a gift that another person could receive as well, but forgiveness and forsaking is my way to help you free your hands from the death grip you had on something or someone that was squeezing the life force out of you because you have refused to forgive and let go. Free your hands, they were meant for faith and flying, not for festering, fearing, fighting, and floundering.

*I promise you the view and life I have to give you is a million times better than the view from whatever **P.O.L.E.** you have perched yourself on.*

*Fasting, biblically speaking, is often used when referring to the physical act of abstaining from food all together, or from abstaining from certain foods as Daniel chose to do when he was taken captive. However, I want to talk to you about other types of fasting, types that will help you climb off a **P.O.L.E.** you might not even realize you are actually stuck to right now. A **P.O.L.E.** that is keeping you from stepping fully into your freedom and your purpose in life.*

Look at your day, where you spend your money and your time is what you value most in life. Where do I end up on the list? How fulfilled does your life feel at the end of each day? Were you busy? Were you blessed? Were you running from distraction to distraction or were you running to Me? Did we sit together, talk together, sing together, drive together, go walking together, help someone together, did you seek Me first in all you did?

Did your kids see my face and my heart because of your relationship with Me? Did you introduce Me to your friends? Did you hear My words, feel My touch, and know that I was with you all day? Or was I an afterthought, a checklist, a five-minute "email" type of prayer, where you sent me your "honey do/ God-do" list that you knew I could handle, so you wrote it out, hit send, and then went back to your "real" life.

Did you pick back up all the worries you just sent to Me? Did you leave Me in your bed, or chair, car, or couch, or wherever you think is the place we meet, promising to return tomorrow for our "prayer time" where you will probably drop off another list? Instead of a list, why not come to Me, just lose the list, and listen.

How well you listen to Me, will also indicate how well you are able to listen to others. Are you self-focused or serving focused? Do you check in more with your phone than you do with Me? Are you obsessed with seeing the light from your screen more than you are seeing the light in the eyes of the saints sitting around you?
What is your default state? Are you looking up at others, at Me, or are you looking down? Where your eyes focus, so too the will heart follow, so please look up.

I have so much to share with you. So much joy and hope and love for you. So much praise and pride to gush about when I think of you. You are My child, My beloved, My masterpiece. I sent My son to give up his life, so I could bless and be close to you in yours. And by the way, I don't stay in your chair, your bed, your prayer closet, or wherever you think you left Me last. I come with you whether you speak to Me again that day or not. I'm there, hoping we will speak again, hoping today you will **F.A.S.T.,** *you will Forsake Anything Stopping Transformation from the life of this world to the life I have for you. Hoping to transform you from broken flesh and a tattered heart to a life of freedom, faith, and the ability to fly.*

*Where does your mind wander most? Is it pure, good, hopeful, and just? If it is not – **F.A.S.T.** .. and do it fast! **F.A.S.T.** from complaining and poisonous thinking. Did you know you are actually capable of not needing to find what is wrong with everything, or at least you are capable, yes, physically capable, of not saying it out loud, and of not continuing to think about it? You are to:*

....Take every thought captive to make it obedient to Christ
(2 Corinthians 10:5, NIV)

*   **F.A.S.T.** from looking at social media, which is just a foothold for comparison and offers a space for either pride or resentment, false righteousness, or shame to set in. It is a minefield just waiting to blow up your sense of self and your spirit. What are you looking for as you mindlessly scroll other people's filtered pictures of the filtered life they are presenting. Are you looking to connect?... Really? If you really want to connect....Call them.*

*   Saying you "like" something or making a "comment" about another's life moment, which has already passed as soon as the picture was taken, is not connecting, it is conning you into thinking you made an effort to connect with someone. For a genuine meaningful human connection, you must join them in their present moment. You must bring your presence into their present. Join them in their life, don't spectate and comment from afar. People don't need judges, fans, or followers, they need friends.*

*   You all need real connections. You need "mat" friends! Scripture tells a story about some true "MAT" friends, who took their paralyzed friend on his mat to see Jesus, and they wouldn't stop until they did. These four friends climbed up onto the roof of the house Jesus was teaching at, ripped off tile and tore a hole big enough to lower their friend (still lying on his mat) to the feet of Jesus! These are some literal "Raise- The – Roof" type of friends!*

They didn't send comments, or post notes of well wishes on their friend's door, no they got their face to his place, gathered him up onto his mat and walked him—well, carried him—through his present situation, united in their journey toward healing and toward Christ.

Can you say the same? Are you a "mat" friend, or a "scroll and go" friend? Do people know you are really there for them, or just that you find them interesting enough to comment on and watch time to time from afar? This is not how I designed you to thrive and connect.

Paul warned his faithful family everywhere to never forsake the gathering of souls together under one roof for the purpose of connection and community.

No wonder so many of you are more depressed and isolated, anxious, and restless than ever. You are actively participating in your own demise, your own captivity. You feel like all eyes are on you, and like no one really knows or notices you, all at the same time. Access to the world, but alone in your soul. Crushed in spirit, isolated instead of inspired. Clinging to the **P.O.L.E.** *of social media, looking for direction from the lost.* **F.A.S.T.** *for a month and focus instead on building true "mat" friends who show up for you when you are no longer putting on a show. See who is there for you, who will follow you, when you are no longer seeking "followers":*

Seek first the kingdom, and all will be added
(Matthew 6:33)

Give your entire attention to what God is doing right now,
and don't get worked up about what may or may not
happen tomorrow, God will help you deal with whatever
hard things come up when the time comes.
(Matthew 6:34, MSG)

I know what you need, what your heart desires, and I promise every good thing I have for you will be given to you only in the present moment.

My presence can only be felt in the present, so stop looking, posting, searching, scrolling through other people's past moments, put your phone down and Look up Child! Join Me in a life lived in the present.

To the parents of My little creations, keep your children's eyes, hearts, and minds away from such garbage. Social media is destroying them and their ability to fully and genuinely connect with one another as I created them to be able to do. It is teaching them to glorify themselves, having followers and fans. Self-worship is running rampant, as seen in this odd compulsion to take selfies.

They are now compulsively taking pictures of themselves for no reason, with no one else even in the pictures, just obsessed with themselves and the façade they are trying to create, and yet what are you seeing in your youth now? A huge rise in suicide, rise in disorders and diseases, rise in drug use, rise in sexual activity at younger and younger ages.

If you do not decide what they are and are not allowed to put in front of their faces, the world will happily show them everything they never wanted to see and can never unsee again. Social media is far more destructive to the forming of their identity and psyche than you seem to realize.

Get their eyes off screens and onto smiles, into their senses, and filled up in their spirit. Help them focus on serving with J.O.Y., for Jesus, Others, and Yourself.

Your brain is not made to look at screens, it has the same effect as sedatives do on it, that's why your children look "zombied-out" when you set them in front of a screen, or hand them your phone, they are hypnotized, they are debilitated.

You have altered their brain and it has similar physical effects on their brain as literally drugging your child. How often would you hand your child your screen, phone, tablet, or TV, if you also had to make them swallow a pill at the same time so you could see what you are doing to them? Just because it is common does not mean it is healthy or good for them in any way.

Stop sedating your children, prioritize them. If I blessed you with them, be present for them. Don't drug them because it is easier for you. If every time you handed them a screen, you could see their eyes start to smoke, how often would you do it? If you could see their brain deteriorating, how okay would you be with that?...You wouldn't!

Just because you can't see it, doesn't mean it is not happening, and honestly, you can see it. You can see their attention span change and their mood destabilize when you try to take the screen away from them. Their reaction looks like that of an addict who has been cut off, but you keep supplying them day in and day out. Please, stop and think if what you are doing is best for them, or convenient for you.

Yes, there is a place for technology, just like there is a place for a screwdriver or a ladder. It should be a tool, not an idol. It is meant to be useful, for work, or school, or answering a quick question, helping find your way from place to place, but that is how you are teaching your kids to view the screens in their life. Or is it now their idol, what they worship, what they sit in "awe" in front of for hours at a time. Do they know more about video games and how to make videos of themselves then they do about My Word, My ways, My purpose in their life?

Do they spend more time swiping and scrolling or more time serving? Is it helping them learn to fly, learn to seek Me, is it helping them transform into the person I am calling them to be, a light to the world, a servant to all, a friend to the many? Is it helping them to cultivate the gifts I've planted in them, or have you stuck them up on a **P.O.L.E.***, gave them a screen, and said "Hold this, it will help"?* **F.A.S.T.***!*

F*orsake* **A***nything* **S***topping* **T***ransformation, theirs, and yours. Help them transform from a zombie state to a state of joy with a zest for life and a passion for interacting with others.*

F.A.S.T. *from criticizing yourself and others. Criticizing never helps a situation or a relationship. It usually has the opposite effect than one was hoping for. It cements in the behavior that you don't want and the other person or even you are filled with the feeling of being attacked or shamed. Forgive yourself, forgive the other person, let go.*

Stop holding on so tightly to the criticism. Free your hands and your heart so you can see that behind the criticism is a longing in your heart for something better, what is it? Focus on that.

Criticism is stopping transformation dead in its tracks, it is you digging your heels in about something, wrapping your arms around some **P.O.L.E.** *and not budging until you get what you want and it usually does not work, and does not bring out the best in the relationship. It just leaves you stuck, perched up on your* **P.O.L.E.***, repeating the same complaint over and over and over again, and even if the person finally submits to your constant bashing, you will have torn at the sacred fiber of your relationship, and ripped a hole in the other persons heart and in their trust that they are truly safe around you.*

Criticism is an attack on a person's character or their abilities, and no one wants to be around such a person. Even if what you are saying has merit, you are not their maker, and you don't know their purpose, so you have no idea what is best for them, and how I might be using that very thing in their life to fulfill a greater purpose later. No one feels loved, safe, valued, or understood in an environment filled with criticism.

Having a complaint or having a longing for change is healthy and normal and good to share with loved ones, but you can share a complaint about a specific action, event, or misunderstanding, without attacking the other person's dignity and divinity as My child. You are all here to help each other grow, and transform into your new Christ-like nature, attacking doesn't help anyone attain that goal.

*So **F.A.S.T.** from it. Don't be the cause of any **P.O.L.E.**-clinging in your loved one's lives. Don't be the thing they will need to forsake because you are hindering their ability to transform into the masterpiece I have called them to be. Either fly with them or leave them be, because you all need to be free to fly with Me.*

*I implore each of you to add spiritual fasting to your life. The dedication to **F**orsake **A**nything **S**topping **T**ransformation. Transformation from death to life. Transformation from worship of the flesh to worship of the spirit. From sorrow to joy, from emptiness to fulfillment, from negative words, patterns, and preferences to those of love, light, goodness, faithfulness, gentleness, hope, peace, patience, kindness, and self-control. Transform from stagnant and stuck to vibrant and alive. Transform from bitterness and blame to faith and freedom. Transform from fear of failure to fearless flying. Fasting will help you turn your seeds into flourishing gardens, but you must release the death grip you have on your old ways of doing things for new life to grow and grow abundantly*

F.A.S.T. *from words that hurt, from people who bring you down, or tempt you toward things not of God. Forsake those who draw you toward lewdness, drunkenness, gossip, cruelty, manipulation, deceptiveness, a spirit of lust, or a spirit of division. Forsake those who worship themselves, who use others for their own purposes and pleasure. Forsake those who speak about others or look at others as disposable pornographic objects in any manner.*

Every person you see holds divinity inside them; respect it, honor it, do not cheapen or degrade what I have made. Each person is made in the image and likeness of God, even if they have forgotten and are not honoring themselves, this does not give you permission to dishonor them as well.

You are called to remind them who they are, and how much I love them. **F.A.S.T.** *from division and arguments or competitive spirits that pit brother against brother and sister against sister, setting up a stage where someone wins and someone must lose. This is not how My Kingdom is set up.*

It is set in a collaborative spirit, a win-win setting. Where one rises, all rise together. Join with each other, encourage each other, praise each other and don't be a stumbling block in another's life.

Fast from toxic TV, from the news of this world, a constant stream of fear blaring into your ears and searing your eyes with things you can't unsee. You do not need to know everything, you need to know Me. Do you know more about what is going on in the world than what is going on in My Word?

Where your time is spent tells you where your heart lies. Don't lay on thorns when my way leads you to green pastures and peaceful streams. It is not an act of intelligence to fill yourself with constant knowledge of the working of this broken world, you are in this world but not of this world and Jesus told you:

I have given them your word. And the world hates them because they do not belong to the world, just as I do not. (John 17:14, NLT)

They are not part of this world any more than I am. Make them pure and holy by teaching them your word of truth (John 17: 16-17, NLT)

He said to learn and be obsessed with—be laser focused on—The Word, not the world! **F.A.S.T.** *and focus! What you focus on you follow, what you follow foretells your future. Who or what do you follow? Which channel are you watching? The channel you watch most is the type of channel you will become.*

Be a channel for Me to use, not the world. Who or what do you follow? Who or what is flowing through your mind, your heart, your spirit, your body? Follow the flow and **F.A.S.T.** *from anything that is not flowing in My direction.*

F.A.S.T. *from crutches you use in your life, from alcohol, drugs, food, TV, phones, computers, video games, pornography, sex, news, social media; anything that you turn to when you feel uncomfortable, unsettled, alone, bored, angry, overwhelmed, or fearful. Anything you turn to so that you will "feel better" for a moment, give it to me. Let me transform it. Give yourself the gift of seeing that none of it can control you anymore now that you have fixed your eyes on me.*

*You might not even realize it has a hold on you until you try to give it up, and let it go. The **F.A.S.T.** can feel slow because often times you don't want to let go. A part of you likes the back door to stay open and an escape route to be readily available. Close the door on your past and fly with Me into your future. You can't look back and move forward at the same time.*

Trust and take that first step away from those "creature comforts" you have been worshiping that have led you nowhere, and will continue to lead you nowhere, at least, nowhere you are hoping to go that will bring the change you are seeking:

This is the way; walk in it!
(Isaiah 30:21, NIV)

Find out what is holding you back, see if you can easily stop using or doing each of those things for at least seven days. If you can't, look closer at why and when you are using these crutches.

*Let that be a giant red flag that there is a **P.O.L.E.** in your life that you are clinging to that is stopping your ability to fly. Get professional help if need be, talk to family members, friends, find a group that is clinging to that same **P.O.L.E.**, talk to people of faith. Gather with others who are working on that specific **F.A.S.T.** too.*

And in all things, pray for My power, the power of the Holy Spirit to cover you and strengthen you during this precious process.

Don't worry, not all things you enjoy will you have to give up forever. You physically cannot fast from nourishment forever, you will die.

*And you don't have to fast forever from making love with your spouse, or enjoying a movie on the big screen, having a drink with friends if it is not an addiction for you, but if the thought of giving it up for a week to 21 days is causing deep anxiety, then you need to **F.A.S.T.** all the more. If there is anything you simply cannot **F.A.S.T.** from doing, then you have placed it above God, and have chosen to cling to it as your life source and life force. Your worship is off, and therefore your world is, no doubt, off as well.*

You have put your faith in the futile and the fleeting nature of this world and it will drag you down and leave you as empty and futile as it is, ashes to ashes and dust to dust. If you keep going back to "it," whatever "IT" is for you, then it is NOT WORKING, it cannot fill you, sustain you, lead you.

It is not a life-giving path, a healthy way to live, That's My Job, that's My gift to you, that is why I gave you My son, and why He plainly told you:

I am the way, the truth, and the Life. No one can come to the father except through me.
(John 14:6, NLT)

*Not the bottle, not the pills, not the food, not the screens, not a person, not the news, not the money, not the power, not the platform, not the job, none of it are the way to do life well, to live with a spirit filled with freedom and peace. I AM the way, so **F.A.S.T.**, **F**orsake **A**nything **S**topping **T**ransformation from the clutches of this world and into the place I have prepared for you. From the spirit of the flesh to the spirit of God. You are the Imago Dei, the Image of God! Lean on My strength to guide you through. Be kind and patient with yourself for:*

… those who wait upon God get fresh strength. They spread their wings and soar like eagles. They run and don't get tired, they walk and don't lag behind
(Isaiah 40:31, MSG)

There is a song, On Eagle's Wings, which paints this picture so beautifully with the lyrics:

And He will raise you up on eagles' wings, Bear you on the breath of dawn, Make you to shine like the sun and hold you in the palm of His hand.

That is the life I want to offer you, the freedom I have to give, the strength I long to cover you in. I want to help you fly into a future with Me, a future where you will confidently and boldly experience and exclaim:

Surely goodness and mercy shall follow me all the days of my life: and I will dwell in the house of the Lord forever. (Psalms 23:6, KJV)

*Even in this scripture it is showing how I intend for you to be moving, flying with Me, because it says goodness and mercy will FOLLOW you—so fly, Let Go, **F.A.S.T.**, forsake anything trying to stop your forward movement, your holy transformation, your sanctification and join Me in your abundantly blessed future. It's waiting for you, so come—**F.A.S.T.***

Chapter 5
What Now? W.A.I.T.!

Worship – **A**lways – **I**n – **T**ransition

*But those who WAIT in the Lord will find new
strength. They will fly high on wings like eagles.
They will run and not grow weary.
They will walk and not faint
(Isaiah 40: 31, NLT)*

      Worship **A**lways **I**n **T**ransition... I think my
response to that explanation was, "Yeah, right," and it
was definitely the response I heard out of one of the
women in my church group when I told her what the word
W.A.I.T. meant. I had the toughest time with this
explanation when I first heard it. I guess because when
God speaks He is sending an energy and then I am trying
to filter that energy through my human mind and
translate that into English words.

So, when I got the word on **W.A.I.T.**, I saw it as worship ALWAYS in transition and I thought, How on earth am I supposed to do that? Am I supposed to just go around singing praise songs all day? (Which I love and do often.) Am I supposed to watch sermons of my favorite pastors on YouTube to keep me in worship mode all day, which I also love and do often. How is that going to work?

How am I supposed to make a living, create new friendships, go on new adventures? How am I supposed to make money to support myself if I am "worshiping always," unless I am the one writing the worship songs or giving the sermons, which I do hope to do one day, but for now, no one is paying me for those talents, and the majority of the population are not paid praise and worship song writers or speakers, so what about those people? How does this apply to them? I kept wrestling with the word, until God showed me what He was really trying to say, I had it half right, we should worship always, but the second translation was a bit more helpful. Worship All-WAYS in life, no matter where you are or what you are waiting for.....Worship.

Waiting sucks! Can I say that I think it sucks anyway? I understand that waiting, in and of itself, is a neutral activity. It is the time it takes to get from one place, one event, one dream, one maturation, or one season of life into another. It is a transition from one reality into another and that, in and of itself, just is. But waiting, often times, at least for me, is this sense of discontent. And as I was wallowing in my waiting, God explained to me what my problem was when He responded to me saying:

The feeling of waiting is you wanting to be somewhere else, of not trusting I am God and you are not. It's your pride creeping in when you think that where I have placed you is not where you were really meant to be, and that may be true to some extent, it might not be a place you were meant to stay forever, but it is no doubt the place you were meant to be, NOW.

If you could only worship while you wait for something I have called you to, instead of wallow while you wait, you would not only increase your joy but you would decrease your time spent in that state of discontent. The feeling of waiting is often accompanied by the feeling of discontent. Why is it always somewhere else that is better? The next job, the next relationship, the next town, the next trip. Why is the doing always seen as better than the becoming? The action better than the stillness, the praise music better than the tears? The working better than the waiting? Why is there this incessant need to go, go, go? How are you to give Me your undivided attention and really listen if you are facing every which way but ME! You are running from this place to that place, this device to that device, this dollar to that dollar, always waiting for the next best thing.

I realized as I reflected on His words, it is a very self-centered way I am looking at something. It is me saying to God, I want something, I don't have it, and I'm not going to be happy until I get it. I can still be such a two-year-old in my thinking sometimes, but God showed me what I should be doing while I wait for anything, and He explained that life, all of it, is a transition. The journey from birth to death and back to life with Him is the Holy Transition.

When I saw the word transition I thought it meant a particular life situation that I was going through such as, I don't have a job and I'm waiting to get one, I'm stuck in transition. I don't have a spouse and I want one, so I'm in transition from single to married, or I've lost someone or something that I deeply love and I am grief stricken waiting for joy to return, I am in transition.

And these are all true, they are a transition, but they are minor compared to the Great Transition, from Darkness to Light, from Sinner to Saint, from birth to death to rebirth, from being childish to being child-like in Christ. This is the main thing, this is the Great Transition, going from less of me to more of Him.

This takes time, it takes every day we are given on this earth and whether we want to surrender to it or not, waiting on God is our job

For since the world began, no ear has heard,
and no eye has seen a God like you,
who works for those who wait for him
(Isaiah 64:4, NLT)

The Lord began to speak to me once again and said,

I had a purpose and a plan for you long before you were ever conceived, and My plans and My time for them are nothing like you imagine because:

My thoughts are completely different from yours,... and my ways are far beyond anything you could imagine. For just as the heavens are higher than the earth, so are my ways higher than your ways and my thoughts higher than your thoughts
(Isaiah 55:8-9, NLT)

My perspective is so far above yours that as I watch all things working toward My vision and My purpose for your life and life itself, you feel like everything is falling apart. You are waiting, and the way you perceive waiting will affect your well-being in life. If you could experience waiting the way a pastry chef does, with this same eager confident expectation that the "waiting" is working. The cake will rise, the bread will bake, all the ingredients will come together to form something delicious if you will just wait for it! The chef knows that without the wait time, this would never be possible.

*It is in the **W.A.I.T.**, that the magic works. In those times where you have done all you were called to do, and now you are called to do nothing but let time and temperature take over and do their part, this is when the magic happens.*

The chef knows that if she put all the right ingredients in, and followed all the steps she knew she needed to, the waiting will bring forth the picture she was shown when she began.

It is the same for parents as they await the birth of their child. They know the wait is crucial and a very sacred time. While it may be uncomfortable and a bit anxiety provoking, it is mainly a time of excited expectancy and preparing for what is to come. The expectant parents know the time is needed for this baby to come to full term and be equipped with all the vital organs it needs to give it the best chance to survive outside of the mother's womb.

If the parents rushed this time or demanded the baby be taken out before it's time, they would be endangering their own child's chance at a healthy life. The wait works, it is the necessary ingredient in the making of you, and not just the first nine months.

*Your society does not know how to wait for anything anymore, if it can't be delivered over night, swiped left or right for, or delivered curbside, you are irritated. You've lost your appreciation for the **W.A.I.T**. If you have to wait for it, you seem to lose your want for it. Good things really do come to those who wait. Ask for My help on changing your perspective in the waiting seasons. If I spoke it to you, if I showed you a snapshot of the final vision, that does not mean tomorrow it will be there like a Christmas present under the tree. I'm not Santa, I'm God, and just as I have promised before, I will say to you again:*

But these things I plan won't happen right away. Slowly, steadily, surely, the time approaches when the vision will be fulfilled. If it seems slow, WAIT patiently, for it will surely take place. It will not be delayed
(Habakkuk 2:2-3, NLT)

I am the Creator, the Almighty, the Giver of all Life, The Beginning, and the End. I am the whole process!

*Yet, you seem to only want the beginning and then the end, but your life is in the **W.A.I.T.**. Your life is lived in the transition. The time between the beginning of your existence to the time You come back home to Me. My love is shown over and over in the transition, in the waiting. All the fruits of the spirit, all the living, loving, laughing, learning, all are happening in the "Wait."*

If you could keep a disposition of expectation, that all that is promised to you will be done, instead of holding onto this constant fear that I am not who I say I am, that I cannot do what I told you I would do, that I am not a good God who wants good things for you. If you could release those fears and grab your faith, you would enjoy this life so much more! If you do this, you will experience God's peace, which is far more wonderful than the human mind can understand.

... Peace will guard your hearts and
minds as you live in Christ Jesus
(Philippians 4:7, NLT)

When you can keep the main thing the main thing, then all those other earthly experiences are just opportunities to see if you are moving toward Christ and the gifts of the Spirit that are planted in you or if you are transitioning away from Me instead. If someone watched your day, where and how you spend your time, what would they say you worship if they were asked?

Would they say, "God"? Does everything about you point back to Me? Does your worship point to me? Do people know who lives in you? Do they know your true north? Is there anything about your worship in the world that makes you different, that makes you stand out? Do you make a room uncomfortable at times because you speak up for Me, for goodness, for kindness, for truth, for life, for love

Do you listen in a way that people can sense Me in your eyes, your words, your smile, your touch. Or do people often think, after running into you, "What the HELL is wrong with them"? Or even more accurately, "What the hell got into them." If you are mean, find it funny to put people down or make fun of others as they try to learn, if you enjoy being right versus being righteous and compassionate, you do not know Me. If you use people, toy with people, test people, insult people, cut people off, you are worshiping YOU not ME. Repent.

Remind yourself who is God in your life, and re-connect to ME, to My Son, seek Lady Wisdom, study Scripture to see what types of fruit the Spirit produces in you, and if you can't figure out what kind of fruit you are handing out with your words ,if it is not one of love, joy, peace, patience, kindness, goodness, gentleness, faithfulness, hopefulness, or self-control, then deep dive to figure out why you are handing out poison to your brothers and sisters. Why are you hurting others, even if you are masking it by saying, "I'm just joking"? What are your actions indicating you truly worship?

Worship is the balm to the sorrows and worries of your soul. Worship elevates your energy; worship heightens your senses. Worship is lasering your focus on God and accepting the invitation to come into My presence. Worship is being aware of Me, fully aware of Me. As you become fully aware of My presence, you will be filled with awe at My wonderous love for you. Worship is a mindset, a heart posture, an invitation you are giving for Me to be the only one you want to hear from.

I have known you since before you were born. You were created to worship. Worship is your way to get you through the wait, the transition, the in-between time, your worship will help you heal, your worship will bring you closer to Heaven, your eternal home. Its power is available for you to use always, and in all ways.

I understood what God was saying, but I always have questions... so I asked, "How do we really worship, what does it look like when I am a living example of worship walking?" As I was asking the question, I immediately began to think about a Marvin and Family cartoon strip from long ago in a Sunday paper, when Sunday papers still came to your door and were hours of entertainment for the whole family.

In this particular comic strip Marvin, a toddler, was trying to talk to his mom while she was focused on doing other things, and he kept saying "Mom, Mom," and she would say "I'm listening," but was still doing something else, so he kept saying "Mom!" until she came over to him and said "What? I'm listening!"

He took his hands and put them to her face and said, "Whole face listen." I'll never forget that cartoon strip. "Whole face listen" is what it looks like when we worship God. It is God's way of saying, "Watch Me, Watch Me!"

Worship is about all attention on God! And when all attention is on God, how can we not get swept up into His grace. I think of children, when they are young, and are constantly saying to their parents and anyone who will give them attention, "Watch Me, Watch Me," they will say it over and over until you finally turn and look at them. And what are you allowed to do while watching them? That's right, Nothing!

They want you to do nothing when you watch them, and if you are doing something—talking on the phone, folding laundry, keeping your eyes on your other kids, fixing dinner, anything—what do they say? "You aren't watching me!" That's how I think God feels when we come to Him with anything less than 100% Whole-Face-Listen!

You have to stop all your movement for Him to move. Stop the noise to hear his voice. Sometimes it is necessary to just Be, so He can Do! Leave it be, so He can move the mountain for you. Stop running and rest so He can make a path where there wasn't one. Worship added to anything gives you a focus and a shift in energy to surrender to the power of His presence. To be grateful for what you can already sense Him doing. The more you can focus on God, no matter where you are, the more you can rest in knowing He is here and He is moving.

Worship is a way to maintain my conviction, that my God, the God of Abraham, Isaac, and Jacob has never lost a battle, never defaulted on a promise, and will never leave you nor forsake you. So, when you feel like the wait is too heavy, Worship! Lift your eyes to the heavens and remember where your help comes from.

Then the Lord reminded me of words that were spoken so long ago that still live on today:

I look up to the mountains- Does my help come from there?
My help comes from the Lord, who made the heavens and
the earth!
He will not let you stumble and fall the one who watches
over you will not sleep. Indeed, he who watches over Israel
never tires and never sleeps.
The Lord himself watches over you! The Lord stands
beside you as your protective shade.
The sun will not hurt you by day, nor the moon by night.
The Lord keeps you from all evil and preserves your life.
The Lord keeps watch over you as you come and go,
both Now and Forever
(Psalm 121, NLT)

When I finished reading the Psalm, I could hear the Lord saying:

*These are My promises to you, but you will choose how you **W.A.I.T.**.*

You will choose how you worship, and you must ask yourself when you don't choose to worship while you wait, What's stopping you? So, my question is, are you using this gift of worship? How do you worship Me in your life? What choices do you make that point back to me? Do you choose in all ways to focus on me and to use the gift of your senses to help you stay focused on the Good of God. You are the guard of your soul, of your mind, your eyes, your ears, your heart, your mouth, and your touch. What do you allow into your soul every day through your senses?

Your senses will have a direct effect on our relationship, and on how deeply you can connect with Me. Your worship can easily get sidetracked and take a detour back to the world around you, not realizing you are spending less time with Me and more time in the getting and the doing. Each of your senses can guide you back to Me and each sense is a gift to be used to worship.

The eyes are the windows of your soul, Do you guard what you watch? What do your kids watch? Do you let evil come into your thoughts and into your heart through the things you call entertainment?

A good man produces good deeds from a good heart, and an evil person produced evil deeds from an evil heart. Whatever is in your heart determines what you say
(Luke 6:45, NLT)

And who determines what is in your mind and what has access to your heart? You do! What you allow into your mind will affect the ways of your heart. Do you watch movies or shows that glorify division, destruction, and sexually objectify others? Do you open your mind to the evil of this world by watching evil deeds play out in front of you? Do you diminish the value of human life by watching people get murdered for entertainment?

Have you seen so much death that you are now numb to it, or see it only as fascinating instead of feeling the utter sorrow and despair you should feel when a human life is destroyed by another?

So many of you watch such vile activity in these reality TV shows that are splattered all over the screens of today. Everywhere you look you get fantastic ideas of how to treat others like trash and laugh while it is happening. You watch these shows and then you slowly but surely begin to emulate it in your own actions and words, leaking out that toxic energy into your own life. You are committed to keeping your focus on idols who only find enjoyment in worshiping themselves and manipulating others in the process.

You see these examples play out time and time again, you actively seek it out, program your devices to record this self-worship as it plays out, and then after only a short period of this brain washing, you begin to think this is the reality you can expect in your relationships, or worse, you become the reason for the discord in your own family, in your marriage, your friendships, and the way you look at your fellow man. You will imitate what you watch most. You will imitate what you worship, and what you watch most, you worship most.

Your brain is created to absorb and transform. It wants conformity in what you see and hear and what you are experiencing in life. It will bring that forth, because it thinks you are requesting it, you want it, you like it. I mean, you are in fact choosing to watch it, so you do want it in your life. Unfortunately, life will begin to imitate art, so guard your eyes from that which does not bring forth good in your life. I beg you to turn off this brainwashing, life-wasting, heart-hardening evil, and destruction, and Watch Me! Whole-Face-Listen! I can show up in movies, I can show up in shows, but you will have to be intentional in finding such shows. You have to protect yourself, because what you put into you will come out of you! What you take into your mind will go into your heart.

What you tell yourself you are okay watching; your mind thinks you are okay experiencing.

Put good things in front of you. Seek out life-giving ways to see the world. Worship with eyes of love. Ask yourself, if Jesus was looking out at the world through your eyes, would He like what He was watching? Would he enjoy watching the frivolous sex, the murder, the slander, the underbelly of human darkness? Could He stomach the horror you laugh at? Could He find peace in the cruelty of others that the shows you watch portray? Would Jesus ever want you to pick what He has to watch again? Jesus didn't come into the world to find people who enjoyed doing evil to others, who enjoyed watching evil be done.

His heart broke to see death, destruction, unfair judgement, condescension, and cruelty. He did not pick up a rock with the others to stone someone, or even stand around to watch it happen, but you do! He stopped the evil; He stopped the hurt. He worshipped with his eyes and He brought forth goodness, love, and righteousness because He kept His vision clean and clear and forever focused on His Father. What channel are you watching? A channel of God, a vessel of love, or channels of hate, hurt, and humiliation toward others?
Get your eyes cleared, turn off that which does not lead you to Me. It is not hard to do. You are choosing what you will stand before and watch, whether in real life or from the screens you sit in front of. Choose wisely. Choose carefully what you worship, and how you are seen by others as you worship in the world.

Be a channel worthy of watching, one that points back to the source of all life, one that points back to Me. You witness by your worship:

Anyone who is willing to hear should listen to the Spirit and understand what the Spirit is saying to the churches (Revelation 2: 11, NLT)

What do you listen to? How do you let your ears worship in all ways? You are always listening. Listening to yourself, listening to others, to the media, and hopefully listening to Me? Who and what do you surround yourself with that is allowed to speak over you? What you listen to, and who you listen to, will become the soundtrack of your mind. The words you hear most are the words you will repeat the most. Whose words do you have on repeat? Whose voice do you hear the most? What do you actively tune into to feed your mind? Because what you tune into is what you will turn into. Let your ears be filled with words of worship, words that tell you who I say you are, and who I say all My children are in My eyes! You are My beloved; you are My masterpiece!

The music, the podcasts, the conversations, all the sound waves that you allow around yourself are tuning you, and turning you, into something. What are you tuning into? What are you turning into? If you listen to gossip, cattiness, sarcastic and cynical people, guess what will start to flow from you in a very short amount of time?

If you listen to someone who spoke words of guilt, shame, condemnation, judgement, and unworthiness over you, guess how you will live out your life? You will live up to the beliefs you hold, even if those beliefs were meant to hold you down. What you listen to has a massive impact on what you believe and how you feel inside, it will color the lens through which you see the world. Let your ears be filled with worship! Words that remind you how wonderful, precious, priceless, and perfect you are to Me. How sacred your body is, how carefully I wove you together, and how I blessed you with a plan and a purpose for your life. You are a child of the Most High God, you are royalty, so tune into that and make sure the sounds that come out of your mouth raise the vibrations in others and call forth their highest good.

Remind them of this message:

*Therefore, as God's chose people, holy and dearly loved,
clothe yourselves with compassion, kindness, humility,
gentleness, and patience
(Colossians 3:12, NIV)*

*When you speak, speak life and you will, in all you
do, be the light that always, and in all ways, points back
to me. How do you worship me with your sense of touch?
Are you open to being my healing hands with an open
heart? Do you make sure that anytime you place your
hands on another person you do it in love or not at all? Do
you honor the temple of other souls or do you use other
people as pawns for your pleasure? Do you see them as
holy or as objects to use as you need and then dispose of
when they no longer serve your purpose? Do you worship
Me in the touch you give to the world? Are your hands
gentle, are they helpful? Do you come along side those who
are struggling and offer to lend a helping hand, a shoulder
to cry on, a neck to cling to? Do you offer legs that will keep
a firm foundation when someone can't stand, or feet to
walk with them when they don't think they can take
another step? Do people feel Me through you? Do you let
Me use all of you to convey all of Me. Honor one another, be
there for one another, and .....*

*love one another as I have loved you
(John 13:34, KJV)*

*When they see you, let them see Me. When they feel
your touch, let it be My love pouring into their hearts,
lighting them up with the warmth of My power and the joy
that comes from being in My presence. Bring peace to all
you hold, bring comfort to all who allow you into their
sacred space, for when you are touching another person,
you are touching the Imago Dei, the image bearer of God.
So, if someone has allowed you access to them, let it be a
touch of love, or leave them be.*

You have no right to physically manipulate or denigrate the body of another person. They are not dolls in your playhouse for you to put where you want and make them do what you want. They are my children meant for my purpose, to engage with and worship Me, not you, so treat them as such. Speak softly, touch gently, listen compassionately, watch closely and worship in all ways, that all may know I am the Lord of your life and the worship of your soul. I want your worship just as you are. Trust Me in all the in-between times, wait for Me, I will not delay. Worship Me in your joy and in your tears, worship Me in your bursts of laughter or your bouts of fear. I am here and I am with you always, and in all ways.

No matter where you are in life, if you will wait on Me and keep your eyes focused and captivated by My awe, I will show up everywhere. The more you look, the more you will see My miracles, and if you can get to the point where you are looking for Me always, you will see Me show up in all ways! I am in everything. I am here waiting for you to experience Me.

Fix your eyes upon Me no matter the situation and train your heart to seek Me first, to know I am in the mess as much as the masterpiece. I am in the bread line, as much as I am in the buffet line. I am in the tears of joy as much as the tears of sorrow and frustration.

Worship Me always and come to me in all your ways, You are worth the wait. Know that I love you and hold to My promise that:

Those Who WAIT on the Lord will find new strength. They will fly high on wings like eagles. They will run and not grow weary. They will walk and not faint
(Isaiah 40:31, NLT)

Chapter 6
What's the P.L.A.N., Lord?

Practice – **L**ifegiving – **A**ctions – **N**ow

*"For I know the PLANs I have for you", says the Lord.
"They are plans for good and not disaster, to give you a
future and a hope"*

(Jeremiah 29:11, NLT)

*I AM THE **P.L.A.N.***

*I have given you the answers that will bring forth
everlasting life. I have given you answers on how to
navigate yourself in this world. I sent you My son to model
how to live this life. The **P.L.A.N.** is to <u>practice</u> what He
modeled. I want you to practice all the lifegiving answers
He spoke about and demonstrated then, now.*

*You are called to work the **P.L.A.N.** by asking the Holy Spirit into your life to help guide you as you practice living in life-giving ways:*

....He will teach you everything and will remind you of
everything I myself have told you
(John 14:26, NLT)

He will help you know if you are living in a life-giving way, speaking in a life-giving way, "loving" in a life-giving way, or if you are living in a way that deforms, demeans, and destroys life because:

... you have received the Holy
Spirit, and he lives within you, you don't need anyone to
teach you what is true. For the Spirit teaches you all
things, and what he teaches is true – it is not a lie.
(1 John 2: 27, NLT)

So many of you have your own plans and ideas about how life should go and often times it seems that your plans are to run yourself into a ditch over and over again refusing to release the steering wheel. You seem hell-bent to have control and to create your own plans for life so much so that you would rather be holding onto the wheel as you drive yourself into a wall, then let me lead your life to a place of goodness and prosperity, a place where your gifts would flourish and you could be blessed as you bless others.

For I know the plans I have for you, ...They are plans for
good and not disaster, to give you a future and a hope
(Jeremiah 29:11, NLT)

I will come and do for you all the
good things I have promised, and
I will bring you home again
(Jeremiah 29:10, NLT)

*I gave you My son, the **P.L.A.N.** incarnate, because everything He did was an example of how you could **P**ractice **L**ife-giving **A**ctions **N**ow, today. There was no limitation on the truth He demonstrated or the truths I have spoken since the beginning of time.*

Have you not known? Have you not heard? The Lord is the everlasting God.
(Isaiah 40:28, emphasis mine).

I am the Alpha and the Omega, the First and the Last, the Beginning and the End (Revelations 22:13, NLT)

My truths don't change and My ways will bring life abundantly if you would uncuff yourself from the illusion that you are in control and let Me lead. I invite you to:

Taste and see that the Lord is good.
Blessed is the man who trusts in Him!
(Psalm 34:8, NKJV)

Now that we have that settled, let's talk a little bit about your life and the many aspects that make up a fulfilled human life. I made each of you so unique that the particulars of how to cultivate each area will vary, but the areas that make a life grow are the same. I taught you about the Life Garden decades ago and it's time to share this practice with the world here in this book,
so... Go Ahead...

I learned about the Life Garden from my mom over 20 years ago. I had just moved to Los Angeles after graduating from college. I couldn't wait to get out of town and finally move to the big city where all my dreams were sure to come true, as if a change in geography somehow grants dreams and not God, Himself. But I was a kid, fresh out of school, finally independent and ready to take on the world! I believed if I could just get to L.A., my life would finally be all I wanted it to be.

Well, I got to L.A. and it definitely was NOT all I wanted it to be. Life did not show up at my door saying, "Here is everything you wanted," wrapped up perfectly like a welcome-to-the neighborhood present.

No, I became very sad and isolated quickly. I had no friends, no community, no job, an unhealthy relationship, and the only family I had close by was my brother who lived in Pasadena with his wife, who I saw maybe once a week, if they had time.

My eating habits were abysmal, I was drinking too much to numb the loneliness, and life just felt empty but I honestly couldn't understand why. Hadn't I done what I always wanted to do, moved out West, come to Los Angeles... wasn't that enough? No, it wasn't.

One day, as I was crying to my mom over the phone, she began asking me questions about what I was DOING daily to put good things and vital healthy habits into my life. She told me I had to practice daily planting healthy habits, virtues, and values into my life. She explained that it sometimes helps to have a visual representation of what my life looks like now and how well I am doing at growing the areas that I said were important to me.

This is when she introduced to me the idea of the "Life Garden." She encouraged me to go buy a beautiful vase, as well as some colored marbles to put in the bottom fourth of the vase. She told me to go to a craft store and buy 6 fabric flowers that I was drawn to, that made me smile to look at. Each of the six flowers would represent an important area of my life that needed to be cultivated and invested in if I was going to have a full life and feel fulfilled each day.

The six areas of importance to help build a vibrant life for me were:

1) My Spirit (for which I chose the white rose as my representation of this area)

2) My physical health (a purple rose)

3) Work/purpose/prosperity (a Bluebonnet)

4) Friends/family (a pink hydrangea)

5) Fun (a multi-colored flower that just looked fun to me)

6) Love/intimacy/romance (a red rose).

I went and got a flower for each area and then I made a list that represented an action I could practice that would correspond to the flower. The list helped me remember things I could do to earn a flower in that area. I wrote lists for how I can feed my spirit with prayer, praise, finding a church, walking with God in the park, reading scripture, journaling, reading inspiring books, going on spiritual retreats, or volunteering ....

As many things as I could think of that I could do to refresh and water my spirit and earn a flower for the day. I did this with each area and would read over the lists and choose at least one thing to do to fill up my life and my vase. At the end of each day, I would take all the flowers out so when I woke up in the morning the vase was empty again and acted as a reminder that if I didn't prioritize intentionally putting good things into my life, not only would I be staring at an empty vase all day, but worse, I would be staring at an empty life.

To this day I still have a Life Garden on my dining room table, and it doesn't take much for me to be able to see what areas of my life I am leaving out and neglecting because there is a flower laying on the table instead of filling up my vase and my life.

The one flower that I have expanded my understanding on is the red rose, my love/romance flower, which I always believed was to represent my romantic relationship and how I was investing in it.

This rose became a source of sadness for me, since I have been single for 3 years and every day I would see that rose lying beside the vase and never in the vase. I felt a pang of sorrow each time I walked past the table. How could I have a full "garden" if I was single? How could I get my "love" rose without someone else giving me the opportunity to invest in them and earn my rose? I would cry and no longer enjoy looking at my Life Garden as that one lonely rose seemed to magnify what I thought I needed to have a full life... a spouse. But God stepped in and wiped my tears away as He spoke so gently when He said,

You can speak to yourself in loving ways, compliment yourself, speak encouragement to yourself, take yourself out on a date. Start to treat yourself the way you should be treated. How do you expect a partner I would send to you to treat you and say the words that type of person would say to you. As you get used to hearing loving words and being treated in loving ways you will not accept less when a potential "Love" comes into your life. Self-love is the most important love and it needs to flourish before you will be able to accept it from someone else.

So now, I write myself love notes and let myself be open to accepting God's love for me, my love for me, and other people's love for me. Every day I smile as I see my red rose back in its rightful place in my life, and back in my vase.

I hope the Life Garden can be a tool you can use to start to work on the **P.L.A.N.** in a practical way in your life. I hope it gives you a visual of what parts of your life need more attention and practice in acting in a lifegiving way now.

When I find myself in a really dark place and everything seems overwhelming, my Life Garden helps me to focus on trying to earn a flower for the day. If I prayed, drank water or went for a walk, texted a friend or a family member, watched a movie or read a book, told myself I loved me and I was proud of myself for trying at all, and if I managed to do anything for work that day, then I earned all six flowers and somehow I felt a little better about myself knowing that no matter how bad I was feeling, I was still taking steps that would lead me toward a life I did want, a life that was full, and healthy, rich in love and beautiful to look at.

Now the week before I started even working on this chapter, I had a "renewing" of my mind take place that was inspired, or should I say was "instigated," by my amazing life coach, Judy. This woman is such a light and a true vessel of God that I am filled with such deep gratitude that I have been blessed to know her and work with her. I had come to know Judy through the prompting of my brother Brian and my mom, who were worried about me and my "plans," or what they saw as a lack of "plans," for my life and my future.

They had decided that I needed to find a life coach to put a "plan" together for my life. I thought this was an odd suggestion because I did have a plan already that I was envisioning, but frankly, it was really more of an outline, a big picture, then any kind of detailed, written out, month by month, action step by action step type of plan that had a timeline attached to it.

Since my mom and brother had told me this would be a gift they would pay for, I thought, "Why not? I'm so incredibly lonely and isolated right now in my life, I could use someone to talk to for 13 weeks who will be paid to pay attention to me and give me some advice.

I mean how bad could it be to have someone who is dedicated to helping me grow?"

My first five sessions with Judy were basically Judy providing spiritual **C.P.R.** to my heart and soul. **C.P.R.**, as God revealed to me, is **C**hrist **P**owered **R**esuscitation and the way to perform this spiritual **C.P.R.** the way that Judy did so beautifully is to:

C: Create a Loving Space

P: Pray over Me

R: Reframe and rewrite the stories I was telling myself through the eyes of God and how He sees me, what He speaks over me, and the future He holds for me.

She used spiritual **C.P.R.** to love me back to life and she not only practices but exemplifies working the **P.L.A.N.** every time I see her. She is devoted to teaching people how to **P.L.A.N.**, how to actually **P**ractice **L**ifegiving **A**ctions **N**ow. I had no idea all the skills and talents that Judy had when I chose her as my life coach. I had no idea just how successful she was, or how many people she had helped to take their broken businesses and busted bank accounts and turn them into booming and blossoming blessings for themselves and the community.

She had repeatedly taken people's messes and helped them turn it into millions. She had detailed plans on how to do this step by step, and she spoke at conferences all the time about how to implement these life-giving steps into people's lives and businesses, but I had no clue. I had chosen Judy because I liked her presence and the soothing nature of her voice on the introduction video she made. I loved that she had a deep unshakable faith and an abounding peace that emanated from her when we first met.

As our sessions went along, Judy let me lead us wherever I needed to go, and often times the thing I wanted most was just her amazing hugs and her powerful prayers that she spoke over me. She was pouring life-giving answers over me, letting the Holy Spirit speak through her and guide her on how to love me into a place where I would one day be ready to take action steps to go after my dreams. By the fifth session, I was curious about this amazing mentor who sat with me week after week so I started to research who she was and what she usually does with clients.

I was shocked, in awe, and somewhat embarrassed that this woman with all of this business expertise at executing plans and exceeding expectations in her own life and the lives of the business owners who hire her daily to help their businesses succeed, was patiently and joyfully sitting here with me.

I was someone who had no job at the time, wanted others to bless me financially, and was throwing myself a major pity party. She never judged me, never made me feel ashamed, she simply kept working the **P.L.A.N.** with me, to **P**ractice **L**ife-giving **A**ctions **N**ow, and I am so thankful she did.

However, I did have a "come to Jesus" with myself after discovering all the many talents and the depth of experience she had to give. I realized I couldn't afford to waste another minute not tapping into it. I needed to get to work, for real. Hugs were great and prayers are necessary, but action was required if I wanted my dreams to become a reality, and I did. I came into our following session with a list of questions for her, some about her personally, some about her experience in the book industry and the business building industry, and some about how to help me get to work.

Judy lit up as I read all the questions, as if she had been waiting for this moment when I would come to her and say, "Okay, what's the **P.L.A.N.**!? How do I take my dreams and turn them into reality? How do I take one manuscript and touch millions?" Judy laughed and said she wanted me to write out my **P.L.A.N.**, write out what steps I needed to take and a timeline for how long it would take me to accomplish each step. She told me that having a **P.L.A.N.** would be vital to fulfilling my purpose.

I was working on the previous chapter when all of this took place, and when I came home from our session I sat down to write out my two plans. One was my timeline for completing my Master's program, and the other was my timeline for completing this book.

I was confused on how I could come up with a timeline on how quickly God would show up and write with me, so I went straight to the source and prayed about it. I asked God how long is the journey going to take to complete this book?

I got my answer back immediately, one chapter a month, and I had ten more chapters to go! I tried to renegotiate with God that maybe this could go a little faster since my finances were dwindling and my patience for staying in this town was at its end, but the answer was the same.

I don't know why I continue to argue with God that my idea of a timeline, which is always NOW, is way better than His timeline. So now I know, one chapter over one month and the next chapter up was this one. As I was figuring out my actual writing plan, the next lesson I was going to be learning would be how to work the **P.L.A.N.** in my life. How I could and would be **P**racticing **L**ife-giving **A**ctions **N**ow.

This had already been an eye-opening month, as I started a new part-time job as a substitute teacher for middle school and high school classes. A job I never, ever, ever would have seen myself taking.

I am not a huge fan of being around a lot of kids, especially if I am not even related to them. I relish the sound of silence, I love one-on one connections and working in public school with 25-30 kids at once, who mostly do not want to be there, are struggling with their own issues, and definitely do not want to be quiet, was a surreal place for me to find myself.

Saying all that, I still felt like I was being called to do this job. Yes I felt annoyed, but I also felt anointed to be in this job at this time and with these kids. I was struggling daily with the frustration I was feeling toward the kids and all the while I was working on writing about the **P.L.A.N.** about how to **P**ractice **L**ife-giving **A**ctions **N**ow.

I prayed and prayed on how to balance showing compassion while still giving corrections. How to show kindness, love, and encouragement while still leading, guiding, and teaching them respect—toward themselves, towards one another, and towards me.

I thought I was so compassionate, all-loving, such a good person, but I wasn't feeling like compassion and kindness were flowing from me as I stood in the front of a class trying to maintain some semblance of order. I felt like I was having to be harsh to get the kids under control. I would come to see Judy and tell her all the crazy stories of the things the kids would do or say and how I would respond. Judy would listen as I went on and on about what was "wrong with these kids today," until she finally looked me in the eyes and said, "Jen, you aren't being very compassionate with these kids at all".

I was a little taken aback because I see myself as so sensitive, compassionate, kind, empathetic and an all-around sweet person. I pride myself on it (that's part of the problem I would find out later). I went to the river after our session to process everything we had talked about.

I had specifically asked Judy to share with me what my blind spots were when she saw them, and then when she did, my internal voice replied, "Nuh-uh!" when I was faced with a truth that directly opposed my own ego's view of myself. Now, it is one thing to have a person point out a part of your personality that they think needs addressing and improving in your life, but it is another thing when God backs them up and speaks the same thing knowing full well that He knows everything about me. So, this was what God shared with me about my blind spots:

Part of your identity is to believe that you are all heart and completely compassionate, but what if you are not? What if what you desire to be is the destination but not the place you stand right now. What if you are deeply lacking compassion for anyone who doesn't align with your values, or even if they don't align with what you believe to be are My values.

It's not your place to judge and shame what I am doing in another person's life. It IS your job to love them, pray for the best in them, and have faith in Me that I do know what I am doing with each person you see.

You are a wonderful person with a beautiful heart, but you are not God, and you do not know all you would need to know about another person to ever judge them accurately.

I love how much you see and appreciate your own uniqueness now because I know that this has been a long hard struggle for you, but I do not see you extending that same love and grace to others who I also made uniquely different from you.

You want to know your blind spot, here it is…. you lack the amount of compassion you think you have and you hold so much pride in thinking that you are a "good person" by your outward actions. You are blind to see how and when you are lacking My light in you.

You are still trying to decide who, when and how much love and understanding you are willing to share with someone you don't totally align with. You are constantly deciding if you think they are "worthy" to receive your love. That is above your paygrade, and I will tell you that no one is worthy to receive My love..

For all have sinned and fallen short of the Glory of God (Romans 3:23)

…And all are worth it to Me! I loved the world so much that I sent my only son to die so that you may have everlasting life. All the people you see deserve to be treated with love and understanding, because they are all My children, and because I am worthy of your love and honor, they are worthy, and you are worthy.

You are not compassionate all the time, but I Am.

You are not loving all the time, but I Am.

You are not merciful all the time, but I Am.

You cannot will yourself to be gentle and kind all the time, but you can accept my gentleness and kindness, which will soften your heart and produce those fruits in you effortlessly.

I AM the gift of Life.

*I am the **P.L.A.N.***

Everything about me is life-giving, and my presence is always working in the present, in the now.

*Work the **P.L.A.N.***

***P**ractice **L**ife-giving **A**ctions **N**ow!*

Practice accepting Me now, practice watching Me, practice saying My words, practice following My example, practice loving others the way I do. Practice loving yourself and accepting yourself the way I love and accept you. As you fill your cup with My grace and mercy, with My love and kindness, you will overflow and pour out blessings onto others with your presence too. Practice life-giving thoughts.

Fix your thoughts on what is true, honorable and right. Think about things that are perfect and lovely and admirable. Think about things that are excellent and worthy of praise. Keep putting into practice all you have learned from me and heard from me, and saw me doing, and the God of peace will be with you
(Philippians 4:8-9, NLT)

Practice life-giving actions in all areas of your life. Use the Life Garden technique to help you focus. Everything you do either gives life of destroys it. Whether it is an action toward yourself or another, whether it is a physical, emotional, or spiritual action, always remember that:

Whatever you eat or drink or whatever you do,
you must do all for the glory of God
(1 Corinthians 10:31, NLT)

Remember too, that what is pleasurable does not always bring Me glory. Just because it feels good to you does not mean it is good for you. I created pleasure, I want you to have pleasure in your life, but pleasure that is not from Me, while it may feel good, will not lead you towards good, or towards Me. Pleasure can be destructive if it becomes your compass for life. I have warned about this over and over:

People who take this path will consider nothing sacred, they will be unloving and unforgiving: They will slander others and have no self- control.

They will be cruel and have no interest in what is good. They will betray their friends, be reckless, be puffed up with pride and love pleasure rather than God
(2 Tim 3: 2-4, modified)

Instead of pleasure as your compass to follow in life, the P.L.A.N. was always to use ME, use Love. I wanted you to:

Continue to love one another, for love comes from God. Anyone who loves is born of God and knows God. But anyone who does not love does not know God-
For God is Love
(1 John 4:7-8, NLT)

Love is not just what I do, it is WHO I AM.

I am the way, the truth and the life
(John 14:6, NLT)

I am the P.L.A.N. and I have given you a map to help you determine if you are following Me, if you are working My P.L.A.N. of Love, because if you are in love, you are in Me.

Love is Patient, Are you?

Love is Kind, Are you?

Love is not jealous or boastful or   proud or rude ...
Can you say the same?

Love does not demand its own way...
But you do.

Love is not irritable, and keeps no record of when it has
been wronged

Have you let go of your running list of how terrible others have been to you, who hurt you, how they hurt you, and how long they should pay for what they did?

Love is never glad about injustice, but rejoices whenever the truth wins out, Love never gives up, never loses faith, is always hopeful, and endures through every circumstance.
Love will last forever....
(1 Cor 13:4-8, NLT)

*If you want to know how well you are working the **P.L.A.N.**, replace the word "Love" with your name and see if it fits. The places where you feel convicted that what you are saying is not even remotely true is where you need to refocus your energy and try again. Consider a different way, consider My way, the way of Love and Life. See if it brings about a better outcome than what you have been previously trying in your life. Use the Life Garden to help you focus on each area of your life and practice a life-giving action instead.*

*Love is Life, and the **P.L.A.N.** has always been the same. It is simple and beautiful and it will change your life and the lives of those around you if you will remember to*

Love each other. Just as I have loved you,
You should Love one another
(John 13:34, NLT)

*Don't get tired of doing good. Don't get discouraged and
give up, for you will reap a harvest of
blessing at the appropriate time
(Galatians 6:9)*

*I Am the **P.L.A.N.** and the **P.L.A.N.** is now in your
hands. You choose whether to **P**ractice **L**ife-giving **A**ctions
Now, or not. I hope you choose love; I hope you choose life;
I hope you choose Me, but the choice, my child, is always
and will always be yours. So, choose this day whose
P.L.A.N.s you will follow, Mine or Yours?*

Chapter 7:
F.O.R.K. IT!

Follow- **O**ur- **R**ighteous- **K**ing

Put up a signpost where the roads FORK
(Ezekiel11:19, GNT)

I love to dance. I think it was an inherited trait from both my parents. I was probably dancing before I was born, since my mom taught dance class during the time she was pregnant with my brothers and I, and as long as I can remember, my parents have danced together in the kitchen, so I was probably in the middle of some of their slow dances before I ever made my official appearance.

In my family, music and dancing have always been an ever present and cherished way for us to engage and enjoy time together. I danced in my mom and dad's arms until I could stand and walk, then I would stand on my Dad's feet and he would rock us back and forth to the rhythm of the music coming from the record player. I once told him, after he mentioned what a wonderful dancer I was with him, that I learned his rhythm before I ever learned mine.

As I grew up, my whole family would dance together in the living room, both of my brothers and my Dad are phenomenal leads to dance with, and my mom taught all of us at some point the different dances that go with different types of music. I have such fond memories of all the places all over the world that we have danced together and I will cherish them always.

My favorite thing about dancing with a great lead is that I can get lost in the music and I no longer have to think about which direction we are going, who is around us, how we look, or what steps we are doing, all I have to do is trust and follow. I can fully relax, lay my head on my leads shoulder, take a deep breath, and just let go. It's one of the most freeing, safe, fun, exciting, intimate ways to share a moment with someone.

Since I grew up with such great leads to dance with, I was a bit shellshocked when I would try to dance with other people who had no clue what they were doing, much less how to lead me. We would step on each other's toes, feel awkward trying to get in the same rhythm and find the right timing for our steps. I have been dropped while they tried to dip me having no skill in performing that move correctly.

I have had people try to push and pull me around the dance floor, drape themselves drunkenly over me to try to hold themselves up, trip over me, and lose the connection entirely when they tried to spin me out and back without knowing how to keep the proper guiding grip for what they wanted me to do.

Dancing with an inept lead is not only embarrassing, it's dangerous and can be painful, so I try to be a little more discerning these days when I choose my "dance" partners, not just on the dance floor, but in life.

As much as I love dancing with others, as well as being a proud "car dancer," "chair dancer," "church dancer," and a "dancing-with-myself dancer," I have never given a thought to what it would be like to dance with Jesus.

J.C. is my best friend, and every other "best friend" I have ever had in my life, I have danced with at some point, yet I never thought it strange that I had never danced with Him. Maybe I wasn't as close as I thought I was, maybe I didn't want to let Him that close to me, maybe I didn't think He even danced. Too holy for dancing, too busy for dancing, making too many plans for me and my life. Maybe He had to teach me more important lessons before we set out to do the work He has for me, so He doesn't have time to stop everything to just hold me and dance with me.

I don't know why, but even though I never thought to ask Him to dance with me, He had that exact thing on His mind, and when He showed up and asked me to dance, I was beside myself. Forever changed. I would say it was like nothing I have ever experienced before, except that God does show up to me and we have spent time together in such a profound way that when He showed up this time, I was not so shocked, because I know who He is, and what He looks like.

This is the story of my dance to remember and of how **F**ollowing **O**ur **R**ighteous **K**ing has touched my heart, changed my understanding, and refocused my direction in how I handle myself, how I handle others, and how grateful I am for how God is guiding me every step of the way....

Lately, I seem to wake up every day between 4:30 and 6:30 in the morning. I still don't always get up, but I am much better about being obedient, and I usually walk across the hall to my office, whisper "Good Morning," to the day, turn on my salt rock lamp, lay out my prayer pillow, place my prayer blanket on top of it, and talk with God.

That's my typical morning, but this morning, I was in the middle of a prayer fast, and since the lesson of this month for me was **F.O.R.K.**, God had been working on me in so many different areas: from which road/decision will I choose when I come to a major fork in my life, to putting down my literal fork, abstaining from eating and to practice instead feeding off of and focusing on God alone for my strength.

He had been showing me so much about the reasons and motivations of why I eat, and about what food was supposed to be intended for, as well as, how far from that intention I had fallen. He showed me how I was idolizing food, putting way more thought into it than into Him. He was showing me that Jesus fasted to strengthen himself and ready himself to go into the test he was about to be confronted by. His fast was a time of physical purification. Fasting does not weaken the body, it strengthens it, and burns the excess fat of your life away and helps to embolden your spirit by reminding your flesh it is in not in charge of your life, God is.

The Holy Spirit compelled Jesus to go into the desert and fast. This was a refining process; it was the first thing Jesus was asked to do when the Holy Spirit came upon Him after being baptized. The first thing He modeled to all humanity was that the human body needs NOTHING external to survive this day but God, the Breath of Life. He was modeling that thinking about food is a waste of time. It is putting something higher than God in your life if you are constantly worried about feeding yourself, satisfying yourself, your needs, your wants.

I realized I was getting more excited about what I would eat today than how God wanted me to serve that day. I love that Jesus showed us this body does not run on food alone and that food is something that will be offered as a gift to share with other people as a way to have community and not some sort of self-soothing, self-gratifying, hourly dependence that we have made it out to be. God wants a clean and pure vessel, and if I am stuffed with junk food and bloated on my own internal cravings, I can't hear and feel all God is trying to say to me. God had no intention of being in competition with food for our focus and devotion in life. He knows we need it; He'll bring it.

I was amazed that I had never understood that story of the desert and the 40 day fast in this light, as a model of how much lower on the importance scale the fork really is, and that I needed to lay it on the altar of sacrifice to God, not create an alter for it as if it were my God. I am not to be bound to my physical cravings and let them lead my life. It is my goal one day to do a 40-day fast, but so far seven days seems to be where I am at. I have to feed off of God, off of every word He breathes over my life.

He humbled me when He began to probe deeper into my heart and ask me to be honest about what I was feeding off of in life before I came into this time of fasting. Not just the physical food I was putting into my body, my vessel that belonged to Him, but what emotions, what energy, what words I was filling up on and then feeding to others. God said:

Take a forkful of humility and stick it in your mouth instead of speaking out in self-righteous judgement. What are you feeding others? What's on your fork to give to the hungry of spirit, the hurt, the lost, the sick, the lonely, the disturbed? When they come into your presence what are you filled with to feed them?

Do you take MY Life and give it freely? Loving and listening, inspiring, and encouraging, healing, and helping? Do you feed them a huge forkful of acceptance and compassion, or do you jab them with a fork of criticism and judgement, force- feeding condemnation into their already broken and malnourished souls? You will only have to feed others what you have stored up in your heart.

Check your "pantry," what do you have on the shelves of your heart? Maybe it's time to clear out some food that is not serving you and definitely not fit for you to serve others.   Are you full of yourself yet? When you feed off YOU, you get sick! In the head, in the heart, and in your spirit. Have you taken every gift I gave you and used it to feed yourself, to satisfy your own desires?

Things that were meant as gifts for others, to feed others, you took and used for yourself:

You're cheating on God if all you want is your own way, flirting with the world every chance you get, you end up enemies of God and his way. And do you supposed God doesn't care? The proverb has it that "he's a fiercely jealous lover."

And what he gives in love is far better than anything else you'll find. It's common knowledge that "God goes against the willful proud; God gives grace to the willing humble." So let God work his will in you. Yell a loud no to the Devil and watch him make himself scarce. Say a quiet yes to God and he'll be there in no time. Quit dabbling in sin. Purify your inner life. Quit playing the field. Hit bottom and cry your eyes out.
(James 4: 4-12, MSG)

Watch what you put on your **F.O.R.K.** in life. What you feed off of, and what you feed others.

Don't feed off of judgment, bitterness, depression, greed, lust, worry, anger, criticism, or self-righteousness. Feed off of love. If you are confused on what that looks like in a practical sense it means that when you are with another person you are to be intentionally kind, and unbelievably patient with their words and with their actions. You are excited about the opportunities and connections the person is experiencing and never jealous about it or try to one up their story with one of your own. You should never look down on one another or see your life through the lens of a bloated ego. You should never be intentionally rude to another, even if they "deserve it" in your mind. The seat of judgement is not for you

Don't hit back; discover beauty in everyone. If you've got it in you, get along with everybody. Don't insist on getting even; that's not for you to do.
"I'll do the judging," …. "I'll take care of it."
(Romans 12:17-18, MSG)

When you are with someone, consider what would be good for both of you, instead of always insisting it's my way or the highway. That type of thinking has left you in a very lonely position many times in your life. The other has just as much right to fulfill and honor their purpose as you do. Don't demand you own way.

Grow up! It's only a child who thinks there is only one way a situation should be handled.

There are billions of ways a situation can be approached, because every one of you are unique and have your own way, your own flavor, your own music that you need to add to this life! Don't dim your light but also, never ever dim the light in another. When you love someone, you take care of yourself so you will not be easily irritated, or moody with one another.

Love delights in others, it is not irritated with them and it doesn't run around throwing people's faults and failures back in their face. It does not manipulate a person through coercion or bullying, it simply keeps no record of the missteps of another.

Like I said, it's a dance, and you will always be thankful if you let love lead because it never gives up on you, never loses faith in the masterpiece you are, and keeps hope hidden in its heart praying that you will continue to choose to love each other over and over. Love promises to stay strong through all the easy steps and the through all the hard ones. As long as you dance, the Lord of Love will lead.

And if all of this is too much to remember, it has also been said like this:

Love is patient and kind.
Love is not jealous or boastful or proud or rude.
Love does not demand its own way.
Love is not irritable
and keeps no record of when it has been wronged.
It is never glad about injustice
but rejoices whenever the truth wins out.
Love never gives up, never loses faith, is always hopeful,
and endures through every circumstance.
Love Never Fails
(1 Corinthians 13: 4-8, NLT)

So,

*...Love each other as if your life depended on it. Love
makes up for practically anything
(1 Peter 4:8, MSG)*

*Your ability to follow me all relies on what you are feeding
yourself.*

So, on this morning, day four of my fast, feeding
myself nothing but blessed water and God's loving words
and presence to strengthen me, I was laying on my bed
thinking about all of this, and decided I wanted to have
my prayer time here instead of in the office, so I sat up,
closed my eyes and started to pray. All of a sudden, I
thought, I really feel like singing, I want to listen to Cody
Carnes song, *Nothing Else,* so I pulled it up on my phone
and hit "play."

As I swayed and listened with my eyes closed,
Jesus appeared, we were now standing on a dance floor
with a soft light on Him, I was astounded. He held his
hand out and asked me if I wanted to dance. I took His
hand and He pulled me to Him, I placed my head on His
shoulder and melted into His arms.

I was crying as I sang to him, "I'm sorry when I
just go through the motions, I'm sorry when I forgot that
you're enough, take me back to where we started, I open
up my heart to you." He led me all across the dance floor,
he lifted me high up over his head and his eyes were so
hypnotically beautiful and loving that it was hard to
accept the adoring way he was looking into my eyes, yet
also so captivating and transparent that I couldn't look
away.

He lowered me and placed me back in front of him
as we just kept looking at each other with my arms
wrapped around his neck. He took one hand and opened

it for me to place my palm back in his and I saw the scar from where the nail had pierced him.

I started bawling as I touched the scar, I apologized over and over for what was done to Him, and every time I had driven a nail into His heart by pushing Him away. He just shrugged and said, "It's okay, I wanted to".

I couldn't comprehend his answer and with tears running down my face, I asked "WHY?" and he smiled and said, "Because I love you, I've always loved you." I just about lost it, I crumpled at His feet and sobbed. How could this holy and heavenly being love me so much, and know me so intimately that He came here to ask me to dance with Him? To let the world fade away and get lost in his eyes, his smile, his arms.

He looked at me and said:

Get to know me intimately, just as I know you. I know you intimately, every thought and every whisper, every want, every need. I love to watch you dance, I love holding you when you cry. I'm always here, walking with you, guiding you, staying on this same path, and even as you run away at times, I stay with you. I follow you into your darkness and chaos. I follow you down your dangerous paths, not to Judge you, but to be right there when you reach for Me. Immediately I will lift you up out of your pain and ask you again if you would like to dance with Me. Follow My lead for your life.

There is so much beauty in the moves I have planned for you, so much joy, and peace, goodness and mercy, wisdom and understanding. I want to whisper them all into your ear and into your life. I have to be close to you if you are to hear My whispers of love.

Trust me that even when I spin you, and you feel like you can't see straight, or when I dip you and the world looks upside down, know I will never drop you, never hurt you, and never let you dance alone. So, they didn't want to dance with you, Well I do!

Dancing is supposed to be fun, but you tense up every time I try to spin you, and even start to wonder if the "devil" has cut in sometimes! It's just me spinning you and showing you my "divine dips" most of the time, not to say I can stop you from Dancing with the devil if you so choose to, I do not force you or demand you to dance with me, I just continue to ask you,…. "Wanna dance?" It will be a dance to remember, I promise. God's moves are better than any other moves you've ever seen.

I created the music, the steps, the other dancers, the night, the dance floor... all of it, so of course I know how to make it all move like magic.

When we dance, I get to hold you close, so close our spirits are one, that is why the Holy Spirit can physically move you. The two have become one. When you allow the Holy Spirit to dance with Jesus, to recognize for you that this is our Righteous King extending the invitation to get to know you. The Holy Spirit guides you to the **F.O.R.K.** *in the road of life daily to let you decide do you want to dance with Jesus or go dancing with your old selfish ways, selfish patterns, and step toward the evil lure of dancing instead for this world. Both Jesus and the devil have an interest in leading you in your life. J.C. wants to lead you to a life lived abundantly; with all the blessings of the spirit you can accept. Evil is hoping to dance you right into deception, destruction, depression, and death. The world WILL dance with you if you don't intentionally choose to dance with Me!*

As He finished sharing this invitation with me, I realized I have wanted so many things in my life lately that I felt had alluded me, so many prayers I had prayed that seemed unanswered.

So many cravings I have chased after, so many places I have looked for answers to the pain of loneliness in my heart, but as I danced with Him, all of it faded away. I wasn't dancing with Jesus and thinking to myself, "Man, I really would love a date right now," or "I really would love to be held right now by someone else." I wasn't thinking, "I sure do need more money right now, or I'm hungry let's go eat Jesus."

I wasn't thinking, "When am I going to move out of this town, or do you know how bad they hurt me!?" I didn't care about any of it. Those thoughts were gone, I was hypnotized, I was immersed in His love. I had His arms wrapped around me, rocking me, singing with me, talking to me, moving me, becoming one with me. All I had to do was follow Him.

I am aware most people do not get to have actual visions and encounters with Jesus. I know how lucky I am, and I have no idea why He chose me to reveal Himself in such a face-to-face way, but I love it. I don't have the words to explain the feeling of being held, picked up, hugged, rocked, and physically pulled closer by Jesus, but if I could describe it, it would be a melting peace, an exciting calm, a feeling of seeing everything I need right in front of me, of being fulfilled in every way, and having it click in my head that all the other dances I was trying to dance in my life were a joke, and a waste of time compared to this dance. I didn't want the song to end, and when it did, I quickly played another one, and kept dancing with Him.

I have no idea how long I stayed in that sacred vision, but the feeling has not left me. It was as if Jesus was telling me:

Before you know it, a sense of God's wholeness,
everything coming together for good,
will come and settle you down.
It's wonderful what happens when Christ
displaces worry at the center of your life
(Philippians 4:7, MSG)

I have been given a gift, the gift of knowing that Jesus is real, alive, and well, and can show up however, whenever, and wherever He wants to in my life. He can even cut in and ask me to dance right in the middle of my prayer time, to slow everything down, erase every need I thought was so important and fill me with something greater: His love, His comfort, His security, His acceptance.

I had felt so lonely in my life these past three years, frankly, more like my whole life, but when He wrapped his arms around me and I felt it as real as I could feel any other person hug me, it changed me. When I saw his eyes, his smile, nestled my head into his shoulder, put my hand on his heart, felt him twirl me, spin me, lift me up over his head like I was a little kid again, I can rest in that feeling. I can rest knowing He is here, present, and leading my dance of life if I will just keep choosing to stay close and follow him. I don't need to run around anymore wondering where I will find love, affection, money, food, clothes, a job, friends, none of it. Jesus wrapped his arms around me and said "I got you! Do you trust me?" and I said, "Let's do this!".

I know I am being called to some very big things in this life and will get the opportunity to "dance" with a lot of people I would never have been able to get on the same dance floor with if it was not for God. I no longer wonder if I will meet the love of my life, I already did! He met me on the dance floor and asked for my hand, and I have never felt the same. All I want to do is listen and move when His hand moves me. I want to remember that

Since the Master honors you with a body,
honor him with your body
(1 Cor 6:13, MSG)

I want to make sure I am feeding my mind, my heart, my body, my emotions, my soul the right "food." It's so important to check what I am feeding myself daily, and now to ask myself, was any of that important when I was in Jesus' arms? If it wasn't important then, it probably isn't important now. When someone hurts my feelings, I can go back into the Master's arms and I could care less what that person said or did.

When God shows me a move He wants me to make, I could care less now what the outcome will be, or the response to it. It was simply a part of my dance, and I am already onto the next step. He doesn't ask me to do things so I will get something from it, He asks because He wants to grow something with it, and it does not always mean He will be revealing what that is to me. He dances with every one of us who have heard the call and it is often times a very private intimate dance that a crowd is not meant to watch.

The steps He teaches me in the dark, the hours of spiritual practices and combinations of compassion and wisdom he wants me to learn are both simple and hard at the same time, and I'm so glad my training isn't done in front of an audience.

There were so many personal and uncomfortable situations that happened this month as I devoted myself to this lesson of learning about the **F.O.R.K.**s in my life.

The question in each of these situations was the same though: What road do I take? How do I handle this situation with the grace and love that Jesus is showing me? How do I speak with love, or do I decide not to speak at all for the sake of love? How do I forgive the impact that others have had on me and continue to show up and love them? How do I honor the people God has chosen to bring into my life? How do I reframe what I think about situations? How do I stop ruminating on the hurt? Jesus gave me the best answer,.... "Just Dance With Me..."and

Forget all that- it is nothing compared to what I am about to do. For I am about to do a brand-new thing. See, I have already begun! Do you not see it? I will make a pathway through the wilderness for my people to come home. I will create rivers for them in the desert!
(Isaiah 43: 18 -19, NLT)

God spoke to me again saying:

Having a great lead in life is everything, and I am the perfect lead, but I have to warn you, I have moves that you aren't familiar with. Don't be afraid when we get to the hard steps, I will walk you through them and gently guide you if you keep your eyes fixed on me, your heart open to feel me as I lead you. You always seem to fight me on those more complicated moves. You get upset and worried you don't have the ability to master them, you walk away, you cry, you get frustrated, never realizing it's actually an amazing step I'm teaching you.

Just because it is hard, doesn't mean it's not awesome! And once we get those steps down, the next time we do it, you are smiling and feeling excited because you learned this one already, and you get more confident in your ability to follow me.

I love that. I love seeing you understand that I am going to move you in ways that will blow your mind, because this isn't a dance of the head, it's a dance of the soul.Remember to hold tight to Me, look into My eyes, feel My hand on your back, place your palm into mine, and trust that I am still in control. I am still on the throne, I am still all good, righteous to my core, and the only lead that knows the dance you were born to dance. Follow me, **F.O.R.K.** *IT! You have everything to lose if you choose to sit it out in life. So, with all of me, I ask for all of you ......Will you Dance with Me?*

It is amazing that it becomes quite difficult to focus on other things and other people when you have a calling on your life, an excitement about where you are going, an anticipation for the dance you are dancing. You just don't care what happens when God whispers, *"I got you! I will take the lead. I will guide you. You can put your head on my shoulder, breath in My divinity, and watch as I change the world through you."*

You want to put down your fork and listen to what God wants, you want to give up self-satisfying activities in whatever form they come in for you, you want to take risks and chances to see what twists and divine dips God is going to lead you through. You want to encourage other people to listen to the music in their heart and ask God to come dance with them. You want people to experience what you have experienced. You want everyone to be held like you were held, where your brain seems to stops functioning but your spirit is so filled with wonder at what is to come and your vision becomes even clearer.

This Christmas season, God asked to dance with me and it was the greatest gift I've ever received besides getting the honor to write this book with Him! He has shown me visions of what is to come, and I have no idea what the steps to make it all actually happen will be but thank God I'm not the one who is in the lead.

He also wanted me to ask you to be open when he extends His hand to you and says *Can I have this dance? Do you trust me?* Will you respond to His invitation to dance with, "I can't. I don't know those steps. I know what I know, and if I do those steps in life, even if it's killing me, at least I know the outcome and the moves?"

Can you release control of your life and humbly say, "Show me the steps, Lord. Lead me in each step, make me aware of the subtle feeling of your hand on my back gently guiding me and telling me what our next move will be?" Will you let God lead you, will you dance with Him?

Whenever the road **F.O.R.K.**s and you must choose to dance with the world or dance with God, I hope you will remember to say "**F.O.R.K** it!" and follow the Lead of Love... **F**ollow **O**ur **R**ighteous **K**ing

Chapter 8

G.R.O.W Up and Get to W.O.R.K.

Get - **R**id - **O**f – **W**orry

Instead, by speaking the truth in love, we will **GROW**
up completely and become one with the head,
that is, one with the Messiah.
(Ephesians 4:15, ISV)

&

Worldly – **O**pportunities – **R**equiring – **K**indness

Commit your WORK to the Lord and
then your plans will succeed.
(Proverbs 16:3, NLT)

This year started off with revelation, regurgitation, and ungodly defecation. I know, gross, and it was not how I planned on kicking off the year either. It was eye-opening, funny, painful, and disgusting. I think I may have gotten food poisoning on one hand, and on the other, I think my gluttonous nature jumped up and helped contribute to this "Holy Shit" moment, as a friend of mine so lovingly called it when I told her what had happened.

You see, when this year began, I was alone in a hotel room celebrating my birthday and New Year's Eve, since they fell on the same day. For the most part, I am not a big fan of my birthday, and this year I was not going to stay home in a town I have been dying to get out of since the moment I set foot back in it. I also wasn't going to spend it ALONE and at home which would have made me feel even worse, so I packed a bag and headed to the beach, my favorite place to see the sunrise and feel like my hope for a better tomorrow is rising with it.

When I got to my initial room, I walked in and my heart just sank. It was so small and dingy. I might as well have opened the door to the connecting room because I could hear every word and sound. The tears started to well up and I knew I would rather sleep in my car than sleep in here, so I went back up to the desk and told them I was going to be celebrating my birthday this weekend and did they have anything else available that would be high enough up that I wouldn't have to hear all the craziness that was about to happen as the New Year's Eve festivities began.

After what seemed like five minutes of excessive typing, the front desk receptionist looked up and said they did have a "condo" available up in the towers, but since it was a holiday it would cost a bit more. When she told me how much more it would be, I about fell over.

I barely had a job, I was in debt, on the verge of tears, and honestly, I didn't care about all of the logical reasons why I probably shouldn't give her my credit card at that moment.

I was already feeling so sad and alone in the world realizing that no one— except my parents—had even asked me what I would like to do for my birthday or care enough to make certain I wouldn't be celebrating this day all alone. I guess God had other plans for me, because that is exactly what happened, and it hurt.

I was bitter and ranting in my mind about everyone and everything. It wasn't my best look, so in my desperation to show myself a "good time" I booked the room, and then had to sit and wait for hours because they were short staffed and hadn't cleaned it yet. My bitterness and self-centeredness were growing by the second, but what else could I do? I prayed this room would be worth every penny I didn't have but had just paid to the hotel to get to stay there.

When I finally got the key, they told me it was the top floor, center condo, facing the ocean with two balconies: one off the living room and one off the master bedroom! When the elevator doors opened and I walked into my room I was so relieved and excited, THIS was exactly what I wanted! The view would have been amazing with nothing blocking my sight. I would have been able to see the sunrise from my bed if I wanted to!

I keep saying "would have" because at the very moment I arrived at the beach, so did this thick all-encompassing fog and I couldn't see six feet in front of me off the balcony. I was literally up in the clouds. I could hear the roar of the ocean, I knew it was there, and I could feel the electricity of it but I couldn't see it. I realized this had to be God's odd birthday present to me, to remind me what faith looks like.

As sure as I know that the ocean is there, not a doubt in my mind about it, I also know my Father is here, omnipresent, wrapped around me, completely absorbing me, and even when it feels like I can't see Him, He is much closer than I ever imagined. I laughed at what a tangible metaphor for faith He had placed in my lap.

That He is surrounding me, even if what I thought it would look like, what I hoped it would look like, what I paid good money for it to look like, was not what it looked right now. So, I prayed for him to show me what he wanted me to see, because clearly it was not the ocean, nor the sunrise. 2022 was coming to an end, I couldn't see 6 feet in front of me, and I was okay with that.

God then laid it on my heart that I would start the upcoming year off with a 21day prayer fast. I promptly reminded Him that I had only done seven days of fasting before, so I wasn't sure about this. He let me know, if I wanted to **G.R.O.W.** up, I needed to do new things to get new results, and that He wasn't interested in my past abilities. He had something new for my future and wanted to know if I was interested in playing a new game?

This new game is really a repackaged one that I still struggle with, but He called it "What Else Could I Think?" He said that **G.R.O.W**. means to **G**et **R**id **O**f **W**orry for starters, and that when a worried or "poor me" thought came into my head during this birthday celebration weekend, I would have to come up with five other thoughts I could think instead of only focusing on the situation at hand. I went walking on the beach even in the fog, and just as I thought, the beach was still there, even if I couldn't see it from my balcony! Shocker, I know.

The Lord began to speak to me about growing up, and that worrying and whining are learned habits, they are often passed down and are generational curses that can and need to be broken!

So instead of me worrying or wallowing....What Else Could I think?! He showed me the power my mind has to be changed and that **G.R.O.W.T.H.** always begins in the dark. He even showed me that for **G.R.O.W.T.H**. to happen I have to **G**et **R**id **O**f **W**orthless **T**hinking **H**abits! In the dark of the mind, my life manifests for the better or for the worse.

He started to share with me all the ways I needed to **G.R.O.W.** up and what I needed to get rid of to make this happen for my life, as well as how this 21-day prayer fast would help to facilitate this pruning and "cleaning out" of the waste in my life.

I had no idea that this "cleaning out" was going to be painfully literal and abrupt. I knew I would start the prayer fast on January 2, because I was driving back from the beach and returning home, so on January 1, my messed-up mind decided that if I was going to embark on this journey of no food and only water and tea for 21 days, I better stock up now, as if I was a bear getting ready for winter or something.

I had even spent the majority of my birthday reading all the chapters of this book so I would have thought all that wisdom and understanding about food and fasting would have sunk in, but no. I am the slowest, most stubborn student when it comes to my attachment to food apparently.

I spent all of January 1st finishing up my gourmet meal that was left over from my birthday dinner the night before, as well as the half bottle of champagne I decided I would celebrate the new year by making mimosas with it to get the morning off to good start. After finishing the meal and the rest of the bottle, I thought what would really go well on top of mimosas, lobster bisque, and half of a ribeye steak with bearnaise sauce on top was... a pina colada... yup, that was my bright idea.

Oh, but it didn't stop there, since the football games were on that Sunday, I also thought I should order as my last day of eating for a while, a huge peperoni pizza with ranch! I reached for the hotel phone and called room service to have them send it up, all the while, my stomach and my spirit are telling me not to eat any more, that I'm going to get sick. Did that stop me? Absolutely not. I ran straight for it; I got my pizza, heated up two slices, and started in on the first one. I opened up the container of ranch and it was green colored.

Did that make me think maybe I should call down and check to make sure they intended for the ranch to be green? Nope, not at all. I stuck my finger in it, and it tasted like ranch to me, so I pressed on in my mission to eat all the things I wanted to before I went into a fast to help "purify my body and clean out my spirit".

My stomach was now really talking to me and telling me to stop eating the pizza, I had enough food and it was hurting me. Once again I didn't listen because I had already heated up the second piece and I wasn't going to waste it! After I wolfed down the second piece, I knew that was it. I put the pizza in the fridge and curled up on the couch to watch the rest of the game. I thought I had gotten away with this incredible mistreatment of my stomach as I went to bed that night. I ended the night praying that I would now be ready for the cleaning out that was to come in these next 21 days.

To my surprise a little after midnight, I was rudely awaked by a churning in my stomach that I was not unfamiliar with, and I had the realization that this cleaning that God promised me was about to happen right now! And not in a slow and peaceful way, but a doubled over, retching, four-letter-word-urgent-prayer, type of way. I got so sick, and I mean every which way that I could.

My stomach is very sensitive. I have had to deal with many excruciatingly painful bouts in the bathroom over the years when food doesn't sit right in my system. However, this night I knew, not only was this going to be another painful potty moment, but somehow I was about to start vomiting too.

Needless to say, I was completely cleaned out before the sun rose over my first day of the fast. It was a disgusting blessing, and it made it quite simple to not want to eat anything anyway those first few days, and even as the weeks of the fast went by and I thought about food that I obsessively wanted to eat, I would picture that "Holy Shit" moment and ask myself if I would like to be cleaned out that way again or would I prefer to try it this way!

Now that my body was completely cleaned out, it was time to go to work on my mind, where all of my stumbling blocks come from anyway. I got home that evening and I went up to my office, there laying on my desk were prayer beads I had just received for Christmas from my niece and nephew.

I thought they were cool looking when I got them for a gift, but I wasn't quite sure what I was supposed to do with them, because I don't pray ritualistic prayers when I talk to God, I just talk to Him like I would any other best friend.

God prompted me to go get them, as they were going to help me **G.R.O.W.** up, and remind me daily that God is here helping me. He said to count the beads and there were 18, but they also had this beautiful clear crystal that completed the chain and so when I touched the top of the crystal, the bottom of the crystal and finally holding the center of the crystal it came out to 21... 21 days to fast, and 21 touchstones that would be accompanied by scriptures that I would feed off of each day.

When I first got the word **G.R.O.W.** and the meaning of **G**et **R**id **O**f **W**orry, I thought that was going to be the whole message, but it was not. **G.R.O.W**. turned into a list of ways God needed to prune me. Here are the multiple ways He used this word to guide me towards the Holy Spirit and to be able to hear Him even clearer. He said:

*G*et *R*id *O*f *W*orry

*G*et *R*id *O*f *W*hining – *Whining is just vocalizing your worries and it's not helping you*

*G*et *R*id *O*f *W*allowing

*G*et *R*id *O*f *W*ine

*G*et *R*id *O*f *W*eight

*G*et *R*id *O*f *W*aste

*G*et *R*id *O*f *W*oulda-coulda-shoulda, *and remember to ask, "What else could you think?"*

*G*et *R*id *O*f *W*ishing *and start working, it takes effort to change*

*G*et *R*id *O*f *W*ishy-washy *decision making*

*G*et *R*id *O*f *W*andering *– be Intentional*

G.R.O.W. out of it! You have to take the lessons you have been shown, the experiences and habits you have formed and instead of growing more used to them, take this year to get excited about growing out of them. See it as a gift, not something to be ashamed of.

*If you **G.R.O.W**. from it, if you foster growth because of it, then it was a blessing. Don't be so stubborn that you are unwilling to **G.R.O.W**. up and **G.R.O.W**. out of it.*

I can't bring you to the people and the places I am calling you to without first deepening your foundation, growing your conviction, growing your strength, adjusting your habits, changing your mind, and your thought patterns.

I have to recreate you before I can show you how to execute the vision laid before you. If I say move, you move. If I say run, you run. If I say stop doing something, you stop. If I can trust you to follow, I can expand what I can trust you with. You still have so much growth left to do, and so much growth you have already done. Be proud of yourself. Be grateful you had eyes to see, a heart to follow, ears to listen, and enough space to make room for me to fully move in and move through your life.

Grow out of the pain. Grow out of the negative. Grow out of the addictions. Grow out of the depression. Grow out of the labels. Grow out of the loneliness. Grow out of all the crap you have covered yourself with and into the Woman of God you are called to be!

*Don't Give up, **G.R.O.W.** Up! **G.R.O.W.** up and instead of running to other things or driving yourself crazy with your destructive thinking, come talk to me about it. I will guide your way, I will bring you to the truth, I will give you life. That's what I came for. I want you to replace all your "worries" with "ways" that I could work it out. You have to **G.R.O.W.** out of being more and more like YOU so that you can **G.R.O.W.** to be more and more like Me! Grow out of your sadness and into my Joy!*

For the Joy of Lord will is your strength
(Nehemiah 8:10, NLT)

G.R.O.W. *out of your bitterness and into My compassion.*

G.R.O.W. *out of your doubt and anxiety, and into My wisdom and understanding.*

G.R.O.W. *out of your selfishness and into My servanthood.*

G.R.O.W. *out of your worry into My wonder.*

G.R.O.W. *out of your debt and into My abundance.*

As He finished speaking to me, He told me to go look up "worry" in the dictionary, the actual hardbound Webster's Dictionary that was on my shelf. I thought to myself, "I already know what worry means, I'm an expert at it, I was raised to perfect it." I had no idea what I was about to discover.

I went over to my bookshelves, dusted off the old dictionary, creaked it open and started looking under W. When I came to the word "worry," I stopped and stared, my mouth dropped open as I read the very first definition of the word "worry," which was defined as to "strangle or to choke." The definitions continued: "to harass by tearing; biting, or snapping especially at the throat," "to touch or disturb something repeatedly," and lastly, "to torment."

I couldn't believe it. Had I been strangling and choking myself all these years and thinking it was quite normal? Had I allowed people to "choke and strangle" me with their words believing it was a way to show they cared about me? My mind was blown open at the words on the page. No wonder God wanted me to **G**et **R**id **O**f **W**orry in myself or from anyone around me, it was literally killing me and restricting the life force from flowing as it was created to do. God spoke to me further about how important this was to Him and He shared this with me:

Your Calling is in progress. You cannot be distracted by anyone or anything that isn't lifting you towards your purpose, your calling, your life with Me. I'm refining you. I'm pruning you.

I am changing and transforming anything in you that could trip you up later. I can't have anyone, ANYONE, speaking anything but life, belief, faith, and encouragement over you. Anything else is unacceptable and will not be tolerated any longer.

Encouragement is always welcomed and needed, but criticism and worry spoken over you or near you need to be banished or kept to a minimum and addressed immediately, honestly, and with humble transparency, and with genuine love. Remember people who "worry" about you, often do it from the intention of love and from the fears in their own hearts. Have compassion for those people. Even as they try to speak fear over you, you will only speak words of honor and kindness over them and over yourself.

Don't let anyone "choke" you and don't you dare "choke" yourself ever again. May it cause great alarm from now on when you feel that grip of worry tighten around your heart and in your throat as the Spirit behind worry tries to paralyze you from moving towards all I have called you to be, cutting off your ability to move, speak, and even breathe freely.

No More! The spirit of worry is broken off of you and can no longer sneak in without you noticing what it is trying to do. Instead of letting worry come right in and set up camp, you will look up to Me. Remember not to look at the worries below you but to the ways I have always taken care of you, and the ways I am working it out for you even now.

As the prayer fast continued and the days each brought a lesson or new insight, I began having dreams, and in one dream God wanted me to grow the lens of how I was looking at the world, at myself, and where He had placed me. He needed me to **G.R.O.W.** out of my short-sightedness and see the bigger picture, but I couldn't seem to see with my vision solely focused on what I perceived were the obstacles or "rocks" in my life.

I had a dream where God showed me how I have to expand my vision. In the dream I was staring at rocks by the ocean and that was all I could see.

All of these rock formations were jagged and had worn areas with not much color or depth to them. He had me look up and expand my view to see where I actually was. Yes, I was on a rock, but that wasn't the only place I was. I was on a rock by the ocean, surrounded by a stunning sunset and so many beautiful colors that accompanied it.

The beauty and the colors in the scenery all around me were always there but I couldn't see them because I was so insistent on focusing on the rocks. It was all right there but I couldn't see it. Then God spoke to me about his omnipresence, His ability to be in all places, in all things, at all times. He described it like the cloud or the fog at the beach during my birthday weekend, and how it had touched and surrounded everything and everyone.

He was engulfing the entire planet with His all-encompassing love and almighty power. He explained that while He is that vast and incomprehensible to our human minds, He is also beautifully personal and when we talk or pray to God, He becomes more pronounced right there with us, and the light comes down from heaven much like the sun rays that come through the clouds and look like "light from Heaven" that shine directly into you.

His light filling you and I, permeating and connecting God to us. God to you and you to God. "Beam me up" is exactly what it looks like!

He began to speak to me again, saying:

I'm still surrounding everything; My presence is infinite. You were given the gift to be able to **G.R.O.W.** *in power by tapping into what was always there. I want you to plug into Me.*

I am the unlimited source that is meant to help you **G.R.O.W.** *up: up towards me, towards your highest self, up into your soul and out of your body.*

Your body should be used to express the power and love you are receiving from Me, and not only something you use to soak up the world by using people, places, and things to try to fill you up and give you the peace that you can never seem to find when you try to take the path of the flesh instead of the path of the Spirit.

Each one of you is created to have a blessed life and not a stressed life, but somehow you think if you don't have a stressed life, you can't reach the blessed life.

You struggle and you hustle and say out loud to yourself and to each other how "insane" your days are, as if that was how I intended your life to be, that it is normal. It is NOT NORMAL to be in the state of "insanity." It is literally cause for someone to step in and have an intervention with you.

I'm trying to give you that intervention right now. If you think your life, your work, your family, or any relationships you have are "insane," then something needs to change and fast. There is a slowing down and a reprioritization that needs to be happening so your sanity can return and you can hear My voice again bringing you to a place and a pace of peace that will bear the right fruit in your life. Frantic is not a fruit of the Spirit, I know the world has somehow tricked you into believing that, but let Me state again, "FRANTIC"IS NOT A FRUIT OF MY KINGDOM!

I want to return all of you to a pace that is lifegiving, not life-draining. Have faith that a life and calling exists for you that will not feel insane but will feel fulfilling and fun, full of wonder does not worry, gratitude not griping and grasping, filled purpose and abundance not debt and a sinking feeling of emptiness.

If you would seek first what I want you to do, what My plans and purposes are for your life, all those things you think you need will either fade away or will be provided for.

Aren't you tired of chasing money? When will it be enough for you? Do you even have a target number you are running toward, and who will you be when you finally get to that number? Where did you even get that number from anyway? Will your soul feel secure at that number? Will your salvation be solidified? Will the people you want to appreciate you and see your value finally recognize it? And then what?

How will your life and legacy be fulfilled after you have gathered up all these riches and grasped tightly to them as if they can save you? Money can't save you. It is a tool, not a balm for the hole in your soul that believes the lie that if you made enough money, you would then be worth something.

Jesus had no money, no home, no pantry filled with food, no garage stuffed with things, and yet He was so filled with joy, peace, patience, kindness, goodness, self-control, and a passion-filled purpose for his life that people with tons of money and with no money came to Him to get what He had. To the human eye, He technically had nothing. He had grown out of the idea that things and money brought security, importance, love, or approval.

He warned over and over that you can't chase after Him and money, you will love one and despise the other. The amazing thing is that if you chase after Him the gifts of abundance will naturally follow. They will flow to you so they can flow through you. But if you consistently worry about how much money you can make, you choke the flow of life in you.

Many times, the more you have, the tighter you hold to it instead of becoming more and more generous with it. It's not YOUR money, it's My money, you are the steward of My blessings, not the source of your own blessings.

When you become self-righteous and judgmental instead of grateful and generous, you are turning from me and turning toward your own self-worship.

Pride always goes before the fall.
(Proverbs 16:18, modified)

I am a generous God who gives and gives as an example of what you should be doing. Do not hold onto your riches as if they are a security blanket, they can't buy your life another day, they can't fix the relationships you are wrecking because you have decided that making money is more important than making time.

They can't buy you peace in your soul that lasts, and it certainly can't buy you salvation and power that I want to give you. Money can't buy it because I give it freely.

I gave you life and blessings freely, and now so many of you analyze and calculate whether someone else deserves to be blessed by you? Calculating if this person in need deserves your help that you have been blessed to be in a position to do something about. GROW UP! Where did you get such a hardened fearful heart? What do you think you will lose by helping another?

....Truly I tell you, whatever you did for the least of these brothers and sisters of Mine, you did for me.
(Matthew 25: 40, NIV)

***G**et **R**id **O**f **W**orry, it's choking the life out of you and causing hurt and shame in others who humbly come to you and ask for your help. You will be a corpse walking before you realize it because of that kind of hardened heart and restricted flow of life and blessings that was meant to flow THROUGH you, and not just flow TO you.*

Grow out of your limitations. You have placed all of these requirements on your life that I never intended to be there. You are fighting to keep a life you don't even want. Grow out of it! You are more than you think you are. You don't even know all the gifts I have placed inside of you that you have yet to uncover. You have to try new things, you have to grow in new ways, get out of your comfort zone, blow past the walls you have set up around yourself. Get comfortably uncomfortable with not knowing where I am leading you.

Just because something is not comfortable for you, does not mean you are not called to do it.

Don't Give up, **G.R.O.W.** *up! Grow out of holding yourself back and grow into pressing forward to run your race with excitement and faith.*

Staying with it – That's what is required. Stay with it to the end. You won't be sorry; you will be saved.
(Luke 21:19, MSG)

If you spent as much mental energy on growing up as you do on making excuses for why you are giving up, you would be amazed how far we could go together.

I didn't know what to say to that. I felt like God was holding this incredibly uncomfortable—but necessary—mirror up to my face and saying, *"This was not what I wanted for you. Is this what you still want for you?"* I didn't want to chase after worthless things. I didn't want to waste any more time holding on to things I clearly needed to get rid of if I was going to move toward the calling on my life.

I looked at the list of all the things I needed to get rid of and I thought, "Okay, okay, I did that, I can do that, I'm doing that...." I still felt stuck, but I know what God's word says to do when I feel this way.

....If you want to know what God wants you to do- ask him, and he will gladly tell you
(James 1: 5, NLT)

So, I went for a jog, and I kept talking to God, telling him "Okay Lord, so I know all the things I need to get rid of, but then what? How do I grow out of the pruning?"

God responded:

*I'll tell you, but you aren't going to like it, because you already know what to do. If you want to know what to do, how to **G.R.O.W.** up, **G**o -**R**ead- **O**ur- **W**ord. See, I put the remedy right there in the question! Our Word— the Word of God—spoken directly through the prophets, spoken through My Son, and spoken through the body of Christ, the Church, and the Apostles. We are one united body. When Jesus gave His life, He completed the circle. He brought us back together so It Is Finished, and there is no separation.*

These are no longer just My words, or their words, they are OUR words and I want you to use them more. I want you to speak Jesus through Jen! Use Godly replies and use the Word to figure out how to respond to uncomfortable conversations, texts messages, emails, or any other way you choose to communicate with others. Intertwine so deeply the way you speak with the way I speak. I want to use your personality, your style, your sense of humor, all of it. I just want it to be marinated in Me so that the taste of your words are life-giving and create a hunger in others to learn where you get your recipe, your flavor for life, from. Make them curious enough to ask where your life and faith grew out of?

*And when they start to ask these questions, you can wink and smile as you hand them a copy of the "playbook" and say you have to **G.R.O.W.** Up, **G**et **R**id **O**f **W**orry and **G**o **R**ead **O**ur **W**ord!*

*Real growth begins by getting rid of those worthless thinking habits and replacing them with the seeds of abundant life. Where can such seeds be found so that they can begin to take root and grow? They can be found when you **G**o **R**ead **O**ur **W**ord.*

Through the Word we are put together and shaped for the tasks God has for us
(2 Timothy 3:17, MSG).

So don't lose a minute in building on what you've been given, complementing your basic faith with good character, spiritual understanding, alert discipline, passionate patience, reverent wonder, warm friendliness, and generous love, each dimension fitting into and developing the others. With these qualities active and growing in your lives, no grass will grow under your feet, no day will pass without its reward as you mature in your experience of our Master Jesus
(2 Peter 1:5-8, MSG)

Summing Up: Be agreeable, be sympathetic, be loving, be compassionate, be humble. That goes for all of you. No exceptions, no retaliation. No sharp-tongued sarcasm. Instead, bless—that's your job, to bless. You'll be a blessing and also get a blessing. Whoever wants to embrace life and see the day fill up with good, Here's what you do: Say nothing evil or hurtful; Snub evil and cultivate good; run after peace for all you're worth. God looks on all this with approval, listening and responding well to what He's asked; But He turns his back on those who do evil things
(1 Peter 3:8 -12, MSG)

If you don't know what you're doing, pray to the Father. He loves to help. You'll get his help and won't be condescended to when you ask for it. Ask boldly, believingly, without a second thought. People who "worry their prayers" are like wind- whipped waves. Don't think you're going to get anything from the Master that way, adrift at sea, keeping all your options open
(James 1:5-6, MSG)

G.R.O.W. *Up and get to* **W.O.R.K.***!*

      Go **R**epresent **O**ur **W**ay. *The way that leads to everlasting life.* **G**o **R**epresent **O**ur **W**ay *of loving each other.* **G**o **R**epresent **O**ur **W**ay *of radical generosity.* **G**o **R**epresent **O**ur **W**ay *of speaking to one another. Grow your world so you can show more people what freedom in God looks like. When they see you, do you seem to represent something a little bit different? Do people look at you and think you are radiating a light that the world seems to be lacking?*

      Go **R**epresent **O**ur **W**ay *of being a friend, a neighbor, a sister, a brother, a wife, a husband, a mother, a daughter. The way we live life should look otherworldly because you are no longer of this world, but merely in this world.*

G.R.O.W. *in your understanding of Me, though you will never truly understand Me because*

My thoughts are not your thoughts,
My ways are not your ways.
(Isaiah 55:8, NLT)

      G.R.O.W. *into the nature of the Holy Spirit that resides in you and works through you. And more than anything, BE INTENTIONAL. Be intentional in your thoughts, choose them wisely. Put My words in your mind and heart so they will effortlessly flow back out of you* *when they are needed. Choose to get rid of worry and actively choose to pray about ways in which*

I am working all things out for the good of those who love me and are called to my purpose.
(Romans 8:28, modified)

*Be intentional with the formations of your friendships, **G**et **R**id **O**f **W**oulda-coulda-shoulda and look at what is. Discern who they really are when they interact with you. Don't pour your heart out to every person right away, see what their intentions are for each of you. The light cannot be yoked with the dark, goodness has no business with evil when joining together to work for the kingdom.*

If God's not in it, You don't want it, I promise.

*Also be intentional about your self-care - **G**et **R**id **O**f **W**eight and waste in your body that is keeping you from serving your purpose to the best of your ability. Be intentional with your finances, don't throw your money around, steward it, think about how you are using it and does each purchase have a purpose? Does it bring you closer to God or to each other? It is cash for the Kingdom or cash for more trash.*

*Be intentional about your work and **G**et **R**id **O**f **W**ishing. It takes real effort to grow up. I can't change you without your willingness to be changed. My gifts are free but they must be accepted for my grace and power to be fully activated in you. Get a clear vision about the directions I am leading you to grow, and then commit yourself to letting me transform you spiritually from the inside out. Be intentional with your words, **G**et **R**id **O**f **W**hining and self-pity.*

For I did not give you a spirit of timidity, but of Power, love, and self-control
(2nd Tim 1:7, Modified)

Let me work my ways into you so I can work your ways out of you! The pity party way of life is immature and self-centered. It's fine to have concerns and take steps to correct those concerns, but the wallowing, worrying, and whining is wasting precious time. Get up, **G.R.O.W.** *up, do what you can about it,* **G***o* **R***ead* **O***ur* **W***ord, pray, and come talk to me about it.*

Be intentional about looking at the bigger picture. Widen your perspective. Open your spiritual eyes to see what only I can show you. Believe it before you see it. Faith comes through hearing My word about what is, not by first seeing what is. Look for where I want you to serve others.

For even the Son of Man came here not to be served
but to serve others
(Mathew 20:28, NLT)

This is your **W.O.R.K** *in this world. Your* **W***orldly* **O***pportunity* **R***equiring* **K***indness. You are to become more obsessed with how you can serve others than how others can serve you. Stop eating all you can and start feeding others. Grow up and become a speaker-servant, one who feeds people the living Word of God. One who feeds them hope, truth, love, compassion, joy, and healing. I have placed in you the gift of healing and the gift of words, the gift of humor and the gift of encouragement, so use them, grow into your gifts. Every one of you have sacred and special gifts I've blessed you with and they are all desperately needed in this world!*

There is no plan B to the masterpiece I created when I crafted each of you and purposed you with your unique way of expressing Me in this world through your gifts. There is so much **W.O.R.K.** *out there right now, so many* **W***orldly* **O***pportunities* **R***equiring* **K***indness.*

You don't need one more dollar to do this **W.O.R.K.** *I have given you everything you need to begin; two eyes to see the opportunities all around you, two willing hands to stretch out to the hurting, two feet ready to move toward that which I have called you, two ears longing to hear how you can help another, one heart filled with compassion, and a mouth filled with encouragement and loving, honoring words of faith, hope and love. You have all you need, so get to* **W.O.R.K.***!*

Will you be faithful in the small **W.O.R.K.***, the daily* **W.O.R.K.** *that only you and I will know about, so that I can enlarge your territory? Will you have an attitude of gratitude on your lips and an honoring spirit working in your heart? Work at honoring everyone where they are at, for the simple but profound fact that they are my image bearer.*

Honor Me in them even if they don't confess to know Me at all, or even curse My name, blaming Me for the pain life has brought to them. They are still My children, and nothing they can do will ever change that. I made them. I love them. I want them, even if they are going through their own "prodigal" season right now. Let Me run to them with your two feet, wrap My love around them with your two arms, and welcome them home, through your loving words. This is your calling, This is your **W.O.R.K.**

Go into all the world and preach the Good News to everyone, everywhere.
(Mark 16:15, NLT)

G.R.O.W. *Up and Get to* **W.O.R.K.***!*

Chapter 9
S.I.N.K or S.W.I.M.
You Choose

Stuck – **In** – **N**ot – **K**nowing

or

Spirit - **W**ork – **In** – **M**e

But when he looked around at the high waves, he was terrified and began to SINK. "Save me Lord!" he shouted. Instantly Jesus reached out his hand and grabbed him, "You don't have much faith", Jesus said "Why did you doubt me?"
(Matthew 14:31, NLT)

When Simon Peter heard it was the Lord, He put on his tunic and jumped into the water to SWIM ashore
(John 21:7, NLT)

"Swimmers, take your mark!"

These are instructions every swimmer who has ever competed in a race is familiar with. This is the signal to prepare yourself that the race that has been set before you is about to begin. All of the preparation, all of the morning practices, all of the instructions the coach has taught you comes together in this one moment.

When swimmers "take their mark," it is a posture that they take on the starting blocks. A posture where they bend at the hips, flex at the knees, position their fingertips to balance their weight as they lean forward with their head up, eyes focused on the lane in front of them. They are relaxed but ready, excited, and controlled. It is an attentively intense state, where your ears burn as they tune in and prepare themselves for the sound of the buzzer to go off and the race to begin. The posture is meant to get the swimmer in the best position to spring into action, to dive in. It is a position of harnessed power when a swimmer takes their mark.

Before the race began, before you ever stepped up onto those starting blocks, the lanes were already set out for you. The race that you would be swimming in was already chosen. Even the lane number and the heat number you would be swimming in, were all predetermined. If you are chosen for a team race, your team members are also already chosen for you by the coach. You won't have to fight for your lane. You won't have to push people out of the way to get into a certain heat or on a certain block. It has all been laid out before you, and this is how it is with God and His purpose for your life. He has laid it all out for you.

No one else can swim your race, but you do get to decide if you want to swim in the race or not. Up on those blocks, there is a wide-open lane of opportunity set up just for you. Even if you swim with a team for a relay race, the lane is open for you when your time comes to dive in.

While each person effects the race as a whole, just like each part of the body of Christ effects the entirety of it, when it is your turn, your time to swim and do your part, the lane is all yours. It is wide open for you to offer up all you have been given—all your strengths, your gifts, your training, and your focus—to swim this race. It is always an open lane when God calls you to the race.

When God calls us to the race He has chosen for us, he too says "Take your mark," but this is not a command, it is an invitation to all the gifts he wants to give you. It is a choice to no longer take the "mark" of this world and its selfish ways, but instead to say I will take YOUR "mark," God. When you take God's mark, you take on the heart posture of eager submission. You open yourself to allow the Holy Spirit to take the lead. You take the mark symbolizing that you no longer swim for yourself, or for the world, but you are on a new team now. You now swim for—and with—God.

Everyone who is on the blocks is on the team. You don't get an invitation, a lane, and an appointed race time, without first joining the team. And you certainly won't get placed on those blocks if you haven't learned to swim yet. Your coach will have already assessed your gifts, determined your best stroke, identified your strengths, and he will have spent hours coaching you, honing your techniques, and letting you practice diving off the blocks, and repeating the "take your mark" position over and over until it becomes your natural ready state. God is the same way; He does not throw you into a race He has not equipped you for.

For God is working in you, giving you the desire and the power to do what pleases him
(Philippians 2:13, NLT)

Those he predestined, he also called, those he called, he also justified, those he justified, he also glorified
(Romans 8: 30, NIV)

While God completely equips, justifies, and glorifies you in the races He sets out for you, ensuring victory in the purposes He has planned.

He in no way ensures or equips you for all the "races" you set out for yourself. You randomly try to dive into things He never called you to and then find yourself crying and praying and mad that you are now drowning, or at least that has been my story, time, and time again.

If I were to try diving off the blocks without knowing how to swim, or if I ignorantly try to "figure it out" by what I saw other people doing without having actually taken any swim lessons for myself, that would be an obvious recipe for disaster. Yet, we do this with our lives all the time when we jump into waters we have no clue how to handle without a life-saving device or a coach to hold onto.

Have you ever seen someone trying to swim who doesn't actually know how to swim? They are in the water doing all they can to make up some sort of stroke, that not only looks all kinds of wrong, but is completely inefficient and exhausting as half their body is dragging behind them while the other half flails, thrashes, and gasps for breath, frantically turning their head side to side but never putting it in the water at all. They are dog paddling their way through the water, their head barely staying above the waterline, and calling that swimming. You aren't swimming, you are only sustaining yourself enough to not drown.

As a Lifeguard, I watched over a lot of people who "kinda" knew how to swim, or at least had learned how to not die while playing in the water, as long as the water was calm, and they could touch the bottom if they needed to. I felt so bad watching over them all, and I wanted to give them simple pointers that would have made their time in the water not only safer, but much more relaxed, less exhausting, and a lot more fun.

A few simple pointers on the proper way to breathe through their stroke. How to use their legs to power them through the water. How to adjust their hip position so they wouldn't sink, or how to hold their hands to give them more surface area to help them move further with each stroke would have completely changed how they felt physically.

It would have changed how they appeared on the outside, and would have exponentially helped them not only get where they are trying to go with much more speed and accuracy, but also with increased strength and confidence. As I thought about watching over all those people below me, I heard God say

That's how I feel watching so many of you thrash and gasp and struggle in your lives. Saddened that even though I sent the Holy Spirit, to not just give you pointers on the techniques that would help you, but the power to be able to do it, you have refused to accept Him. Insisting you already know how and that "You got this," when clearly, you don't "got this."

I sent Him to give you clarity and make your spirit strong while you swim in the many waters you will face in life, but you have to let Him show you, guide you, and teach you the ways that will work best for you. Yes, He will bring discipline to your life, and that will require engaging muscles you hadn't had to use when you took your own mark in your life and tried to "just make it work."

When you live a life like that, on your own power, your goal isn't really to learn how to master swimming because you don't know how to do that anyway without instructions, your life goal becomes not drowning and to come up with some semblance of a stroke that will let you survive, and not one that will help you thrive. You hope it will get you by without really having to try, and that's how most of you look as you live out your lives.

This is not how I created you. I created you to **S.W.I.M.***! Can you humble yourself enough to realize you need to take your Mark, to say the words,* **S***pirit* **W***ork* **I***n* **M***e. I can't* **S.W.I.M.** *in this world without you. You have to let Him take control over everything you had previously been doing to just keep your head above water and trust that He knows what you need to learn to live the life you were called to live, as a champion for the Kingdom.*

Your inspiration will have to change. How you breathe in the world has to change. You will no longer be gasping and trashing your head around with no direction or rhythm.

No, now you will have an intention behind your breath, a relaxation and rhythm in your breath. Your inspiration and exhalation will change. He will train you to keep your eyes focused, no longer looking all over with legs and arms flailing.

I have sent a "swimmers manual," Scriptures for success. How to **S.W.I.M.** *in this world without drowning. My holy and living Word was sent to help you with each stroke. I sent instructions on how to control your body, your breath, your focus, your rhythm, and it is all time-tested and God approved. It has been proven to work 100% of the time.*

Heaven and earth will disappear,
but my words will remain forever
(Matthew 24: 35, NLT)

My Word will bring you life, and save you from sinking, from drowning. Yes, it takes discipline and I know you shrink back from those words. Most of you think discipline equals restriction and that I am keeping you from something, but your discipline is My way of saving you FOR something! I have a purpose and plan for you, and it's awesome.

As you learn each of the disciplines, the life you live, the "strokes" you use, not only get easier, but they become enjoyable, and then they become your second nature. The old habits and ways of doing things will no longer feel right when you are taken over by the Spirit and have dedicated your life to the new race I have set before you.

Professional swimmers do not think about every single part of their body when they swim, nor do they think, "kick, pull, breathe, kick, pull, breathe" as they move down their lane, they just swim! All of it is no longer a separate, confusing, uncoordinated part of a stroke. It all moves as one fluid motion that has immense power, direction, and drive. And while they can see the other swimmers out of the corner of their eye, they know they will mess up their rhythm, lengthen their time, and alter their direction if they were turn their head completely to focus on someone else's race instead of focusing on their own race, in their own lane, where they are headed and what they need to do to finish strong.

But forgetting all that, some of you are still refusing to accept that it takes hours of practice to learn how to swim and dive safely and skillfully. If you still choose, as many of you do in life, to try swimming or diving with zero instruction or preparation, your "best case" scenario is that you will exhaust yourself, look like a crazy person, and barely get where you are trying to go. Unfortunately, the "worst-case" scenario happens more often; you break your neck and are paralyzed for life by diving into places where you should never dive, or you kill yourself before you ever got the chance to swim your race.

The same things that could kill you when used in the wrong place at the wrong time, in the wrong way, can also catapult you to the next level when used in the right way and at the right time.

Diving, when done properly, is the most powerful launching skill you can use to not only get you off the blocks quickly, but also set the pace for your whole race.

To dive properly when racing, you jump out and slightly up, keeping a relatively shallow dive that propels you forward with the least amount of energy needed to glide under the water and then you use your legs to dolphin kick under the water as far as possible so that when you finally rise to the surface you are in your full spirit mode. The race has begun! But what happens if you dive down and in? The race has now ended before you even got one stroke in. You just dove headfirst into a concrete bottom of a pool and you ended your race before you even started because you refused to assess the situation you were in, to discern the depth of water, or see if there were any dangers in the area.

You refused to ask someone with experience if there was a proper technique or best practice when entering the water. If you could have put away your pride and humbled yourself to the fact that you don't know everything. If you had been open enough to seek out instruction on how to learn to dive, it would have been something you would have been able to use to help you instead of hurt you.

I wish I could have had this realization decades ago, and I am seriously surprised it took me this long because, just like the dancing I mentioned in an earlier chapter, swimming and being in and around the water was something I was a part of since before I was born! It's literally in my DNA!

My mom was born and raised in the Virgin Islands surrounded by water and in the water almost daily. Still to this day, she is happiest when she has a body of water, any body of water really, that she can stare at or dip her toes in especially around sunset. These days she settles for the pool in my parents' backyard to bring her this needed daily dose of water in her life.

While my mom settles more for just being near the water, my dad has been an avid swimmer all his life and taught both my brothers and me how to swim before we even had walking down pat! And because of that, I don't recall the first time I saw the ocean, played in a pool, learned how to swim, or learned how to dive because I was so young when my dad and my coaches taught me.

It is a blessing when your family instills in you skills that could save your life, like swimming, or being introduced to God and His ways at an early age, and my family did their best to do both. While I was like a fish in water from a very young age, a water baby in every sense of the word, I was definitely a much slower learner when it came to applying many of the principles of swimming and diving to my walk with God, and my relationships with other people.

I have been a notorious, look-before-I–leap and dive-before-I-discern type of person my whole life, up until this chapter was written and this life lesson was revealed in such a way I could fully grasp it and begin to apply it in my life. God rubbed some **D.I.R.T.** on my eyes to reveal what I had been blind to all these years, and that deeper insight definitely renewed my thinking!
I could finally see what I was doing, and how I was ending so many "races" He had given to me because of my impatience and my pride. By diving in headfirst and refusing to wait on God's timing, I was not only destroying my chances at new relationships or new opportunities, but I was also destroying my purpose just like that! I was disqualifying myself over and over, and blaming it on the race, the officials, the buzzer, the other swimmers... it was clearly NOT me! No way, I was not going to take the blame for why I kept fouling out.

I was repeatedly refusing to wait on God's timing and refusing to use God's techniques for how to best approach my race, my purpose, and my relationships. I was finding myself sidelined over and over again. I had a coach, I had the Holy Spirit, and I had joined the team, but I wasn't acting like it.

I was welcome to participate with the team, but I wanted to do what I wanted to do, when I wanted to do it, and it was ruining my life, destroying my relationships, wrecking my races, and confusing my soul.

At this point in my life, I had found myself sidelined and sad, desperate, and quickly coming to the realization that it was impossible that EVERY life race that I was disqualified from was always someone or something else's fault. I clearly had to be doing something wrong, because I was the only constant factor in every single circumstance.

Luckily, my coach, the Big H.S. (Holy Spirit) Himself, is a comforter, an advocate, a counselor, and an encourager. He will leave the whole team to come sit next to me and give me a pep talk to help me not only connect fully with Him and my teammates, but also to get me back in the race, and set me up for victory.

Every team needs a coach. Every successful swimmer has a coach, and every successful "kid of the Kingdom" has Christ as their head coach and the Holy Spirit as their own personal coach. You can join the team and never learn to really swim. When you accept Jesus as your "head coach," the one who signs you up and makes a way for you, you are in! It's done! He wants EVERYONE on the team, and there is room for everyone on Team Jesus.

Even if you never swim in a race, or work on your stroke, you still get to come to the pizza party at the end of the season, which I believe is the equivalent of Heaven on earth for most kids! You are guaranteed a spot in the picture and invited over to His house to celebrate and make it your own. You are accepted, wanted, loved, and chosen. While all these things are 100% true for the swim team, and of the Kingdom of God, that is not all there is to joining the team. You have to "take your mark," you have to accept the race that God set before you, you have to climb onto the blocks, and intentionally decide to **S.W.I.M.**! That's what the team is made for, to **S.W.I.M.**!

And to do that effectively, you have to ask for the "mark," the gift of the Holy Spirit. By saying "**S**pirit **W**ork **I**n **M**e" you activate your personal coach and allow Him to come alive and start your training, your instructions on the proper way to best swim your race, to best live out your life! He can't wait to teach you, encourage you, lavish gifts on you. Gifts that are all paid for and included in your membership when you joined the team, but you have to accept them, you have to claim them.

When I was very young, the "six and under" group of the swim team had a massive gap between the skill level of those of us who had been swimming since we were two and those who joined the team that summer and had never been swimming before in their life.

Sometimes, on days when we would have a swim meet and it was a new swimmer's turn to get up on the blocks, they would climb up, but never take their mark, and certainly not dive in. At six years old, and in regard to the swim team, it's kind of adorable and your heart goes out to the kid that is just standing there thinking that the starting block WAS the main event! They were just so excited about the diving blocks, not realizing the blocks were the starting point for their race and not the destination.

So many Christians seem to be in the same position. They accepted Jesus and joined the team. He was the way to get to the starting blocks, to have a lane, to have a race that was chosen for them to win at, but God didn't intend for you to just stay there. He sent you a personal coach. He sent the Holy Spirit to teach you how to **S.W.I.M,** not how to **S.I.N.K.**

He didn't want you to get **S**tuck **I**n **N**ot **K**nowing that you were made for more. **S**tuck **I**n **N**ot **K**nowing that there were gifts that you had access to that would strengthen you and equip you for your race. Jesus gets you on the blocks, the Holy Spirit helps you win the race by swimming with you, training you, and empowering you! If you only stand on the blocks, if you only accept Jesus as your Savior, that is wonderful! You are saved. You are going to that pizza party in the sky, but you missed the joy of the opportunity to **S.W.I.M.** your race.

You missed the chance to see the strength that you possess when the Spirit is at work in you. You missed your chance to enjoy the feel of the water as you completely immerse yourself in your gifts and talents that were given to you to help the whole team win, and to experience the full expression of what you as an individual and as a member of the team were created to do—to **S.W.I.M.**

God began to explain:

*So many people have refused to accept that they are really on the team, so they **S.I.N.K.**. They feel their **S**oul **I**s **N**ot **K**nown, not wanted, not seen, not empowered, and with that feeling of disconnect comes discord in every part of their life. Notice that I said, they **"FEEL"** not known, not that they **"ARE"** not known.*

YOU ARE KNOWN

I have known every one of you since before you were born. Every hair on your head, every breath you take is accounted for and your name is recorded in the Book of Life, Yes...

Rejoice because your names are registered in Heaven (Luke10:20, NLT)

You are on the team, and I know you; I see you, but that does not mean YOU know that, or that you allow yourself to fully believe it and feel it completely. The devil's playbook is still the same, it's so old, and yet still works on your spirit in such damaging ways if you don't abide in me, rest in me, remain in me, and let me be your source, your safety, your fortress, your shield. The devil comes like a thief and

The thief's purpose is to steal, and kill, and destroy (John 10:10, NLT)

He delights in whispering lies to you.

There is no truth in him. When he lies, it is consistent with his character; for he is a liar and the father of lies (John 8: 44, NLT)

so, he does what comes naturally to him; he whispers into your soul any chance he can get, and instills fear where there should be none, and you **S.I.N.K**. *into despair. You start to believe that your* **Soul Is Not Known** *and that you are all alone in this world.*

Nothing will leave you more vulnerable or more prone to devaluing and degrading yourself faster than believing that you have no one who cares for you, and nothing to care about. You are built to be known, to be understood, and I know you.

Even if that is hard for you to comprehend, or if you never even heard that was possible, let me tell you now, it is true, and it grieves me to watch you **S.I.N.K**. *into depression, anxiety, and addiction.*

You **S.I.N.K**. *into abusive relationships, grasping at anything or anyone you can grab ahold of—except Me—on your way down. Yet everything you grasp at only weighs you down and causes you to sink deeper and faster, or worse, it causes you to pull others down with you. Have you ever seen a drowning person who is approached by another swimmer who is not skilled in rescuing drowning victims? That concerned and well-intending person never saw what was coming.*

*The drowning victim will not only grab onto them for dear life, but they will also push the other person under the water as they try to hold themselves up as long as possible. Now we have not one, but two people in a possibly life-threatening situation. This is what I see in so many of your relationships. You are grabbing onto people who are ill-equipped to pull you up. All of their advice or coping mechanisms they offer are useless, and only good for pulling you further in the wrong direction. Instead of helping you to reach up, they push and pull you down, further, and further. Only by reaching up, by asking "**S**pirit **W**ork **I**n **M**e, give me Your power to learn how to **S.W.I.M,**" only then will you begin to rise. It's*

...not by might, nor by power,
but by my Spirit
(Zechariah 4:6, NIV)

...that you will conquer the pain pulling you down!

When you can accept the help that comes from Christ, through the gift of the Holy Spirit, you are known forever, you have a friend that will never leave. You are on the TEAM! You are in the family.

*All who have the Holy Spirit working in them are on the **S.W.I.M.** Team, the Christ Crew, the Heavenly Homies, the God Squad!*

*You are known, you are wanted, you have a place and purpose on this team. If you can embrace this beautiful gift of a faith-filled family, you will have people around you when you start to feel like you are sinking who will be able to remind you that you have everything it takes to **S.W.I.M.** as you call out "**S**pirit **W**ork **I**n **M**e!". And if life becomes too much and you do start to **S.I.N.K.**, you start to feel like you can't move, can't pray, can't breathe, or discern which direction you should be swimming in anymore, you will have teammates who can come along side you, hook arms with you and **S.W.I.M.** up with you. You will all rise together as you keep listening for the voice that is calling you up, calling you back to safety.*

*Don't **S**tay **I**n **N**ot **K**nowing, leaving all the gifts the Holy Spirit wanted to give you undiscovered, not realizing that all these gifts are meant for you and have your name on them. You **S.I.N.K.** into depression or anxiety, you **S.I.N.K.** into debt, into a poverty mentality, into victimhood, **S**tubbornly **I**nsisting **N**ot **K**nowing that you are more than a conqueror, destined to live out your divinity through Christ.*

*So many of you are refusing to accept that you not only have a "coach" who knows all things and has supernatural power to help you overcome any obstacle, but is also a comforter, an advocate, an encourager, a wise counselor, and a friend. So many of you have joined the team, but then **S.I.N.K.** back to your old ways of doing things before you joined. You are refusing to take your mark as a new creation, ready to do a new thing.*

The Holy Spirit can teach you all things, he has the gift of Wisdom to give you to help you discern the new information and new races in which you will find yourself. He has the gift of knowledge to help you understand things you could not have known otherwise.

*He offers the gift of faith, to empower you to **F**ollow **A**n **I**nner **T**ruth **H**ome, to have an inner compass that is stronger than any data that could be collected, or diagnosis that could be given.*

Faith is the gift to believe in things that are not seen or understood in the natural, and you are free to ask for more of it! It's yours! You can ask for your gift of healings and the gift of miracles.

Yes, the Holy Spirit is just waiting to give you all of these gifts when you are ready to open your hands and hearts to ask for them, to claim them.

There is a gift of prophecy at your disposal to be able to see what is to come and speak encouragement into another person so that they may achieve all that is in them! He has the gift of your heavenly language that is just for you and the Lord. It is your own private way to let your soul speak and intercede for you, to build yourself up in the spirit when your own understanding and words fail. This is something everyone can have if you ask for it.

So many people are frightened or unsure of the gifts that are their inheritance when they were born into the Spirit, so they are left unopened. Who would ever leave a gift unopened that had your name written right on the tag? A gift that your own Father had left for you and told you that He had these gifts to give you? Who would just walk by and leave these gifts unopened and untouched... lots of people apparently.

*Lots of people look at the gifts I have for them, and their heart starts to **S.I.N.K.** as they **S**tubbornly **I**nsist **N**ot **K**nowing that these gifts are for them. They stay **S**tuck **I**n **N**ot **K**nowing that they are my child, that I love to lavish gifts on them, I have created for each of them amazing gifts that would help them as they live out their Kingdom calling here on Earth.*

On earth, as it is in heaven
(Matthew 6:10, NLT)

I want all these heavenly gifts to be used on earth to help you, to help others, to expand my vision, to let my Kingdom come, and my will be done.

*My love comes through you and my work is accomplished through you. You are my kingdom on earth, so take every gift and use it as part of your testimony to the power you have when you **S.W.I.M.** in my love, when you let the Holy Spirit work in you.*

*All these gifts are yours to help you **S.W.I.M.** your race., but you do have to SEEK them out.*

Seek first the kingdom of God and his righteousness and all these things will be added to you
(Matthew 6: 33, ESV)

As God's voice quieted, and I sat reflecting on what it would be like to "seek the kingdom," I thought about these gifts that are ours, these treasures that are immersed in the waters of the spirit of the kingdom and I remembered childhood swim team parties where the coaches would throw money into the pool while all the kids waited outside, and when it was time, they would invite us in and tell us that there were treasures underneath the water and we could keep as much as we could find. The deeper we were able to dive, the more gifts, i.e., money, that we would discover.

157

I think the kingdom of heaven and the gifts of the spirit are like that swim team party. There are so many treasures waiting at different depths for us to discover, and while it takes a greater amount of strength, energy, determination, intention, and focus to get to those deeper levels, the rewards were also greater.

God said to me...

That is absolutely true, the greater the depths, the greater the treasures, but it does require that you get in and take an active role to seek out the treasure, and then DIVE for it! You will remain empty if you choose to sit on the edge of the pool of life, on the edge of the Kingdom of heaven, and refuse to dive in and claim what is waiting for you. The scripture says "SEEK," but what does seeking even look like? It is an earnest, urgent, intentional, active, and full body search for something.

*It is getting to the bottom of the pool and discerning if what you saw at the surface is turning out to be trash or treasure. Was it a marble or money, garbage, or gold? You have to be willing to **D.I.V.E.** for it. A successful **D.I.V.E.** for something of value requires you to **D**iscern – **I**nvestigate – **V**alidate - **E**xcavate.*

Discern with the Holy Spirit if this is even a place that you should be swimming, much less diving, in the first place. When trying to find friends or a spouse, maybe deep diving at a dive bar is not going to produce the treasures you are looking for. Some waters, and some relationships, are not suitable for diving. Either they are too shallow to be handle your dive, or the rip tide is too strong, i.e.,...your temptations are too strong, so you shouldn't be diving in that area to begin with.

***D**iscern, ask for the gift of wisdom in that first step. If you get a Yes, this is a safe place to dive and has the potential to hold treasure for you," then start to **I**nvestigate, look around and see what you find.*

*Take a closer look. Ask yourself questions. Look it over and if it seems like it could add value to your life and your purpose, stop and ask the Holy Spirit to **V**alidate what you are investigating. Pursue slowly, carefully, and wait for His validation. Wait for the Yes, that this is a gift from God placed there for you, whether it was an actual item, a job, a relationship, a house, a new city to move to, or any choice that is needed to be made. Seek His validation only.*

*When you seek everyone's validation, you will get confused. Remember, one person's trash is another's treasure, so just because someone else might think they would benefit from it, does not mean you will. Actively seek the Spirit's validation that it will be a blessing in YOUR life and a help to YOUR pursuit of the purpose God's calling you into. Keep your **S**piritual **W**orth **I**n **M**ind, but also keep the **S**piritual **W**orth **I**n **M**ind of whatever, or whomever, you are swimming after.*

*Ask yourself, "Is it (or are they) even worth swimming toward?" Don't **S.I.N.K**. below your spiritual worth for fool's gold, cheap thrills, comfort that lacks commitment, or pleasure that is sure to pass, because it is never worth it. But once you do get that validation from the Holy Spirit, when you get the "yes, this has worth for you," then you can **E**xcavate it. You should dig it up with care and take it with you, cherish it, honor it, make it a part of who you are and who it is you represent. It will increase your worth to the kingdom as you dig up all the gifts God has buried in you.*

*Excavate your soul, dig deep, **D.I.V.E**. deep, with the Holy Spirit as your "metal" detector and your value appraiser. He will tell you whether you are onto a treasure or if you are wasting your time digging up trash. He will be able to tell you how much worth something holds for you, as well as advise you on what is junk that needs to be discarded.*

A lot of times you forget you have this friend, this **D.I.V.E.** *coach, and you try to search for things to help you ease the pain and difficulty of life through your own power, your own poor attempts to discern things for yourself. You begin to* **S.I.N.K.** *because you feel your* **S***oul* **I***s* **N***ot* **K***nown, that you are alone in this world with no one to connect with, to help you, to comfort you, so you try to connect without your true "treasure detector" to help you discern value from vanity, divinity from destruction.*

The sinking feeling closes in on you over and over again. You keep digging up junk and because you are grabbing at anything and becoming one with it without the Holy Spirit's discernment to tell you if it has worth to you or not, you are weighted down even more. Trying to swim up and out of it now starts to feel impossible.

I watch you as you try to take it upon yourself to **D.I.V.E.** *for things you think will help you feel better, settling for trash instead of treasure. You* **D.I.V.E.** *for new friends, new relationships, new drinks, new drugs, new jobs, and new experiences. Instead of asking the Holy Spirit if this is really best for you or if it's even something safe for you to dive for, you choose to dive blindly, unaware of the dangers lurking in the darkness.*

Some waters, just like some relationships, won't have the depth needed to handle a headfirst dive and if you would have asked for discernment about it prior to diving straight in, you could have saved yourself and the other person the pain and confusion of diving too deep, too fast, and too soon. You are self-sabotaging your opportunities to connect with people at the depths they were made for. Not everyone has the depths you possess. Not everyone has done the work, invested, or prioritized spending the time to **D.I.V.E.** *into their own soul to be able to go deeper and deeper in their understanding of themselves, their relationship with Me, and their relationship with the world around them.*

You have to learn to respect where they are at in their discovery process or they will never feel safe around you because you are forever pushing boundaries they did not willingly ask to have pushed, so they will not only push back to protect themselves, but they will also push you away to ensure their psychological safety is kept intact.

The other way you are wreaking havoc on new relationships without realizing it is by trying to use the "cannonball approach" as your attempt to make a "splash" in a new environment, a new group, or with a new person as your way of making sure that you will be noticed. You are not realizing that what you want to do— make a real and sacred connection with another person, or with the group—will never happen when you take that destructive approach to relationships versus a gentler approach.

As God shared with me what I had been blindly doing over and over again and then coming back to Him crying about why I just couldn't seem to make friends in this town. I was sticking to the premise that it couldn't be my fault, it was clearly "this whole town's fault" that there were no places or people with whom I resonated. I was positive the obvious solution was just to hold on until I could move to a place where the people were "better quality."

I was sitting with my life coach crying as I told her what I perceived as the "truth" about the people in the city I was living in and all of my issues with them and how fake, unwelcoming, and unfriendly almost ALL of them seemed to be.

I told her all the ways I was trying so hard to make new friends, join new churches, go to new small groups, join a new Bible study, sign up for what I thought was going to be a dinner party for eight random individuals and not four couples plus me, I was putting myself out there.

I was really trying, and yet, I kept getting the feeling that I had to be doing something wrong, because a lot of people's response to me seemed to be a pushback, especially among the women's group that I was so excited to join.

The ladies were very nice to me when they met me, but after only two gatherings, I sat at the coffee table, where the church bulletin said they meet "every Saturday at 9:00," alone. No one came, no one texted, no one called to say the meeting had been cancelled. I just sat there, sinking into my own sadness, feeling completely alone and unwelcome.

Judy sat and listened. She honestly couldn't figure it out either from the way I was telling my version of the story. She could see how hard I was trying. She knew how big my heart was and how deeply I wanted to connect and make friends in this town since I was going to have to live here for at least another two years.

As the tears flowed, she took my hands and prayed over me. This woman has the best prayers ever. I can't even remember what all she even says, but I can feel the Holy Spirit covering us and comforting me when she prays, and I love it. After she ended the prayer, she looked at me and said, "the word I'm hearing for you is EASE. Ease into these new experiences, ease into these new friendships, ease into each new group."

I wiped my tears and felt a feeling of relief wash over me as I agreed to be at ease in my spirit and at ease that God knew what he was doing, even if I clearly did not. As I drove home, I thought, "God just four-letter-worded me again!" He told me **E.A.S.E.** means to **E**nter **A**nother's **S**pace **E**mpathetically. He told me I was using the worst approach possible to try to join a group, and when He showed me the image of me "cannonballing" into a pool filled with people I wanted meet, I got it!

For all of you who don't know what it means to cannonball into a pool, it means to jump into a pool, usually around people, and tuck your knees to your chest, wrap your arms around yourself, and make your center of gravity as compact as you can to ensure the biggest splash as possible upon entry. And frankly, I HATE when people cannonball anywhere near me when I am in the pool, especially if it's a small pool! I was shocked to realize this is what I was doing every time I tried to join a new group!

I must have walked around my office for an hour after this realization blew my mind, holding my head and saying out loud to myself... "Oh my God, Ohhh my God." I've been cannonballing people I wanted to get to know, and then was shocked that they kept leaving, or seemed defensive or annoyed around me! After I finally calmed down a bit, got past the shame and embarrassment of how I had been acting and moved into complete gratitude for this revelation, God continued with his loving correction:

The cannonball approach to introducing yourself is not welcome or appreciated! No matter what kind of person you are, your entry matters. Nobody—well most people, and especially most women—do not like to be splashed, and they certainly don't like to be "surprise splashed," which is what often happens with the cannonball approach introduction.

E. A.S.E. *in when it comes to people, **E**nter **A**nother's **S**pace **E**mpathetically. How do you think they will respond to your approach? How do you respond to that approach?*

*When you **E.A.S.E.** in, it takes into account what is already happening with that person or that group in the moment, and it acknowledges that you see value in them, in what they are doing, and in how they are living their life before you entered into the picture.*

When you "cannonball" a person or group, you destroy the rhythm they have created, essentially devaluing what they have found comfortable, and probably enjoyable, before ever asking them or observing where you may or may not fit into that rhythm. You instead demanded to be the center of attention.

Cannonballing is an incredibly self-centered and usually unappreciated way to introduce yourself to a new person, group, or environment. You won't get the response you were hoping for, unless the response you were hoping for was to upset and piss off a group of people who were quite content before you showed up.

They are now soaked, have chlorine in their drinks, their hair is ruined, their eyes are bothered, and their sunglasses now need cleaning. You have made a mess and although you were just trying to show them how much fun you are, or to make sure they notice you so you wouldn't be left out, you did it without thinking about the other people involved. They noticed you alright! They noticed you were self-centered, unaware of others, and lacking empathy for the situation at hand before you arrived.

*If you want to have different results, choose a different approach: **E.A.S.E.** in. Don't disrupt a group by trying to join it. Join a group and see if it is seeking to have a different experience. Forced change rarely lasts, and if that change comes in the form of a person, i.e., you, and the change was never asked for or welcomed, that person will find themselves either aggressively, or passive aggressively, shown to the door. The circle of connection that you tried to break into, instead of join into, will quickly begin to close around that broken space you made, and you will find yourself on the outside of the circle with the sinking feeling that once again your **S**oul **I**s **N**ot **K**nown. You are misunderstood and no closer to the connection you were longing to form when jumped in the first place.*

*You go from group to group "cannonballing," getting the same result, and then blaming them for "not getting you," not being "your kind of people." They are exactly your kind of people! The kind of people who don't like being intruded upon, don't like their life rhythm messed with without being asked, don't like a show-off or someone demanding to be the center of attention. It's your approach, not YOU, that is causing the friction, and frankly, everyone is not going to be "your people," but you would be able to find that out with a lot less drama, damage, and hurt, if you would simply **E.A.S.E.** in, check it out, and then, just as gently, **E.A.S.E.** yourself out of it (**E**xit **A**nother's **S**pace **E**mpathetically) if this isn't where your gifts will thrive best.*

I just couldn't believe I had been a cannonballing jerk! I pictured myself sitting at that coffee table alone, and began to see it as a small pool that I had just cannonballed myself into and then came up asking, "hey, where did everyone go?" and I realized as I asked myself, "Where would I have gone if that had happened to me"?

I would have been pissed because now I have to get out of the pool to go clean off my sunglasses from the splattered water stains that were now making it hard to see clearly. I have to go get a new drink, since mine is essentially ruined. I need to go find my towel to wipe my face off, and find a brush to fix my hair as my frustration continues to rise because even though it is a pool party, I had spent 45 minutes fixing my hair as I had no intention of getting it wet and was sure no one would be so rude as to come splash me in my face and ruin it! Can I get an "amen," ladies? It made total sense why I was sitting there alone now... girls don't like to be splashed in the face, and they don't like watered down chlorinated drinks either, so they leave. WOW.

So obvious, and yet I was completely oblivious to what I was doing! I would never ever actually cannonball into a real pool, because I hate that and it's rude, but yet, I was cannonballing every new relationship and every new group I was trying to join.

I took Judy and God's advice and implemented the **E.A.S.E.** in approach immediately. I also took to heart the advice what the Holy Spirit spoke through Judy:

*When it comes to your walk with God, working with the Holy Spirit, and seeking all of the gifts of the Kingdom that our yours, DIVE IN! The waters are safe to swim in and deep enough that DIVING won't hurt you, but will propel you to the treasures below but, when it comes to people, **E.A.S.E.** in. **E**nter **A**nother's **S**pace **E**mpathetically, as you **S.W.I.M**. toward them.*

*Keep both yours and their **S**piritual **W**orth **I**n **M**ind, and never **S.I.N.K.** back into the bondage that Christ freed you from by **S**tubbornly **I**nsisting **N**ot **K**nowing that you are a child of God Almighty. You are selected, saved, and set apart for prosperity and purpose from this moment on. If you don't take the mark God gave you, you won't be honored by the mark you will leave behind in this lifetime. You will continue to be upset, frustrated, and confused as to why your ways aren't working. But when you take on God's mark for you, He erases all of the mistakes that came before, cleaning your slate so that no previous races matter, only the race He has now set before you.*

And with that, I encourage you, swimmers take your mark! Accept God's Spirit in you. Let it change you, transform you, teach you and guide you. Let the world know by your markings what team you **S.W.I.M.** for, and who **S.W.I.M.S** with you. If you want to leave a mark in this world, you must get up on the blocks, accept that you are chosen and assigned, posture yourself to wait on the Lord with eager anticipation, and when the time is right and the buzzer sounds, **D.I.V.E.** in and **S.W.I.M.** FOR IT!

Chapter 10
I was M.A.D.E. For It!

Maker's - **A**lmighty – **D**ivinity – **E**mbodied

This is the day the Lord has MADE.
We will rejoice and be glad in it
(Psalm118:24, NLT)

"This is the day the Lord has made; we will rejoice and be glad in it." How many times have I heard that scripture? Well over a thousand times I'm sure. It is one that has made its way onto T-shirts, mugs, posters, wall art, song lyrics, you name it, that scripture is out there. And even though I have heard it thousands of times, it was not until this month that the Lord revealed to me the immense power and assumption that I had never thought about before.

At the beginning of this month, I had what I like to call a "Christ compulsion." You know when you get this internal nudge that just won't go away until you do whatever it is that the Spirit is asking of you? Well, this compulsion was that I read Psalm 118, all of it, every day, for the next 31 days. I read it over and over.

As I read it, the words I kept adding were "And I was made for it!" So, as I read "this is the day that the Lord has made," I added, "And I WAS **M.A.D.E.** FOR IT!" This created a new level of understanding that blew open my perspective of how I approached each new day that came.

*All things are possible because you are the **M**aker's **A**lmighty **D**ivinity **E**mbodied! So, you were **M.A.D.E.** for it, whatever "it" is that comes your way today. Because you have Me in you, you are a new creation, with a new design, that was made just for you. Your calling has been tailor **M.A.D.E.** for you and to you. You will fit it, and it will fit you perfectly. No matter what you walk into now, you will be able to say, "**M**y **A**wesome **D**esign **E**mpowers me to do anything this day brings because this is the day that the Lord has made and I was **M.A.D.E.** for it, and you were **M.A.D.E.** for it!"*

As the Lord gave me this awesome pep talk, he showed me how intentionally he **M.A.D.E.** me. Revealing to me all that my awesome design can now do because I have my **M**aker's **A**lmighty **D**ivinity **E**mbodied. This mind blowing, incomprehensible, gift allows the supernatural to be natural in my life. It super charges each new endeavor. Super charges my body and elevates me for what I was **M.A.D.E.** to do.

I knew this month I would be "made" to do things that were out of my comfort zone so I could live this lesson and not just write about it. I could feel the Holy Spirit pushing me to serve at my church, even though I wasn't sure how long I would be a part of it.

I had this confidence that could only be from God as I walked in and announced to the woman who coordinated volunteers that I needed to serve, and just like that, I reached for what God had been calling me to and was welcomed with open arms.

I signed up and did my first day as a greeter at the door to welcome everyone as they came in for the service. Right before service was about to start, I opened the door for the pastor's wife, I smiled, and said in my awful but delightful French accent, "Enchantè Madame," she laughed and said, "Oh Jen, you are perfect for this role," and she was right, I was **M.A.D.E.** for it!

I also had been convicted about starting a new women's bible study on my own, but I have never ever been one to be a hostess for anything. It makes me extremely uncomfortable for some reason, so I would rather just mingle in and out of other people's groups when I want with no commitment, but the Holy Spirit would not let this go.

I knew this month, I would have to create this group and put myself out there but this time knowing this is all in God's hands, it's not my group, it's His group. I am simply **M.A.D.E.** for it! I'm **M.A.D.E.** to be a part of it, to listen and follow His prompting as I meet new souls who are also seeking to live out what God has **M.A.D.E.** them for!

So, I did it and no one showed up the first week. I still kept my commitment and went because this was not only made for others, but I realized, it was first and foremost, **M.A.D.E.** for me! It was carved out time for me to be out in public reading, praying, and talking to anyone I met about what God was up to in my life! Knowing I was **M.A.D.E.** for it, and it was **M.A.D.E.** for me, helped me to let go of all the expectations and disappointments I would have had if the first meeting didn't go as I envisioned

I had to lay the outcome at God's feet, accepting that I am only responsible to obey Him and not responsible for the outcome that flows from my obedience. With that revelation came a peace that surpassed all understanding as I reached toward the life He was calling me to live out.

This month I was also called to fast again, and the focus was on Easter, and the fact that this is what Jesus was **M.A.D.E.** for. He was **M.A.D.E.** to rise, so I named the fast "The **M.A.D.E.** to Rise Fast..." which I found humorous since most fasting days can feel pretty slow, as if time seems to be standing still somehow. This fast was going to be 18 days and would end on Good Friday. It would be a Good Friday indeed, and a welcomed feast for Easter!

I am amazed every time I am given the spiritual power to be able to pray with my body, as I do when I fast. I dropped in physical weight, but I increase in spiritual weight. The strength in me can only be attributed to the Holy Spirit, because on my own, left to my own fleshly nature, I am a complete glutton.

I don't know what is in me that craves crap and will eat and eat and eat. It's crazy to see how the Spirit works, how He swoops in, picks me up and takes me into His presence. He fills me with new desires to want to focus solely on God and what He wants for my life. I can feel Him filling me from the inside out with this contentment and peace that makes my spirit soar, and I am permeated with a peaceful joy that I want to experience every day. **My Awesome Design Enables** me to do so much more than I would ever have hoped or imagined was even possible on my own.

I am my **M**aker's **A**lmighty **D**ivinity **E**mbodied, and nothing lets me experience that power more than when I surrender everything to Him; when I empty my dreams, my cravings, my stomach, my desires, and my heart for Him alone to fill.

At those moments, when it seems to the world that I have nothing that it would value, these are the same moments when I could not ask for more. I am filled with the Spirit, and in Him, I am complete.

Can I just take a second and have that concept sink into your heart and mind, as it has been sinking into mine. My limited brain cannot fully comprehend this concept even though that was exactly what God spoke from the beginning of time: that He **M.A.D.E.** me, He created me, He breathed His spirit into me. His Spirit.

Jesus said the same thing. Over and over, Jesus said he was going to be sending the Holy Spirit to dwell in us, but I don't think we can ever fully grasp this amazing concept. That our bodies were created to be a host of a spirit, and the Spirit of God at that! Do you know what each of us could do in this world if we fully accepted and activated His power to take us over? ANYTHING! The impossible no longer exists.

Embrace the fact that if God made this day for us, then He also **M.A.D.E.** us for it! We were written into the script with supernatural power already included as a way we can live our lives! All of the miracles we've heard that Jesus did were meant to be a part of our lives as well. God has never stopped speaking, and never stopped moving in and through us. The more we clear out our vessel, our mind, and our body, the more He can move into those parts of us we had not been open to surrendering. The more we can submit, the more He can equip us and show us all we are **M.A.D.E.** to be able to do for Him!

Here are some of the abilities of this tailor-made design He created when He **M.A.D.E.** each of us. Remind yourself by saying these words when doubts begin to choke your dreams:

My **A**wesome **D**esign **E**mpowers me!

My **A**wesome **D**esign **E**nables me!

My **A**wesome **D**esign **E**xcites me!

My **A**wesome **D**esign **E**quips me!

My **A**wesome **D**esign **E**ncourages me!

My **A**wesome **D**esign **E**ndures for me!

My **A**wesome **D**esign **E**nergizes me!

My **A**wesome **D**esign **E**mpathizes for me!

My **A**wesome **D**esign **E**mbraces others!

My **A**wesome **D**esign **E**difies all I meet!

And because of all of that, **M**y **A**wesome **D**esign **E**nsures that as long as God is in me, working through me, I will succeed at whatever He has called me to do.

The Lord began to speak to me saying:

*These are things you are **M.A.D.E.** for; they were a part of your design when I had you in mind before time ever existed. Because I am eternal, you are eternal in spirit. You come from me, and you will return to me.*

*This time in your body is your chance to experience the power I have to create, and to love, through you in bodily form. You are the missing piece for a problem out in the world, a passion, a process, a ministry, a relationship. Ask yourself, "What do I seem to be **M.A.D.E.** for?" Even if it's not necessarily something you want to be, it could still be what you are **M.A.D.E.** to be.*

*I didn't check in with all your fleshly wants when I created you, but I did make you in such a way that when you do follow Me and My design for your life, you will start to WANT to do the things you were **M.A.D.E.** to do!*

And God is able to make every grace overflow to you, so that in every way, always having everything you need, you may excel in every good work (2 Cor 9:8, NLT)

I reflected on His words and realized how true they are, that not everything you were **M.A.D.E.** to do will be something you initially want to do. But as you step out in faith, God will equip and empower you to be able to do it! Even Jesus, in the Garden of Gethsemane, was asking to not have to do something he was **M.A.D.E.** for, something God **M.A.D.E.** him to be able to do. He didn't want to go to the cross if it was His choice. He didn't want to be tortured, separated from the Father, and covered with sin that was not his own. He was **M.A.D.E.** to rise again, that was His calling and His purpose, but that didn't mean He didn't have reservations about the plan.

He cried out to His Father and then surrendered to what God's will was, and God empowered him and equipped him with the strength to recognize that this was what he was **M.A.D.E.** for. No one else could do this but Him. He was **M.A.D.E.** for it! He was **M.A.D.E.** to rise. The Lord continued to explain to me:

And just like Jesus, I want you to bring all of your fears, concerns, doubts, grief, all of it, bring it to Me and I will embolden your spirit with the reassurance that if I called you to this place, at this time, with this purpose, then I will equip you with the knowledge, skill, and burning desire to do it.

*I will empower you to start it, endure it, and finish it! Because you were **M.A.D.E.** for it, intrinsically built for it! The passions and fascinations you uniquely hold, the annoyances, or the hurt you feel with the injustices you see in your family, neighborhood, church, or the world, that resonate in you so deeply that you get "worked up" about it, and feel like it is just not right - this is unique to you because I **M.A.D.E.** you for it! To bring a light to it.*

*I **M.A.D.E.** you to be a solution to the problems you see. You were **M.A.D.E.** to heal the hurt with Me! Better yet, I exist to accomplish this through you! Embrace it, step forward and say to yourself, even if all you can do is whisper it at first, "I am **M.A.D.E.** for it!*

*I am **M.A.D.E.** for THIS! This is the day the Lord has made and because my **M**aker's **A**lmighty **D**ivinity **E**mbodies me, equips me, and empowers me; I am literally **M.A.D.E.** for it!"*

*Walk tall in this knowledge. Fully embrace it. Lift your eyes to the world and meet it head on. Look for ways to help, heal, serve, and love one another. Know that just as my Son, Jesus, was made to **R.I.S.E.**, to **R**eturn **I**n **S**pirit **E**ternally, you were also meant to **R.I.S.E.** and to shine! With the Holy Spirit now in you, you can **R.I.S.E.** You can **R**each **I**n **S**upernatural **E**xpectancy! Reach for the dreams I have placed in your heart, trusting that if I said it, it is done! I am a dependable God!*

The One who called you is completely dependable.
If he said it, he'll do it!
(1 Thessalonians 5:24, MSG)

*So, reach for Me! Reach for your dreams, not looking at the world and what you can only take in with your senses, but **R**each **I**n **S**upernatural **E**xpectancy, that if I said it, it is done! Work like you already know it will happen.*

Create the group, start the class, write the song, start the painting, create the movie, invest in the business, leave the job, marry the person, love with all your heart, move to the mountains, find a church to serve in, not for what you will get out of it, but because of all you were gifted with to be able to give to it!

R.I.S.E. *into the position you were* ***M.A.D.E.*** *for! Grab hold of the plans I laid out for you and start to* ***R.I.S.E.*** *again! You were* ***M.A.D.E.*** *to* ***R.I.S.E.****, if you would let go of all that is holding you down. Cut away every bitter root and toxic connection that is keeping you stuck. As the dead weight falls away, you will* ***R.I.S.E.*** *effortlessly. Only then can I open the doors for you that are easily available at these higher levels of your spirit, but you have to reach for them!*

Reach for me, knowing I have always been reaching for you. Like the prodigal son, I started running after you before you ever knew to look up and run after me!

You didn't choose me. I chose you
(John 15:16, NLT)

Because I chose you, I have called you to look up, ***R.I.S.E.*** *up! You were not meant to live life looking down. I am watching so many of you today in this constant posture that I did not create you for, one where you are looking down all day! Head up, eyes up, live up!!* ***R.I.S.E.*** *UP! You are enamored with your own devices and your own selves. You are hurting your body as you maintain this bent over, head down posture. That posture traditionally symbolized shame, defeat, and hopelessness, or it is a display of reverence to Me... are you praying as you stare at your phone all day? I already know the answer... no response necessary. Put away your devices and raise your eyes to the world I have laid out before you.*

*I **M.A.D.E.** you with eyes to look out into the world and **R.I.S.E.** up to help the hurt and the lost, not to serve yourself and numb your brain with a false life lived through a screen helping no one, not even yourself to grow in mind, body, or spirit. It's a tool, not a God you worship, and it is destroying your mind, your heart, your relationships with yourself, others and with ME! Not to mention the harm and disfigurement to your physical body!*

***R.I.S.E.** up and remind people to start to look up again, engage again, be interested in the other God created souls surrounding you! Honor each other's presence. You were **M.A.D.E.** for it! Live a life with your head up, your spirits up, and your heart filled up with the joy and encouragement of knowing that you are here to do something! There is a quote I inspired through Woodrow Wilson that explains this purpose in your life beautifully.*

He said, "You are not here merely to make a living. You are here in order to enable the world to live more amply, with greater vision, with a finer spirit of hope and achievement. You are here to enrich the world, and you impoverish yourself if you forget that errand."
–Woodrow Wilson

*Because you were **M.A.D.E.** for it!!*

As the Holy Spirit convicted me with how I needed to be living my life, He also put these lyrics into my heart, and maybe one day this will be a song that we can sing that will inspire hope, encouragement, and reignite a fire in each of our souls as we step forth into a new day.

I Was M.A.D.E. For it

I was part of the plan
before the plan was placed
I'm no stranger to my Father,
No, He knows my face.
He knows my name, knows my number,
Every breath that I take,
He knit me all together
And he made no mistake
So, every morning as I pray,
I smile as I say
This is the day that the Lord has made
And I was MADE for it-
Yes I was made for it,
Oh, I was made for it,
Yea I was made for it!

It doesn't matter if you feel it,
if you "like "it, you agree
I can't be caught up in your drama
when He's running after me.
I am wanted, I am chosen, I'm anointed
Yes, I'm called
And with God upon the mound
You know I'm swinging for them all

So, I step into this moment,
yeah I bow my head and pray
Can't nobody dare to stop me
when I remind myself and say
This is the day – Hey
This is the day – Hey
This is the day that the Lord has made
And I was MADE for it,
Yes I was made for it,
Oh, I was made for it,
Yes I was made for it!

RUB SOME D.I.R.T. ON IT.....

Come on, this is the day,
Yes, this is the day
What? This is the day
That the Lord has made,
And YOU WERE MADE FOR IT!
Yea, YOU were Made for it
Oh, you were MADE for It
Yes, you were made for it!

If you're struggling to hear me,
To see just what I mean,
Let me point you to the Bible,
To Psalm 118.

Chapter 11
Stop Slamming the D.O.O.R.!

Depends - **O**n - **O**ne - **R**esponse

And so, I tell you, keep on asking, and you will be given what you ask for. Keep on looking, and you will find. Keep on knocking, and the DOOR will be opened. For everyone who asks, receives. Everyone who seeks finds. And the DOOR is opened to everyone who knocks.
(Luke 11:9-10, NLT)

Have you ever experienced what I like to call a divine- déjà-vu-door? A door that God showed you in a previous season, but now has arrived, and you recognize it as the door from the vision standing open, extending the invitation for you to live out what was once only a prophetic dream.

As you move one step closer, you watch yourself as an observer and know that the next stage of your life all hinges on this **D.O.O.R.** you stand before... your life now **D**epends **O**n **O**ne **R**esponse, the next response you choose to take toward the open door of life that has been laid out before you.

This is where I sit, this is my life as I walk through **D.O.O.R.** after **D.O.O.R.** with the writing of each chapter in this book. So many doors opening, so many different ways to understand the importance of the doors in our lives, both literally and metaphorically and God pulled no punches this month as he continues to prune me and refine me, take me to task, hold up that Holy mirror and ask the hard questions, that somehow still feel filled with goodness and mercy. His loving hand guiding me toward the calling He has for me.

I am so excited to be a part of this whole inspired experience. I feel like I am walking through a movie, through divinely designed doors just for me. When I try to wrap my brain around the fact that the King of the world is talking to me, writing to me, singing to me, guiding me personally... I am beyond humbled and honored, and honestly, even though I know this to be true, it still feels surreal. I wish I could report that I wake up every day with this confidence and unbridled excitement that nothing can mess up this moment, but that has not been the case.

As I was working on this chapter, trying to piece together all that I was hearing, I began to go into freak-out mode, well... every month I seem to do this. I am excited and intrigued at the beginning of the month, then crying, and freaking out at the end of the month. I find myself stressing out that everything won't all come together... and every month it does!

You would think after ten months of this rollercoaster I would be tired of it and be confident that God plans on completing what He started, but instead I feel pressure mounting from the inside of me, and this month was no different. I again had somehow forgotten that this is not about how talented a writer I am, deadlines that needed to be met, or a clever message I wanted to give.

This is 100% divinely designed and driven by God, and I am somehow blessed to be along for the ride. Still, it feels like a huge responsibility to be a vessel and an oracle for God, and I don't want to do anything to mess it up!

As my mind was tail spinning with this unnecessary pressure I was putting on myself, I decided I needed to get out of my office and go walking, praying God would begin to speak to me and give me some direction for this chapter, because the month was coming to a close and I had written down in my calendar the day that God would show up to write it.

I know, I do see the humor and boldness in thinking that God works on my timeline, and not the other way around. Since nothing seemed to be happening, I figured I should go out and get some air, maybe He would meet me on my way... and man oh man, did He! Almost as soon as I stepped out my front door, God started to talk to me saying:

You know you can't mess Me or My plans up, right?! It will come to pass. It is happening, whether you come along crying, kicking, and screaming, or you choose to put a little swagger into your step because Who you are carrying in you is worthy of your honor and is more precious than you seem to realize. You are crying and stressing out about our work together doesn't make you a martyr, it makes you a doubter! Everything will come to pass,

The words that come out of my mouth will not come back emptyhanded. They'll do the work I sent them to do, they'll complete the assignment I gave them. So, you'll go out in joy, you'll be led into a whole and complete life.
(Isaiah 55:11-12, MSG)

*I cannot lie. So, do you trust me or not? Believe in me or not? Going back and forth in your mind is going to drive you crazy, but it will not change what I am going to do. You have already stepped through the **D.O.O.R.**, so it is Finished.*

I think my mouth dropped open as the Lord shed a light on my behavior, revealing that while I was saying I had the Spirit of the Lord alone guarding the door to my mind and heart, my behavior was revealing that a different spirit also seemed to have access to those doors. The spirit of fear.

Thank God when He admonishes me, He still somehow has a sense of humor and a deep love that I can always feel, and today, not only did God have love and care for me, but God had jokes apparently... I didn't even know how to respond when God said "Knock knock..." And then promptly answered his own question, *"Who's there,"* Just kidding, but seriously... *WHO IS THERE? Behind the door to your heart?*

I had to reflect on that joking— but deadly serious—question that we all need to ask ourselves: do I REALLY want what God wants for my life or am I still holding onto what I think I want. Have I completely surrendered to Him every area of my life?

Have I checked behind every doorway to my world to make sure the Holy Spirit and no other spirit has control of the access points into me which will influence every action and reaction I take. Do all my **D.O.O.R.**s have the same set of standards for entry? Does the door to my ears have the same protection as the door to my mouth?

Does the door to my heart have the same standards of entry as the door to my sexuality?

Do I allow myself to be tainted because I have not surrendered every door yet, and trust that the Holy Spirit knows me better than I could ever know myself. He loves me more than I seem to love myself, and that He knows what is best for me and what is harmful. Am I trading "access passes" through the door to my heart because of loneliness or boredom, instead of honoring the inheritance I was designed for, my destiny as royalty, as a princess to the King of Heaven?

The Lord spoke up to help me with my questions and said:

*An heiress who finds herself slumming it will never feel right in her soul. RISE UP! Man, the doors! Protect the precious package you have to deliver to the world. A weak area, a weak access point can corrupt the entire castle. Don't taint the temple for temporary trash parading like treasure. Just like Jesus rose up out of the grave on Easter morning, so too must you choose the **D.O.O.R.** of Life, and life more abundantly.*

When this month started, I was preparing for Easter with another prayer fast. I wanted to unlock new doors with prayer and fasting, and what I realized was that Jesus was truly gangster in how He kicked down the door of death, busted open the grave that tried to hold him in, and walked right out like it was nothing. The door to death, Hell, and the grave was completely obliterated when Jesus got up and walked out. From that moment on, no door could stop the spirit from entering.

The destruction of one door was the creation of another—the door to everlasting life. He opened the **D.O.O.R.** of access to God again and put an end to our anxiety and our constant wondering, "Is it going to turn out okay? Do I matter? Will I make a difference? Am I loved? Are you here? Can I stay?"

His answer to that question is always, YES and Amen. Welcome back my prodigal one, I'm so glad you came home.

We finally had a second option—we no longer had to fear the struggle and try to force ourselves through the impossible **D.O.O.R.** of perfection that no one could achieve, instead, Jesus created a better **D.O.O.R.**—a better way—HIM! Jesus is just better... period. Better than any other door this broken world has to offer. There is no door, no hit, no bite, no drink, no bank account, no person, or earthly ecstasy that can satisfy your soul and offer you life everlasting, love everlasting. The invitation has been given, the **D.O.O.R.** has been open, the table is set, and Jesus stands at the doorway saying....

Welcome home, welcome to my world, my kingdom, my way of experiencing this world and the next at the same time! Welcome to the supernatural! I am the door to the other side. I am the invitation to the Holy Spirit. Behind this door is peace, an unending peace.

I am the way, the truth, and the life. No one can come to the Father except through me
(John 14:6, NLT)
The Words that I speak to you aren't mere words. I don't just make them up on my own. The Father who resides in me crafts each word into a divine act
(John 14:10, MSG)

I am the access pass for the God of the Universe, the King of the World, The Great I Am to come dwell in you, never to be locked out again.

I love that "locked doors" meant nothing to Jesus. Trying to comprehend what the disciples must have felt when Jesus walked through the wall after they had made sure all the doors were locked and secured. They must have freaked out!

Jesus doesn't care about my "locked doors" in life, He will walk right through a wall if that's what it takes, and there He will stand, smiling, wanting to talk to me, wanting to bless me, dance with me, walk with me, kiss me with peace on his lips, if I would just be open to accept his invitation to the **D.O.O.R.** to his heart.

There is no door man can lock, that God can't unlock. He doesn't even need a door; He can use the wall or the window to create an access point. He will find a way to get to you. He will keep pursuing you, never giving up on loving you. It is His commitment to us, not our commitment to Him, that He is upholding. He loves us, He has always loved us, and He will never stop loving us all the days of our life. He longs to enter the door to our heart, and let two become one, in a way no other person is able to when He comes inside of us to live and breathe through us. But we have to be willing to let Him open that door, and rejoice that He is the way, He is the **D.O.O.R**. to our freedom, to a passion-filled purpose, to eternity, to unending love, and divine communion.

Why then would we not run to the door the minute we first hear the knock? Why, for many of us, do we sit staring at the door, doing some weird version of the Hokey Pokey... one foot in and one foot out... I know that even now as I work with God in the most intimate and mind-blowing way, I STILL don't do what He asks 100% of the time!

I fall short constantly. I stare at myself, shake my head in disbelief and think, "Really, Jen, seriously, haven't you learned yet?"... No, I haven't, but at least I know what to do when I don't understand something. I go ask Holy Spirit directly and He delights in telling me, even if I don't delight in always hearing the truth in His words, and what that means for me and the rest of my life.

So, when I asked why I wasn't doing what he asked me to do in one particular area, He wasted no time responding with,

"Because you are lazy."

I was shocked! My mouth seems to fall open a lot lately when I go on walks with the Lord, and today was no different. I attempted to plead my case to Him on how I was definitely NOT lazy, but I resigned myself to the fact that He was right, I mean, He's God. Why do I bother arguing when I know the only thing I need to say back to him, is "Yes, and amen!" So here I am, walking with the Lord, and hearing that I am lazy.

When He continued to prune me with convicting questions that I was going to have to face the truth about, He asked.

Well, would you say you are lazy, or disobedient, or both?

Humbling question? What was I finding so difficult about daily walks with the Lord? I could fast for 21 days straight, but I couldn't walk a 5k faithfully? How hard is it to just step through the door to becoming a 5k-a-day type of woman!

Truthfully, His request was every other day, and you would have thought He asked me to climb Mount Everest by the way I was whining and making up every excuse possible for why I couldn't seem to make time to walk with him.

When I prayed about why I was unable, or unwilling, to take walks with Him, He replied

"Because you are lazy, it's okay, it's your nature. You are more of a snuggle on the couch with Me, than a go for-a-run-with-me type of spirit. You like the peace I bring, and you melt into me, and I love that.

*I love sharing that intimacy with you secluded and tucked away, but I need you to move more. I need you to walk through new doors— new rooms, new environments, new jobs, new churches, new relationships. You need to walk through a lot more doors than just your own. But whether you will or you won't, whether you **DO - OR** you don't, well that's your **D.O.O.R.** to choose.*

*It will all **D**epend **O**n **O**ne **R**esponse, the next response you take toward the invitation, which will change your life. If the only door you see all day is your own door, you aren't serving me or others fully. Step beyond your door and shine like I designed you too.*

He continued on:

*You should play a game and see how many new doors you walk through in a day. The more doors you go through, the more lives you can change, touch, and inspire. You bring my Spirit to every new doorway you enter. You bring people my invitation to another way of living life and a different way of treating yourself and others. Start opening **D.O.O.R.**s, instead of slamming them. Gentle gestures give grace a chance to be received.*

*Be gentle, my love. Trust the process, don't force it!. You won't like what you find in rooms you weren't invited into by Me anyway. Focus on your **D.O.O.R.**! Don't get distracted.*

Trust that the right people, right provisions, and right opportunities will be on the other side of your door. You can't force people through your door. You have to trust that I know best who needs to come and who needs to go. Who is in and who is out.

Just because someone has been in your life a long time does not mean they have been good for your life for a long time, or that they have an invitation to the next room I am about to take you into.

You have to trust that the friends you need to support you will be there. Trust that the book will be written. Trust that you are called. Trust that I am the door-opener, and you are not.

*Trust that I love you. When you trust a **D.O.O.R.** will open, you don't exert much effort trying to get it to open. The momentum you have that led you to the door will gracefully guide you through the door. You won't have to be frustrated, twisting, and pulling, pushing, and ramming yourself into it to try to get it to open up, you won't feel like you are banging your head against it trying to make something happen.*

*If you are trying that hard to force a door open, it is not the **D.O.O.R.** for you. When I call you, the doorman has you on the list, He has your name written down, and you are expected. The rope is easily removed for you, the door is opened for you and you are welcome into any room I've called you too.*

If one door isn't opening, look around, see which one I am holding open for you. When you throw yourself into what you are called to do, not trying to always go around opening other people's doors, it will inspire others to pick up their mat and get moving toward their own divinely destined **D.O.O.R.**

Cultivate these things. Immerse yourself in them. The people will all see you mature right before their eyes! Keep a firm grasp on both your character and your teachings. Don't be diverted. Just keep at it. Both you and those who hear you will experience salvation
(1 Timothy 4: 15–16, MSG)

Remember you are not called by people, so why do you keep getting so upset when people don't call you? They didn't call you, So what? I called you! Get off that rollercoaster, that constantly revolving people-pleasing door, and come to the door of the living God! Abide in my heart. Breathe. Rest. Relax. Smile. Because behind THIS **D.O.O.R.** *...is Home.*

Chapter 12
Am I D.O.N.E Yet?

Divine – **O**neness – **N**ever- **E**nds

&

Desired – **O**neness – **N**ever- **E**nds

Your kingdom come, your will be DONE,
on earth as it is in Heaven
(Matthew 6:10, NIV)

I can remember it like it was yesterday. Tears flooded my eyes and poured down my face. I was lost and sad, scared, and frustrated. I laid in bed after a terrifying night of spiritual torment that ended up with me in my bathroom curled up on the bathmat praying for protection as I was getting pummeled by the spirit of suicide raging in me again.

I have had this spirit over me since I was about 12 years old and I never thought it was a spirit, I just assumed it was me, but this time the voice I was hearing was so out of character, even out of alignment with the way I speak, that I knew something was not right, and I held tightly to Jesus's hand as I finally battled that spirit and demanded that it leave me in Jesus' name.

I watched in my mind's eye as this bizarre creature went running out of my home as Jesus and I stood together and closed the door behind it. I was exhausted and scared. I finally fell asleep on the cold floor of my bathroom until early morning. When I awoke, I got up off the floor and got back into my bed, I laid there, and the tears washed over me once more. I didn't want to do this anymore.

I didn't want to fight this battle for my life constantly. I have had to listen to the Devil tell me to just kill myself for decades. "Who would care?" he would hiss. "Who would notice?" He bullied me to just put myself out of my own misery, trying to convince me there wasn't much to my life anyway.

For decades I had endured these flashes of myself dead in different places and it would shake me to my core. I could hear Satan screaming at me, "Haven't you had enough yet!?"and I would yell back "NO!!" So much pain and trauma, deception and betrayal, and loss on every level was occurring all around me. I had lost almost all of my friends because of a cruel demonic spirit of deception and destruction who had spread lies to people I loved, and they believed them, even though deep in their spirit it just didn't sit right that I would ever say or do such things.

Still, I had just been kicked out of the only friend group here in town that I had, and it was devasting. I had also lost my career because of COVID-19 mandates. I had lost my dear professor and friend, Dr. Ray, who was finally helping me to put one foot in front of the other and start on a new path. When he passed away, the program I was studying ended as well. I was overweight and could not get a grip on it.

I hadn't had an intimate relationship in years, and I would go days or weeks without a single hug or loving touch, which left my soul wasting and famished. I had finally returned to my townhouse which had been completely destroyed by a fluke flood from a toilet leak which caused me to have to live out of a suitcase for five months in a hotel room. Everything was piling on, and I was DONE! I was done being tortured; I was done with being hurt. I was done fighting with everything I had to stay alive for a life that seemed to have nothing and no one in it to fight for. It was in that state of mind, that I pulled myself off the bathmat, got into bed, and asked God the question that was really on my mind. "Am I done yet? Can I come Home now?"

Since a very young age, I have always wanted to return to God. I was, somehow, always aware this place, this planet, was not my home. That desire for oneness with God has never ceased in me, so as I put my hands together once again and let the words and tears flow, I begged in earnest for God to take me Home. I knew I was not allowed to take myself out of the game, and it must have been the grace of God over me all these years that stopped me from ever even attempting to take my life, so it had to be His call to let me return to Him and not mine.

After explaining to God all the good I had tried to do, all of the patients I had helped when I worked in Physical Therapy and as a massage therapist. All of the random acts of kindness I had poured out in my life.

All of the people I had forgave, all of the hugs and love I had freely and abundantly given, all of the prayers I had prayed for people, all of the times I had turned the other cheek or picked up a check when I had no money.

All of the times I had smiled through the tears just like He wanted, and pressed on even when I was rejected, dejected, and cast out. I explained that I had really done my best to be His good and faithful—but also seriously flawed— servant, so could I please, please be done already?!

God responded back so clearly and abruptly with:

Nope! We have a book to write.

The directness and conviction of His answer brought the tears to a screeching halt as I just laid there, thinking... "Huh... well... okay... I guess He's not done with me yet." I honestly thought I knew which book He was talking about, and it wasn't this book that you are now holding, it was *The Heart Garden,* which was the story of a vision I had over the course of two nights when Jesus came to me in person and showed me the most beautiful vision of the garden of my heart.

The story was already written but I had run into the most bizarre circumstances as I was trying to get the artist for the book in place. Somehow, I ended up with a professed Satanist (I did not know that at the time) in my house looking over my work and offering to help me. When I found out who the artist was actually working for, I cut off the connection, and this was when all the fallout began.

I didn't understand that when God said we had a book to write, He meant this one. I was grateful to hear him so clearly though, it was undeniable that He was with me, and that I had a very specific calling on my life that He was unfolding, even in the tormented tears.

He let me know in no uncertain terms that **D**esiring **O**neness **N**ever **E**nds, that the longing in me would not go away, but also that His **D**ivine **O**neness **N**ever **E**nds either.

His ability to complete me was inherent to His nature and mine! He was what I was searching for. We were created to be in unity with God. We were created with the never-ending desire for unconditional love, acceptance, purpose, and unity. He is the only thing able to fulfil every desire. This is a daily walk, a daily need, and he will never be **D.O.N.E.** with us! Love is never **D.O.N.E.** loving. Kindness is never done being kind. Hope never stops hoping. Faith never stops strengthening. He cannot, will not, and has no desire to stop being who He is: Love.

No, we will never be **D.O.N.E** with our walk together. Never **D.O.N.E.** deepening our dependence on Him. Never **D.O.N.E.** working side by side on the mission He has laid before each of us, nor we will ever be **D.O.N.E.** with the frustration of this world and its separate state, its brokenness. We are not meant to get to a point where we no longer desire to be one with one another, to not be panged by sorrow when we see a fellow saint cast out and demoralized because they have been built to shine differently then you or I.

God's message has always been the same; until we are all ONE, our work will never be **D.O.N.E.**! When we see a hurt that we have the ability to help, our response to it should be, "I can, I will, and I want to".

There have been so many times when God has said those words to me when I prayed, "Lord can you help me?" In the silence, He would respond back: *"I can, I will, and I want to."* In the silence, love can be heard so clearly, but most people will not allow themselves to get quite enough to listen.

There should be nothing more peaceful than the sound of silence because that's when God speaks! And when God speaks... His words, His message, is beautiful. It is helpful, it is honest. It can be funny. It is enlightening, convicting, life-giving, and life changing.

When He speaks, your world shifts, and you will never be the same again. You cannot unknow what is now known, unsee what He has revealed to your heart to see. Each time, every time, God's promises to you, His wonderful Word, will not return void.

God loves to speak, He is the Word, so if you aren't hearing him, you have turned up the world too loud, and turned down His invitation to come into His presence and talk—really talk—to each other.

For me, one of the most effective ways that I have found to turn down the noise of my world is too fast, so once again, during the writing of this chapter on **D.O.N.E.**, I decided I truly wanted to understand what love looked like and where I was falling short. It didn't take long for me to realize, man, was I falling short. At the beginning of this fast, the Lord told me that I would be spending the entire fast studying 1 Corinthians 13: 4– 7, which is the infamous "love is" Scripture. I have written about it multiple times; I have the verse above my bed on a canvas art piece. All that to say, I am very familiar with it, and yet, I was still not getting it.

The first thing He said was:

Every day, you will take one line of this Scripture to feed off of, to marinate in, to carry with you as your pocket praise, and live out in all your interactions with everyone you meet, but for the first three days of the fast you will stay focused on one line:

LOVE IS PATIENT...

I chimed in immediately with, "Why three days, there are so many good verses and I..." I caught myself, and could almost feel God smiling and shaking His head... jokingly saying, "Wanna make it five?" Wow, I realized, I was so impatient to get onto the next day, the next Scripture, the next chapter, that I could see why I would need three days, 72 hours of saying to myself, "Love is patient, love is patient, love is patient".

As I went out into the world and interacted with people, I was to say, "Jen is patient". As I went to work in the public schools to substitute teach, I was to carry my neon pink "pocket praise" notecard to remind me; Love is Patient, Jen is patient, and my life should burn with a passion for patience.

Every morning, I woke up and looked above my head to the scripture on the wall. I would read it aloud and put my name in place of Love. Jen is patient, Jen is kind, Jen does not envy, or boast, Jen is not proud, Jen is not rude... I kept reading it and thinking, "Oh man, love is always patient, but I'm not.

Love is kind, but I'm not always so kind. Love does not envy, but I seem to have a big problem with it...

I started asking myself, "If God is love, and love flows from the Spirit of God, and if these are the policies and procedures for how I will be able to act when I work with the Holy Spirit, the Spirit of love, then crap... what Spirit have I been working with?!" What spirit has snuck in and set up camp in the corner of my heart that says "It's fine to make those snide remarks, it's fine to one-up someone else, it's fine to take pride in all I have done..." like any of it was due to my own abilities and not God's gifts to me to help me flourish in certain areas.

What spirit was telling me to keep a running tab on how everyone else had messed up, while also excelling at keeping no record of my own missteps? This spirit of destruction, deception, and self-glorification can seem subtle, but it will cause distortion to your insight and a decaying in your soul. What's worse, it loves to watch your demise. Sitting next to a fire with its smug and snarling smile, thrilled you have no clue he is there wreaking havoc, dancing in delight at the slow death of your life.

You are unable to become who you were meant to be because of the smoke from the fires he was setting to your soul. No way to save yourself from a visitor you never knew was there. I realized this verse, however, if we could all faithfully sit and serve under its teaching, would lead us to recognize when a spirit other than love had taken up residence in our hearts. This verse would let us know how we are to act in every situation when the Holy Spirit guides us.

It tells us who we are to be. It is the most succinct instruction for the options we have in our behavior. When we enlist in God's army. When we join God's family and let Him pour His Spirit out over us, He boldly and joyfully proclaims:

Welcome home, in this family we love everyone, period.

The way we love other people may be expressed differently at different times, but as long as we are under His love, working with the Holy Spirit, we are required to be patient. We must be kind. We will not want what is not ours and we will not boast about anything but what God has done for us, because we all know rock bottom sucks and that is where we would all still be if not for the grace of God. If we are going to boast, we will boast about our weakness and His strength and we will never, ever speak rudely to any of His children.

I could hear him so clearly as He spoke to me,

Love is not rude, so why are you? You cannot seek after Me and be self- seeking. Love is not proud. Have nothing to do with pride, for pride always goes before the fall. No, love is not proud, it is actually quite humble. It looks for the beauty and uniqueness in others. It treasures and ponders the other and itself. I gave you two eyes to look out into the world, not two mirrors to stare hypnotically at yourself.

He continued,

You will not be easily angered, it is below your calling, and you will not keep any records of the wrongs of others. You are not the judge, not the jury, and you are certainly not the record keeper of others' struggles. You have enough struggles and shortcomings of your own, all of which have been forgiven, so let it go. Blaming never begins the healing process, it only births bitterness which rots you from the inside out and does none of the intended harm you had hoped the other person would experience by you staying upset with them. Love is not bitter, and you are not made to house the spirit of bitterness without serious spiritual and physical consequences.

So, keep no record of other's wrongs, it will save your life. You will not delight in evil, for the light has nothing to do with the dark, you will rejoice instead in the truth. You will always protect others and build up their spirit, you will keep the faith, you will persevere even when it gets hard.

You will Love one another as I have loved you.
Your Love for one another will prove to the world
that you are my Disciples.
(John 13: 34 -35, NLT)

I stood there realizing that this "love is" verse in Scripture was not just the most popular verse couples choose when they get married, but these were to be everyone's marching orders! If you aren't sure how to react in a situation, go read it again, and do that!

It was amazing as I carried my notecards in my back pocket each day of the fast, how those words began to flow out of me. The Holy Spirit would prompt me to take it out and, without a word, hand it to someone and watch how the Word convicted them. I was amazed to watch how a conversation that was about to harvest the fruit of bitterness could immediately be changed to one that would produce the fruit of peace and forgiveness instead. There is so much power in the word. So many messes that the Messiah has been able to turn into meaningful messages. Each one of us is that mess and each one of us can be that message too.

All of our daily tests can be turned into our continual testimony. God is not **D.O.N.E.** with us. If we are not kind all the time yet, then he is not **D.O.N.E.** pouring out Kindness over us, filling us up over and over with His kindness until the overflow becomes the fruit of our lives; the gifts we give out without any conscious effort to do so. If we are not loving, then God is not **D.O.N.E.** loving us, healing us, and helping us.

Love's never **D.O.N.E.** loving! How could He? He is what He is, and He will never be **D.O.N.E.** loving his beloved, wanting us close. His love never quits.

My heart melted when he whispered to me:

I delight in you, because I am the light in you, and I get a kick out of you and I am doing what we were designed to do, as you let me work through you! You were made to be a vessel to transport my love to the world.

When you allow yourself to be filled up with anything else, it will evaporate before your eyes and before you can figure out what happened, you will be empty again, **D.O.N.E.** *with whatever you were trying to fit into your heart-shaped hole that was designed to house Me.*

I am the key to your lock. I   am the key to your locked heart, your locked mind, your locked life, your locked purpose, and your locked gifts. I made you with this hole, not as a punishment or a torment, but as a promise that we fit together. That hole will be My entry point to make you whole. You are the lock, and I am the key, and together we can open hearts, change lives, shift worlds, perform miracles, inspire change.

When my key is in place, all the notes of your life, the music of your life, the fruits of your life, will begin to flow effortlessly.

I've watched you try key after key after key. Jamming, twisting, forcing, and struggling to make things fit when they don't, they can't. I see you are frustrated. I see you are **D.O.N.E.** *trying, yet you still use people, places, substances, food, screens, jobs, money, anything. You grasp at one "key" and then toss it when it can't unlock your peace. You grab the next one, use it, force it, get angry with it, curse it for not fitting the way you needed it to!*

You have destroyed relationship after relationship because you have labeled your relationship, as your key! And you have been hurt because of your own misunderstanding of how you were made and how the Master locksmith made you to respond to the turn of His hand and nothing else. You keep looking for the right key. The key to your peace, the key to your joy, to grace, to mercy, the key to unlock your patience, your kindness, your purpose, your fulfillment, the key to your calling... the KEY you are looking for is ME!

I can unlock all those dark doors, those empty spaces and places in your life, those empty relationships, all of those places you locked up, swearing you were **D.O.N.E.** *with them, when really what you wanted was for you to be ONE with them, not to be* **D.O.N.E.** *with them. When you couldn't MAKE them fit, couldn't MAKE them be something they were never created to be; you threw them away and blamed them for not fitting, not knowing how to love you the way you wanted to be loved.*

You asked a Vessel, to fill a Vessel. It doesn't work like that. You demanded a blessing become a source, you asked another "lock" to be your "key," it was an unfair and impossible request that was going to inevitably lead to disappointment and the breaking of both locks, as you banged them together confused why the gifts inside you were still not able to be unlocked. I AM THAT KEY, and I am not withholding My love from you. You are MY IDEA! My creation! I want you here to love you and to show you how amazing you truly are to Me. I want to unlock all the love I have poured into you, because love, expressed through humanity, is simply breathtaking.

You are, and always have been, created to be free, to be unlocked, to be open, to be my love walking. For My work with you here is never **D.O.N.E.** *No stone will I leave unturned to discover a way to bring you home again.*

As much as you have cried and tried, pressed, and pulled, begged, and pleaded for me to let you go, let you die; I will not call you home yet, because I love loving you! Stay awhile longer, so I can love you longer. You have to rely on Me as your key, and not another person, to unlock your heart and your dreams. I'm not done molding you, loving you, refining you, cherishing you yet.

Don't let anything disturb the view I had in mind when I created you. You are stunning. Keep yourself well-loved, well cared for, well-spoken to, well-fed, yet still hungry for My love. Desperate for my voice. Restless for the keys of My heart to be the "key" to yours.

Be desperate for My voice to whisper into your ear, My touch to massage and caress your pains away. Be desperate for My ways to move you. Be fixed on and locked into My Spirit, wanting nothing more than to steal away for a private moment alone with Me, as you practice learning how to let love in, and how to then let love out.

Let the door to your heart be unlocked and the river of love flows to you and through you. Learn how to lead in love and learn how to follow as well. Accept love through your whole body. Be healed of every ache and pain, every regret, and every shame. Let love restore the years of your life. Let joy return to the home in your heart. Take one step closer, lean in for one more touch, take that one step closer until you and I are moving as one, unlocking door after door of intimacy and unity, love, and blessings. You were designed for love, to be loved, that is why I call you my Beloved. That's how I make you shine the brightest. When you are filled with Me, you shine, you are stunning, simply radiant. You radiate my loving glow, and it is undeniable. No word will need to be said, you are glowing from the inside out!

But when you try to force something else to be that key in your life, that will be obvious too. There is a cost to trying to use caustic keys as your life source. It will cost you your shine. You should not have to pay the price of stability in your mental, physical, or spiritual health to keep a blessing that is from Me, but you will have to pay a high price if it is a counterfeit key. When you try to make a person your purpose, instead of making My Purpose your purpose, you will get hurt. Don't try to cut into a dance that I am already leading in someone else's life.

There will be a right time and place to dance with others. The perfect time when they, and you, are ready, but if you try to cut in and take the lead, acting like you are the key they need, and not let me be the key, you will find yourself confused why you feel so sick, so drained and tired, frustrated and walking on eggshells trying to not step on their toes while you profess to be leading them. If I am not your lead AND their lead in life, you will get hurt.

*You are not the answer to their prayers, I am. You are not the key to their heart, I am. You are not the love that will lift and break them out of the chains that the spirit of anger and depression have bound them in, I am. You are not their Savoir, I AM. I am the Key, but they have to want to be opened. Be **D.O.N.E.** with trying to "save people," and **D.O.N.E.** with craving to find someone to "save you." I sent the "someone," and it has been **D.O.N.E.**.... We will never have to be apart again. Your desire for oneness is answered only with my ability to be with you, together as One again.*

We will never need to be separated, never will I turn away from you, never will I pour my wrath on you or remove you from my loving presence. The price has been paid. The veil has been torn.

*The covenant has been made. I signed it for you with the sign of the cross, I put a ring on it, and it is **D.O.N.E.**! So be **D.O.N.E.** with the wasted life, the bitter life, the fear-filled life, the life of "ME and Mine," the life of selfishness, pride, gluttony, greed, promiscuous, empty sex without a deep, committed promise of a lifelong love and intimacy as well as provision and protection to be offered with it. Be **D.O.N.E.** with the gripping anger, the fits of rage and impatience.*

*Be **D.O.N.E.** with hoarding the gifts I have unlocked in your life. Be **D.O.N.E.** with thinking you are alone, have no purpose, no plans, and no one who cares about you.*

*Be **D.O.N.E.** with the trinkets and trivial promises of this world. Do not marry yourself to these things, be **D.O.N.E.** with them and run to me! Run to the throne of goodness and mercy. Throw yourself on the altar of My loving kindness and offer up your hand to mine. Let me put a ring on your finger and robe on your shoulders. Let me wash your wounds and raise you up to all I called you to be.*

*Marry Me and you can finally be **D.O.N.E.** with the heartache and frustration. Be **D.O.N.E.** with the wishing and hoping that because something or someone has the "potential" to be a good fit that that means they actually are a good fit. I'm not **D.O.N.E.** lavishing you in love. I'm not **D.O.N.E.** calling you into your purpose. I'm not **D.O.N.E.** taking you from Glory to Glory. I'm not **D.O.N.E.** doing life with you, through you. I'm not **D.O.N.E.** seeing you shine, seeing you smile.*

I gave you a beautiful smile, I wish you would let yourself feel it more. You were meant to be stunning, a light to the world, chasing away darkness with one look. Your smile is the outward expression of our inner connection. Smile like the sun because you are one with the Son. Shine. Pick your head up. You were called for such a time as this.

Love one another as I love you. The message is the same, this IS the way, walk in it.

The way of lovingly living your life. Lovingly working with others, lovingly raising the lost children of this nation. Look up, and love. Try to love every person I bring across your path. People should leave your presence the way you leave mine: uplifted, inspired, encouraged, edified, and blessed.

*Don't ever be **D.O.N.E.** with your assignment. Work hard always with the spirit of love in your heart. Keep praying the prayer I taught you, say it over and over, and may you realize you will never be **D.O.N.E.** again, nor will you ever want to be. Pray this prayer: "Lord, help me become who I need to become, so I can do what you need me to do. Train me in your ways and lead me to the doors that you want me to walk through. Take my hand and never let go. Thank you, Lord, that we will never be **D.O.N.E.** until your heart and mine are joined together as one."*

I have been praying that prayer and then watching that prayer come to life before my eyes, as I become a completely new person. One who can say, with humbled awe, since that day in my bed almost two years ago, I have watched as God has done some amazing things in my life. From writing this book, to bringing new friends into my life, and even changing me physically with these fasts that He enables me to do!

He was definitely not **D.O.N.E.** with me! He has restored the years, and I am no longer begging to die. He broke off the spirit of suicide.

I no longer am tormented with vivid images of my demise, but instead filled with jaw-dropping visions of my future and amazement at the miracles I am watching come through me! I find my joy redeemed, and a strength and peace running through my soul that are not of this world. I find myself excited to live and love and see who God is molding me to be. What words is He inspiring me to speak?

What books is He eager to help me write or what songs will He want me to sing? I am looking forward to meeting all of the pastors He wants me to work with. I get almost giddy with anticipation at what campfires in National Parks He will bring mc to join, or what races he wants me to run in.

I look forward to meeting the hand He wants me to hold, and seeing what roads He wants me to drive down! I'm so grateful He has been more dedicated to making sure I live a life filled and surrounded by love, than I ever did when I tried to steer it with my own hands!

I am the epitome of the truth that Jesus spoke when he said,

> Whoever clings to this life will lose it,
> and whoever loses this life will save it
> (Luke 17:33, NLT)

I have been changed. I have been saved. This is my testimony, and everyone else who has surrendered to His will, His way, His hand, and His heart. Cast off the life you are trying to live and submit to the life He created for you. Come experience His life-saving love and His peace that surpasses all understanding because it is not something that can be understood, it is something that has to be felt deep inside each of us.

He wants all of us to experience being overwhelmed with the completeness of His Love and commitment to us, depicted always as a Bridegroom dedicated and devoted to his Bride.

I am filled with joy and anticipation as He picks me up and carries me over the threshold of my heart. He places a new sign over the door to my heart, and one on the back of my Jeep with streamers surrounding the words:

Just Married! Let the Adventure Begin, never D.O.N.E., forever,...ONE!

Chapter 13

I L.O.S.T. It!

Leaving – **O**ut – **S**piritual – **T**ruths

*For the Son of Man came to seek and
save those who are LOST.
(Luke 19:10, NLT)*

Do you know what you sound like when you are
L.O.S.T.? When you are **L**eaving **O**ut **S**piritual **T**ruths
about yourself or about another person? Do you know
how to spot a **L.O.S.T.** soul? Do you know how to point
them back home? I found myself quite **L.O.S.T.** in the
midst of writing this chapter.

I was **L.O.S.T.** in sadness, anger, disgust, fear, and confusion. I was **L.O.S.T.** in judgement, and I observed in my heart the fight between the spirit of the **L.O.S.T.**, the father of lies, and the Holy Spirit as they waged war for my soul and therefore, my actions.

Thank God the fight has been fixed and the **L.O.S.T.** spirit is just a bully who can't actually hurt me or come in any farther than my thoughts will allow. I didn't realize how the lord of the **L.O.S.T.** is still right there trying to use anything to get my heart to become bitter and cold, resentful, and haughty. I watched over the course of two weeks how my words, my actions, my energy, and my body changed when I allowed myself to get **L.O.S.T.** and **L**eave **O**ut **S**piritual **T**ruths that God had spoken over me, and over all of us.

I was leaving out love, I was leaving out compassion, and I was definitely leaving out forgiveness. I was judging and judging harshly but thank God I know what my knees are for, and I got on them to listen to what my Heavenly Father had to say about the lord of the **L.O.S.T.** and what to look out for in myself and in others. This is the message He shared with me, and it saved my heart and mind from going to a very dark place during this very disturbing time in my life. It helped me be more aware of this spirit in myself and in others, so I can rebuke it, pray over it, and cast it out.

He also reminded me to love myself, and let the Holy Spirit lead me back into the loving arms of truth, back to my Almighty Father's arms. Here are the words He shared with me...

If you speak about another person or a community as "they" or "them," you have declared yourself to be a "judger" of that person or group, and not a journeyer alongside of them. You can't "care" about someone at a distance. You can't know someone from a distance, and that which you do not know, you cannot love.

*When you say "they," "them" or "those people," you who are doing the judging are the **L.O.S.T.** ones, **L**eaving **O**ut **S**piritual **T**ruths about each person in the group; presuming no one person is an original, but instead denying the sacredness that each person inherently holds as My beloved child. How can you dare to say, "THEY ALL do this..." "ARE This..." or "WANT this!."*

*You have no idea what desires I have placed on their hearts or what journey I have sent them on, and for what reason. Are you suggesting that you hold the only valid perception of a person, group, or situation? Are you suggesting that only your feelings about life are valid and no actual truths exist? How blind you are? I only create originals, so if you don't have a particular daughter or son of mine in mind when you make these Blanket (B.S.) Statements. just know that YOU might be the **L.O.S.T.** One and not them.*

Get to know the heart of my children one by one. This world doesn't need any more blanket statements, it needs the personal touch:, the face to face, arm in arm, and heart to heart. Each soul needs to be known, understood, seen, validated and, at times convicted, but even that should be done out of love. Waving your judgmental finger at someone, or worse a group of people, about a "rule" you think they broke, or a sin you've decided was worse than any of yours, doesn't help them. Acting as if you are qualified to throw a stone at them will not help that person feel loved, wanted, or interested in getting to know Me!

*Almost all of you keep trying to drag another "condemned" person to me, as if that's how I work. Dragging another scared, **L.O.S.T.** soul to my feet and demanding I judge them and judge them NOW for whatever you had an issue with. What if you knew my answer to your demand for a "judgement NOW" would be met with, "Okay, I'll start with you first."*

*We will all be on our face before the Lord in Judgement
and Honor one day, and your critical
and condemning ways won't help you one bit
(Romans 14: 11, MSG Modified)*

*I love my children. I know them. I am not surprised
or shocked by their journey. I'm just waiting for them to
come home, to want a better life, a supernatural life with
Me. If any of you think you have been called to "hate" or
"judge" a whole group of people, that is not of Me. I may
call you to LOVE a people, a group, even a nation, but I will
not call you to judge and condemn them. You have never,
and will never, be authorized to do that. Love will cast out
all desire to judge and address the fears beneath it that
are causing such hate in your heart, or such an obsession
with a group of people instead of working on your own
issues, focusing on healing your own wounds, and walking
out the purpose that I have called you to. If hate is present,
the Holy Spirit is not. A **L.O.S.T.** spirit has taken over your
heart. One that enjoys keeping you in the dark, purposely
Leaving **O**ut **S**piritual **T**ruths to see how much darkness
they can cover you with.*

*A **L.O.S.T.** spirit will tell you to be proud that "at
least you aren't that" forgetting to mention that what you
actually deserve is death, hell, and the grave.*

*For all have sinned and fall short of the glory of God
(Romans 3: 23 NIV).*

*And some of the people you are judging aren't even
sinning, they are living out the calling on their life for My
purpose, and My plan. You who judge think YOU Are God,
and that you have the full picture over the span of eternity,
when in reality, you have no clue what I am doing. But
sadly, you are so quick to pick up a torch and take others
to task for simply being on a different path than you.*

Why are you all so obsessed with other people's calling, other people's work and walk with Me, and not even because you want to help, love, or build up their spirit, but just as an object of entertainment, self- sabotage, or vanity. No good comes from comparing your life, and your calling, to another's.

> *Before I formed you in the womb I knew you,*
> *before you were born I set you*
> *(Jeremiah 1:5, NIV)*

*I hand carved you for your purpose, not your neighbors, not your family of origin, not your teammate, not your friend, not your co-worker, not even your spouse, and you still get **L.O.S.T.** down the rabbit hole of comparison and bitterness, and then projected hate and judgement. You think it feels good to judge another, until you realize the price of judging another is disconnection from Me.*

*You have to deny Me in this moment to declare that you are God, and the judgement should be left in your hands and taken from mine. It's no wonder this generation is so **L.O.S.T.** since you have all been programmed through social media to judge, compare, and compete with everyone, everywhere, at all times! Loneliness and isolation are the byproduct of this type of haughty disconnection from the reality that you are all in this together. You are all brothers and sisters, born just as sinful, and desperately in need of a savior. You become more isolated as the **L.O.S.T.** spirit of judgement comes over you because you feel compelled to turn another brother or sister into an object, separate from you.*

You have to distance yourself so you can more easily pass judgement on them. You have to believe that you are somehow inherently better than "they" are. You have to be in a state of self- glorification and pride to behave this way since I already promised that

> *It is mine to avenge; I will repay*
> *(Deuteronomy 32:35 NIV)*

*Christ has paid the price already so you all can look forward to that day and come boldly to the throne of Grace with confidence. Why have you chosen instead to follow a **L.O.S.T.** spirit and leave out these spiritual truths deciding instead that the Heavenly order is wrong, and YOU are God, and the throne of judgement is somehow rightfully yours?*

You will not sit in that seat for long, for

Pride goes before destruction, and
a haughty spirit before a fall
(Proverbs 16:18, NIV)

*I want nothing to do with the proud. I cannot use a haughty heart. There is not room for Me when you are so filled up with you! Your preferences, your dreams, your appetite, your money, your body, your relationships, your time. So **L.O.S.T.** in YOU, there can be no sign of Me anywhere. So be aware of this haughty and **L.O.S.T.** spirit in you, my Beloved.*

*Be careful who you surround yourself with as well. **L.O.S.T**. souls, people who constantly **L**eave **O**ut **S**piritual **T**ruths in their life, will do the same for your life. Instead of building you up, speaking life-giving and loving words over you, they will choke out your light and life source with worry and limitation, condemnation, and criticism. They will be so sly about it, and even pretend or somehow believe that they are doing you a favor by "managing your expectations."*

Have you ever had someone say to you they were just helping you to "manage your expectations?" If you do end up in a conversation with one of these types of people, RUN... there is nothing Biblical about "managing your expectations." God doesn't say to pray and trust in him, BUT don't really think it's going to happen. That is in divine contrast to what He promises.

If you have the faith in a mustard seed, then it can be done. If God began a good work in you, He will be faithful to complete it. What kind of faith or prayer is it, to bring your petitions, desires, and dreams to God, ask Him if it is His will, and then in the next breath let Him know, that you know, He "Probably won't be able to do it?"

In this earthly reality, very few people have multimillion dollar companies, only 5% of authors are truly successful, most singers don't land a record deal, most athletes aren't good enough to play in the pros, and on, and on, and on....

Why would anyone try anything, believe for anything, if they looked at the littered bodies along the way. But the Lord says, "Keep your eyes fixed on Me," and for a good reason. He doesn't want you to look at the waves. He doesn't want you to believe in what someone else was able to do or not able to do. If He called YOU to do it, DO IT! What God breathes on, you had best stand back and watch out, because it is about to take flight! Where is the faith in the person who says they want to help you "manage your expectations?"

You are looking at someone who, in their heart of hearts, believes that you are more likely to fail than to succeed. They are telling you that you should believe more in your ability to fail than in God's ability to succeed. Jesus was able to raise people from the dead, heal the blind, make the lame leap, and cure the incurable.

Has He not made the case that if you are going to "manage" any expectations, manage them toward the IMPOSSIBLE!

Insecure, anxious, depressed and **L.O.S.T.** people want to "manage expectations" because they have been hurt and disappointed so many times that they lost faith that the supernatural is completely natural to God and anyone who is working with Him. It is disheartening to see the vast majority of people in the world making sure that they "manage your expectations." Why is that? Do they mean it in some kind of protective way, that if they can rattle your faith and bring it down to their level of faith, their reality, then they can continue to believe in a God that does not exist, a limited God....

Notice these types of people, the "expectation managers," always call themselves not pessimistic, but realistic. Greatness never came from being realistic and following the patterns the world is presenting as the best options for you. Faith is not saying, "Well this is what I've seen so far, so that's all I can believe for." No, faith is saying, "I've never seen it, but God is still God and He does big things with big prayers." He moves the immovable. He breaks the unbreakable, but it does require that we believe for it, that we insist it will come to pass.

You can't throw up a prayer to God and then stubbornly insist not knowing that He CAN do it. If that is how you were taught to pray, all you will be able to do is sink. But when you learn to say, "Spirit work in me," and you swim for your dreams, the whole ocean can come around you to lift you up with one wave and take you further and faster than you could have ever gone on your own strength. Don't ever manage your expectations with God. Believe in it! Do not allow others to lead you to feeling **L.O.S.T.** by their directions and believing that they already know how your life will go for you! There is a God, and they are not it. They are **L**eaving **O**ut **S**piritual **T**ruths when they try to take your eyes off of God and off of His call on your life. They have forgotten that God is omniscient, He knows everything.

Are you seriously trying to remind God of the stats for being successful at something? Are you trying to remind God what has worked in the past and what hasn't, in your experience? Your experience, no matter how much you think it is, is so finite it's almost embarrassing any of us claim to be experts in anything. God doesn't work under the construct of this world and its probabilities, He is Omnipresent and omnipotent, all-present and all powerful, and someone trying to "manage your expectations" has seriously forgotten that.

You think that GOD can't open the door, can't get you the audition, can't run you into the person you need to meet, find you a job, heal a loved one.... What kind of God are you believing in if your answer to any of these is "Probably not, I'm just managing my expectations." You are basically saying, "God usually disappoints so get ready for another one." That type of faith breaks my heart, and even if He doesn't answer your prayer the way you want, when you want, with whom you want, is it possible He is saying, "I have a better idea! Come and see."

I have been through some painful, heartbreaking, gut-wrenching disappointments. I have believed to the depths of my soul for a prayer to come true, and yes, it does a number on your faith when it doesn't happen how you unwaveringly believed it would. Sometimes, you don't even get a reason why, but maybe we don't need a reason, we need to search for the revealing of a deeper truth inside the pain. Faith is not believing as long as it goes the way we decided it should.

Faith is continuing to believe even when it doesn't turn out how we thought it would, but that doesn't mean you should change from Faith to Fear, hedging your bets when you lay the chips on the table and not going "All In" because of what statistics say. If you have truly prayed about something, been called to it, and felt God's hand on you, then Go BIG or Go HOME!

God is in the business of Big Prayers and Big Dreams. How can He demonstrate His mighty power, His saving grace, His abundant blessings, and His favor on your life, if you aren't praying for anything that you couldn't do yourself if you put out a little effort?

Don't join the sinking ship of disbelief or facing "reality." Don't face reality! Face God! Don't look at the worldly stats, look at God's stats. Don't get **L.O.S.T.** as you look at your dreams. Don't leave out these spiritual truths as you try to calculate in your human mind if God can or can't make it happen. God has never been defeated, but oh how he has been tested, called upon, even asked to step up for a dual! Remember Elijah?

It was 800 prophets of their God, Baal, to 1+, Elijah (and God), and we know who won that one! What would the "realistic" people of the day have said? What would those "expectation managers" have been trying to whisper in Elijah's ear? Yet time and time again God comes through without so much as a wince of wonder if He could do it!

He knocked down walls, sent down fire, parted seas, wiped out armies, restored fortunes, placed babies in barren wombs, healed withered hands in an instant, dropped food from the sky, brought water forth from a rock twice, shut the mouths of lions, changed poisonous water to clean water to drink, won wars where the odds weren't even close, brought the dead to life, healed the sick, exorcised demons and sent them into swine, made the lame leap, gave the blind their sight, kept three men safe in the middle of a fiery furnace, (let's check the stats on that one), and raised his Son from the dead... God is either the God of the impossible or is no God at all. Instead of asking, "Who am I that I could ever achieve anything great?" you should be asking, "Who is HE that can't do anything less than Great?"

I changed my mind, go ahead and please do "manage your expectations," but to His scoreboard, His record, not to your family's, your neighbor's, the world's, or even your own. Check His stats. He came just for you. To seek and save the **L.O.S.T.** He came for all of us who seem to be **L**eaving **O**ut **S**piritual **T**ruths as we look at our own God-given dreams.

I heard God say to me:

*Never forget all that I have spoken over you, and please stop asking **L.O.S.T.** souls for directions in your life. If I don't have their ear and their heart, don't give them yours!*

I warn you now,

> *Do not be unequally yoked with unbelievers. For what partnership has righteousness with lawlessness? Or what fellowship has light with darkness? (2 Corinthians 6:15, ESV)*

*If you are being led by two opposing voices, two opposing forces, you will never be able to fully run toward your calling. When you are tied to someone who is stuck on themselves, and is wandering around **L.O.S.T.**, spewing words that somehow leave out vital spiritual truths that are needed for you to discern if you need to let them go.*

If they are purposely withholding encouraging words that will help you grow, you will wither and become sick. Leave them be and walk toward Me. Some parts of life can only be discovered on a solo journey requiring time alone, just you and me.

*You are called to love and save the **L.O.S.T.** by pointing them back to me, not by sleeping with them. Missionary dating is not my design for a healthy marriage between two committed, loving, and God-honoring souls. Please stop sacrificing your soul to your "savior complex." YOU CAN'T SAVE PEOPLE, I do that! But you can hinder the process of salvation by making what I wanted to be uncomfortable, comfortable.*

*When you shield someone from the full brunt of their rebellious life choices, you don't help them, you promote the continuation of that **L.O.S.T.** soul.*

*When you excuse poor and abusive behavior, a lack of need for growth and maturity, when you turn your head to the fact that they have a complete lack of commitment to Me as the head of their life... when you do this, you are denying Me, and lowering My standards that you say you hold so dearly in your life. That **L.O.S.T.** soul not only won't value Me, but they also won't truly value you or the principles and values you profess to hold.*

And why should they? So far, there have been no consequences for their self-centered behavior. They can still deny Me while subsequently continuing to use you, physically, emotionally, mentally, and spiritually.

*You do a disservice to the ones closest to you if the things you say you value you then diminish in importance when a **L.O.S.T.** soul is around. In that moment, you too are becoming **L.O.S.T.** as well. You are now the one agreeing to **L**eave **O**ut **S**piritual **T**ruths you know about yourself and about Me.*

*Getting **L.O.S.T.** isn't always a major cataclysmic event. It can start in subtle ways, but it will always lead to an internal or external (or both) consequence. You can get **L.O.S.T.** in a behavior that does not suit you, such behaviors that are beneath the calling on your life*

*. When you find yourself feeling **L.O.S.T.**, it means that you have not fully embraced the fact that you are, at ALL times, the temple of the Holy and Living God. My power runs through you, and you should honor Me in all your ways, whether surrounded by a beautiful **L.O.S.T.** soul or not.*

*Always watch out for yourself, notice when you are becoming **L.O.S.T.** in envy, or **L.O.S.T.** in coveting something or someone. When you become **L.O.S.T.** in these things, you are discounting all that I am doing in your life. Discounting the character lessons, I am trying to teach you. I'm molding you so that you can become all you need to become, so that you can do all I am calling you to do.*

*Everyone is so special, precious, and unique to me, and you have no idea what you are really asking for most of the time. You think you simply want that job, that car, that life, that wife, that husband, those fun experiences; you THINK you want them, but if I have not taught you the spiritual truths you will need to take care of and keep those blessings, if you haven't let me mold your character into that of a loving, self-controlled, sacrificing servant and, if I haven't taught you how to steward your gifts well, you will be even more **L.O.S.T.** if I gave you all the blessings you begged me for. If you don't know how to desire the Kingdom of God more than the treasures and pleasures of this world, you will become a **L.O.S.T.** soul.*

*When you keep **L**eaving **O**ut **S**piritual **T**ruths, you become sad, mad, bitter, resentful, and most of all – SELFISH. The **L.O.S.T.** mentality and motto is "I can't worry about you, because I have to get MINE!" When you have let go of Me as your anchor and your compass; when you have abandoned My love, My word, My purpose, when you let go, you are vulnerable for the wind to take you where it pleases. This is where evil, the keeper of the **L.O.S.T.**, the spirit of this world, will snatch you up. And He has a very clear plan for you: to steal your mind, kill your hope, and destroy your calling.*

*The spirit over the **L.O.S.T.** nation is not **L.O.S.T.** at all. He is intentional and driven in his plans to steal as many souls as he can before the day of judgement is at hand.*

He will judge you unfairly, deem you unworthy, and whisper to you that you will never be enough until you prove otherwise. There is no salvation, no safe place in the land of the **L.O.S.T.**. *It is a sick and cruel game that evil plays with your heart, promising to fill it, but He never can. He will have you aiming at an always moving target that is just out of reach. He will parade pictures of other* **L.O.S.T.** *people in front of you and whisper, "See, I have made them happy by playing the game, why aren't you happy?" The tormented thoughts of not being good enough, not having enough, not knowing enough, or not being good-looking enough, scramble your brain until you no longer realize you have been snatched up and are now* **L.O.S.T.**

I am throwing out a lifeline to all who are **L.O.S.T.**. *I'm Here, I'm Here! Grab on, my child. Grab tight to Me, My daughter! Hold fast My Son! I've got you. I can fulfill your deepest desire to feel known, to have a place.*
I am your rock and your refuge. I am your shield of power. I think you are to die for. Sit at the foot of the cross and receive the love I long to give you. You don't have to chase cars, money, jobs, or relationships. Let me flow through you and all I have in mind for you will begin to flow to you. I planted good seeds in you, and you will love the fruits they will bear if you can be patient in the time of planting and pruning.

When you feel **L.O.S.T.**, *you will feel anxious and impatient. Ask yourself in that moment, "What lie am I believing right now that makes me want to act in haste?" Because I, the Lord your God, do not move in haste. I move at a slow and steady pace. While it might appear to the outside world that the fruit was immediate or that you are called an overnight success, you know that the struggle was real, the faith was longsuffering, and the pruning was painful, but it was all was necessary for the fruit to appear in its perfect season.*

It might look as if it came out of nowhere, but I had a plan in place long before you were born for such a time as this. Impatience is a flag to you that you believe you are **L.O.S.T.** *– that the place or experience you want is not going as YOU planned.*

Humble yourself, My child, you have no idea what is going to happen tomorrow, or even in the next hour. Pride will creep up in such subtle ways, and impatience is a good sign you are giving birth to a pride-filled heart. You will begin to think you know better, you deserve better, you should have this or that, and that nothing is enough for you. You seem to be forgetting the price I already paid so that the veil could be torn, and we could once again walk together in the cool of the day like mankind did before the fall.

I let My only son be beaten, whipped, mocked, and spit on. I watched and felt every cry of pain. I let them drive stakes into His hands and jam a sword through His side as they laughed. My Son, who outshines the sun, was crucified by the **L.O.S.T.** *for the* **L.O.S.T.** *I offered him for you. So, the stench of pride on you causes Me to turn My eyes from you. It churns My gut as I can still see My baby boy hanging there while you still think you deserve more than that which has already been paid. Be aware of pride and all who walk under its banner. Heed the scriptures to*

Humble yourselves under the mighty power of God, and at the right time he will lift you up in honor
(1 Peter 5:6, NLT).

Where were you, prideful souls, when I created the moon and the stars? What say did you have on where the ocean should stop on the shore? What part of the trees did you create? Which flowers in the fields did you design and dress in all their splendor?

How heavy was the moon when you placed it a perfect distance from the earth and the sun, and then put it into an orbit that has stayed consistent for all existence? Just like I asked my servant Job so long ago, I ask you now, proud-hearted people, where were you?

*How **L.O.S.T.** you are when you believe that you control your destiny. How **L.O.S.T.** you are when you believe that you control how many days you have on this earth. How **L.O.S.T.** you are when you try to manhandle life instead of submitting to My voice, My guiding hand, the compass of My Word, and the protection of My heart to comfort and lead you all the days of your life. I am a God of order, and plans. Nothing about Me is at a loss.*

*Nothing about Me is able to be **L.O.S.T.** Since I cannot lie, then I am unable to **L**eave **O**ut **S**piritual **T**ruths, for how can I be what I am not? I am the Truth that brings forth all Life. I am the Creator, I know every hair on your head, every bird, every flower, I know you by name and I am outside calling, calling in the night, calling each of you by name, calling you home.*

*You don't have to be **L.O.S.T.** one second longer. You don't have to listen to the Spirit of Lies who is purposely leaving out the truth about how loved you are, how special you are, and how strong I can make you.*

*The **L.O.S.T.** spirit loves leaving out the truth that each person you see is worthy of being treated with kindness and respect no matter how old or young they are. The spirit of the **L.O.S.T.** nation is cruel.*

*He finds joy in telling you that you aren't enough, you aren't capable, you can't have peace, and that you don't deserve love or blessings. The spirit of the **L.O.S.T.** scoffs at the dreams I have given you. He lights fires in your heart, taunting you and lying to you that life is chaotic and that's just the way it is.*

He snarls as he hisses in your ear, "This is as good as it gets for you!" LIES, ALL LIES! Bitterness seeps in and resentment is dancing right behind it. Before you know it, you live in a house full of **L.O.S.T.** *spirits who have now found a warm place to find shelter in you. Get them out! Tell them to flee in Jesus' name, and they must.*

Wake up, open your eyes, learn the truth, pour the Word into your mind night and day. Wash it over your children and all your loved ones. Speak the Word openly and often. It can be trusted as a guiding light to make sure you do not get **L.O.S.T.** *either. Know all the promises I have given to you. Tie them around your heart and use them as a mirror to check your soul. I ask you; do you spend more time looking at an outer mirror than you do with my holy and purifying mirror, My Word? Align your heart with My words, My ways, and My wonderous works and you will never be* **L.O.S.T.** *again.*

Jesus never faltered because He knew the Word, He used the Word; He was the Word –

The Word became flesh and made his dwelling among us. We have seen his glory, the glory of the one and only Son, who came from the Father, Full of grace and truth
(John 1:14, NIV)

Just as His words revealed the truth, your words will be the indicator to tell you and others if you are **L.O.S.T.** *or if you have found your way back home. Peace abounds at home. My mercy flows. My laughter and joy fill every room. My heart cries out like the father in the parable of the prodigal son when it said*

While he was still a long distance away, his father saw him coming. Filled with love and compassion, he ran to his son, embraced him and kissed him
(Luke 15:20, NLT)

And he exclaimed:

We must celebrate with a feast, for this son of mine was
dead and has now returned to life.
He was lost, but now he is found
(Luke 15:23-24, NLT)

This is how it is with Me and My children. I don't wait for you to get yourself right and come all the way to my feet to make you grovel.

No dear one, I RUN to you! I watch for you day and night, I wait for you, and when I see you turn even the slightest bit back home to me, I run to you! I will not leave you. I will not berate you. I want you home with me where you always belonged. My child is home, and Christ's bride has returned. Unity, love, and encouragement are my love languages. I want you so filled with My love that you cannot help but...

Go into all the world and
preach the Good News to everyone
(Mark 16:15, NLT)

*Tell the truth to the **L.O.S.T.** and guide them to Me. Go to your "family" throughout the world and bring them home to Me.*

*Worship together, do life together, pray together, play together, love each other, and bless all those you meet. Do not marry the **L.O.S.T.** but do PRAY for them. Do not tether your life to anyone who isn't after My heart, longing to bring Me into their home as I bring them deeper into My heart.*

*In this day and age, the **L.O.S.T.** have usually heard the truth, and they have actively and defiantly chosen to say, "God? Who needs Him. I am the God of my life, and I will do as I want." "I'm a self-made man," the **L.O.S.T.** will proudly proclaim.*

*They speak toddler language. They act like a tyrant as they run around lording over others with brash bravado, completely **L.O.S.T.**, but still so cocky in their belief that they are not **L.O.S.T.** at all. Reminding everyone else that "this thing or that thing, this person or that person, is MINE." You can hear them ranting about "my money, my house, my stuff, my life, my creation, my relationship, mine, mine, mine." The **L.O.S.T.** scream "MINE" because they do not know or actually believe that everything that they have, right down to the breath they breathe and the brain they use, are all gifts from God. As they shake their fist at Me, they forget, I knitted that fist together and they should use it gratefully instead of being grotesque and grandiose with it.*

As I listened to God warn me and remind me, I became even more grateful for His love. I am so grateful for the Rainbow for the promise that God gave to never again pour out His wrath on us. That he will never destroy what He created on earth and all the sinners that fill it, including me! I'm grateful because I know all of the prideful, judgmental, cynical, critical, condemning, sarcastic, flippant, and disrespectful ways I have talked to and about God over the course of my life, as well as the way I thought it was okay to speak like that to other image bearers, to His other children. I know what I deserve for these things is an incinerating fireball right to the face. I mean seriously, I think most of us wouldn't have made it past the age of three if we got what we deserved for how we treated God, ourselves, and others.

God's rainbow of mercy is my blanket that I snuggle into each morning. His goodness wrapping around me and encouraging me to get closer.

I love that God never turns down snuggle time with me.

Draw near to God, and He will draw near to you.
Cleanse your hands, you sinners, and
purify your hearts, you double-minded
(James 4:8, ESV)

The Lord continued to warn me when He Said:

Beware of the arms you snuggle into, make sure the Holy Spirit is the spirit allowed to whisper into your ear through the person who holds you closest.

*If they do not openly profess, and demonstrate through their daily actions, My way to live and love in this life, then I do not know them and if I do not know them, they will not listen to Me. This type of **L.O.S.T.** person will not listen to anyone unless they want to feed off you.*

*A **L.O.S.T.** person will still be somewhat nice to at least a few people, not because their heart knows anything of true and abiding love, but because their heart and their **L.O.S.T.** spirit still needs to feed itself to grow in strength and it will drain your life if you keep these types of people too close to your physical temple. Flee the place where the spirit of the **L.O.S.T.** slumber. If you have not married them, give thanks for My saving grace over your life, and find a way out!*

*If you have legally married them and made that covenant, then speak clearly, pray constantly, and boldly ask what the intention of this **L.O.S.T.** spirit is for you and your family. What change is this **L.O.S.T.** soul willing to strive for, and what spirit do they believe in? What spirit of anger or spirit of sorrow, spirit of depression or spirit of deception do they let have access to their life and to yours? What **L.O.S.T.** spirit is you allowing over your children, who are so susceptible and sensitive? They don't need to be around confused leaders who bully and force or try to beat them into submission.*

*That is not My way of leading a family. I love each of you into who I need you to be for the purpose I called you to do. I do not beat and berate you out of the person I don't want you to be. That type of abuse would only leave you feeling more **L.O.S.T.** than loved, more left out than lifted up.*

You were called to crush fears, not crush souls; so be careful with your words and with your touch. Is there is a "fear-raiser" or a "soul crusher" in your midst? Remove yourself, or remove them, from your presence.

*My dreams and plans for you are too great and they will need a pure and strong faith to be accomplished. Your dreams will need the activation of the Holy Spirit in you, not a **L.O.S.T.** and scared, sarcastic, haughty, or fearful and bitter spirit. No fruit of that nature can fill you and bring you salvation and peace. Protect your heart, your head, your body, your home, your friends, your children, and the dreams I have placed inside of you. Seek and save the **L.O.S.T.** but do not cleave to them. Point them to the Light. Season their life with my good words and amazing message. Tell them it is a choice that will change them forever, but it is a choice that must be made because*

It is written "as surely as I live" says the Lord, "every knee will bow before me; every tongue will acknowledge God"
(Romans 14:11, NIV)

You're Sons of the Light, Daughters of the Day. We live under wide open skies and know where we stand. So, let's not sleepwalk through life like those others
(2 Thessalonians, 5:5 MSG)

Speak encouraging words to one another. Build up hope so you'll all be together in this, no one left out, no one left behind
(2 Thessalonians 5:11, MSG)

*Be able to say with full confidence, "I am not **L.O.S.T.** ... I once was Lost, but now, I'm Home."*

But if you refuse to serve the Lord, then choose today whom you will serve....
Joshua 24:15, NLT)

But as for Me and My family, we will serve the Lord.
(Joshua 24:15, NLT)

God continued to speak saying:

*You are not **L.O.S.T.**, stop acting like you are. You are allowing someone else to slow down the pace of your own spiritual growth because you are tied to dead weight. If they are not alive in Christ, if they do not have My name on their lips and My fruits in their life, they are dead in sin, in pain, in self-loathing, or in self- glorification. They are filled with lies that they are telling themselves, and if you stand by and say nothing, shake your head or let them use and abuse you to fill the hole in their hearts for a day, a week, a month, or even years, you are dying a little inside every day.*

*A **L.O.S.T.** man will drive a whole family into a ditch. Loose yourself from the **L.O.S.T.** and seek out the saved to do life with. Love is what LOVE really looks like. Find godliness attractive. Don't bargain shop, don't pick a spirit with a beautiful body but a barren soul. No lasting joy is found when a **L.O.S.T.** soul appears; no peace does the **L.O.S.T.** soul carry. Patience and Kindness from this type of spirit is an ACT.*

*The **L.O.S.T.** soul can put on this act for short periods of time, but wearing it is exhausting, because it is not the **L.O.S.T.** soul's true nature. Anger, bitterness, self-centeredness, entitlement, haughtiness, possessiveness, jealousy, and irritation are the natural feelings of the **L.O.S.T.** soul. This is not the Holy Spirit dwelling in the person.*
*You are sharing a bed with someone who is manipulating you. This **L.O.S.T.** soul is clever enough to learn that people like "nice" people, so they act like it at work, or to charm you in the early stages of your relationship, or to manipulate a situation so that they get their needs met, regardless of anyone else involved.*

But if you open your eyes and ears, you will hear the complaining after the mask of "goodness and charm" starts to slip back down to uncover their true underlying snarl.

This spirit is not able to produce the actual fruits that they are pretending to possess. Only the Holy Spirit is built up, energized, and amplified by using its natural gifts of love, joy, peace, patience, kindness, goodness, faithfulness, gentleness, and self-control.

The Holy Spirit does not see others as burdens to deal with, but as blessings to love, listen to, and learn from. Any other spirit is simply trying to copy these gifts as a form of manipulation, but it is a lie, an act. When you are in alignment with My spirit, the gifts I produce not only invigorate you as you bless others, but they are also felt as a blessing to you. You will not feel drained or burdened by displaying the fruits of the Holy Spirit working in you.

*A **L.O.S.T.** soul is a deceptive soul, and it enjoys draining you. Sucking the life out of you, and out of any partner they can use sexually. Engaging in sex before making a covenant with the other person is partially the cause of the blindness you seem to have to be able to identify and then leave this type of destructive soul. You are letting that spirit feed off of you and steal your calling as you offer up your body to this sick spirit who wants nothing more than to take your power to satiate the pit of darkness that they live in.*

I can't bring you into your full calling while you have a snake wrapped around your chest, squeezing your creativity and divine inspiration out of you. I can't bring you into your divine destiny while you still believe that you can drag the dead with you,

Let the spiritually dead bury their own dead!
Your duty is to go preach about the Kingdom of God
(Luke 9:60, NLT)

The thief comes only to steal and kill and destroy; I have come that you may have life and have it in all its fullness. (John 10:10, BSB)

*There is nothing worse than a **L.O.S.T.** and pride-filled spirit. They leave you with the worst type of hangover, and usually sex, bullying, manipulation, and money are their favorite weapons to wage war against your spirit to try to break you and make you stay. Trying to get you to believe you should bend your knee to them and not to Me.*

Trying to make you believe you aren't worth it, you are a drain and don't deserve to be treated as cherished, holy, and chosen.

*They want you to believe that "you get what you get, and you should be grateful for it." The manipulation, emotional gaslighting, the verbal lashings, the biting words, like weapons aimed at you …. ALL **L.O.S.T.**, all wrong! That is what the spirit of the **L.O.S.T.** is actually saying to them. These are the words that they hear the most in their heads. The **L.O.S.T.** rarely even want to spend time soaking and marinating in the words of life and truth. You can see the discomfort in them when they are surrounded by believers and the Word of God. They are very tied to the illusion of power that they think they hold over others.*

*They don't want to improve their actions, their words, their character. They don't want to find the good or the "God" in others. They find a sick joy in making fun of and destroying others. The spirit of the **L.O.S.T.** is a mocking spirit. Its power grows in other's pain and what you feed it will always grow.*

Be careful of people who mock and belittle others, letting others know how "stupid" they are, because you will be next on the list of their discontented and loathsome appetite to deceive, destroy, and deal a death blow to your spirit, and to your calling.

That type of person wants nothing more than to kill your dreams because he can't seem to produce his own, so when he sees the favor of the Lord on your life, he feels compelled to dismiss and diminish it. When he hears what you value, He will disparage it.

He sees your joy and he will judge you as crazy, simple, or stupid. He should do all of you a favor and put on his self- appointed and self-anointed crown so at least everyone will know that he has no God, HE IS HIS GOD.... With none of the power, none of the glory, and none of the fruits of the Spirit.

He is a miserable tyrant, a man in stature but a toddler in spirit.

*The spirit of grace will not rest upon such a face. I cannot use such an arrogant, hateful, manipulative heart. But if they could repent and return to Me, I could do a new thing in even the most depraved and **L.O.S.T.** of souls! Instantly I can humble you. Graciously, I will welcome you home. Diligently I will train you, but you have to put your wants and ways down. Can you remove your crown, oh **L.O.S.T.** one?*

Can you find the strength to humble yourself and kneel before the one true God? Can you accept your assignment to love, and let me be the judge?

Fall in love with love. Have tender hearts and humble minds. Hold yourself accountable to My Word and the standard of love I set out for you. Commit yourself to the journey. Commit yourself to climb with Me. Jesus explained what the journey from lost to found will look like when he said

The person who trusts me will not only do what I'm doing but even greater things because I, on my way to the Father, am giving you the same work to do that I've been doing
(John 14:12, MSG)

I will not leave you orphaned. I'm coming back. In just a little while the world will no longer see me, but you're going to see me because I am alive and you're about to come alive
(John 14:18, MSG)

The Friend, the Holy Spirit whom the Father will send at my request, will make everything plain to you. He will remind you of all the things I have told you.
I'm leaving you well and whole.
That's my parting gift to you. Peace. I don't leave you the way you're used to being left—feeling abandoned, [and L.O.S.T] So don't be upset, don't be distraught
(John 14:25- 27, MSG)

You are blessed when you feel you've lost what is most dear to you. Only then can you be embraced by the One most dear to you
(Matthew 5:4, MSG)

If you feel a **L.O.S.T.** Spirit trying to derail you, discourage you, or worse, trying to lead you away from Me by getting you to doubt yourself or your calling, raise your eyes to the heavens, fill your heart with My power and boldly rebuke this spirit by telling it plainly, "You didn't design me, so you can't define me. You didn't call me, so I didn't answer you.

You didn't save me, so you have no idea what suits me. You aren't the one who broke my chains and set me free, so I am in no way bound to you!"

I have blessed you with a wonderful authority over this earth, to heal the sick, cast out demons, raise the dead, redeem the years, and intercede for another. You have the authority to lavishly use the gifts of the Spirit to have the ability to feel others and become one with the body of Christ.

I have given you the authority to do all of these things, but I never gave you the authority to condemn another masterpiece.

You who disturb the peace I have placed in every heart that belongs to Me, be warned that you will hold no peace in your heart, and you will wander aimless and **L.O.S.T.** *for all eternity if this is the path you choose. If someone wants to know Me, let them come! But a grave warning to anyone who causes someone to run away from me because of YOU! If you work for me, WORK FOR ME!*

Heal the Sick, raise the dead, touch the untouchables, and cast out demons. Give as freely as you have received
(Matthew 10: 8, NLT)

When others are happy, be happy with them. If they are sad, share their sorrow, Live in Harmony with each other. Don't try to act important but enjoy the company of ordinary people. And don't think you know it all.
(Romans 12:15, NLT)

You will have so much to do when you actually get to work that you won't even have time to add "condemn others" to your to-do list for the day.

*So, I ask you, do you want to be **L.O.S.T.** or do you want to be well? Do you want to be healed? Do you want to work with me?*

...I'm after mercy, not religion. I'm here to invite outsiders, not coddle insiders
(Matthew 9:13, MSG)

Become what you believe
(Matthew 9: 29, MSG)

Stay calm; Mind your own business; do your own job
(1 Thessalonians 4:11, MSG)

*You can't be **L.O.S.T.** and lead! You have to know whose you are and where you come from before you can ever lead the **L.O.S.T.** back home. Get lost in love, so that you can effectively love the **L.O.S.T.** Remember, your roots go up, not down, so don't build your home down here, when you were meant to soar on wings like eagles, and find your way back home to Me. You came from Me, you will return to Me. This is not your home. You are on loan to the world from Me, and I have no intention of letting you go.*

How could I when

I'm the vine, and you are the branches. If you abide in Me and I in you, you will bear great fruit. Without Me, you will accomplish nothing
(John 15:5, The Voice)

I'm so thankful for God's grace over my life, for the promises He has made me. I'm grateful that I can now laugh to myself as I think, "If He's the vine then I can't get **L.O.S.T.**, I'm attached! I'm just a branch... hanging out...bearing fruit! Good fruit! I am no longer **L.O.S.T.**, I am **H.O.M.E.** because I now understand and find great joy in proclaiming that **H**e's -**O**nly- **M**y- **E**verything.

Chapter 14

Q.U.I.T IT!

Quiet – **U**nderlying – **I**nner - **T**urmoil

Love never QUITS, never loses faith, is always hopeful, and endures through every circumstance (1 Corinthians 13:7, modified)

This month was a rollercoaster ride of mountaintops of beauty, and valleys of heartbreaks. It was filled with twisting roads of confusion, and finally the healing highway that led me back home.

I started this month saying "I **Q.U.I.T.**, I'm done!" Too much hurt, too much confusion, too much of the Texas summer heat! I packed my bags and headed north.

I had felt a road trip brewing in my heart for weeks after an incident that broke my spirit and revealed truths to me that I had denied for decades. I knew this chapter was coming up, and I was in desperate need to embrace the **Q.U.I.T.** and learn how to finally **Q**uiet **U**nderlying **I**nner **T**urmoil once and for all.

At this point, my mind and heart were churning up storm after storm in my spirit, raging on and on with no signs of letting up... so I left. I had felt called to North Carolina for almost 2 years to go to Elevation Church at Ballentyne and see Steven Furtick preach there. I figured one day I would make a trip up there and after hearing that my cousin had moved to North Carolina a year prior, and was right in the middle of the state, I was excited to get a two-for-one deal of visiting with her again and going to Elevation Church together. I also had a deep desire to go to the mountains, and I didn't care if they were the Smoky Mountains, the Blue Ridge mountains, or the Appalachian Mountains; I just needed to get away and go to the top of a mountain to pray and be restored.

I had packed six new books to take with me on the trip. I was determined to read as many as I could while away, as they were all intended to help me heal these old but fresh wounds that now demanded my attention. These childhood wounds were wreaking havoc on my life, and I had no idea. How do you heal what you don't know is hurting you? How do you **Q.U.I.T.** hurting yourself or letting others hurt you when you don't believe the depth of the devastation it will have on you if you don't learn to **Q.U.I.T.** allowing such behaviors to continue in your life ... Where do I even start?

I knew where to start. It was where I always start with prayer, scripture, and helpful books. I always start with His Word and His love, and this healing journey would be no different. I know He is watching over me and directing my path.

Whether I stumble or sprint towards the wholeness and healing that are my divine right as a chosen child of God, I know He is there, proud of every step I take. So, I put the car in drive and headed out for some "Highway Healing" as I like to call it. Just the road and the radio to soothe my soul. Only a few people knew I was leaving the state, where I was going, and who I was going to stay with, and no one, including me, knew how long I would be gone. God had told me to go, but never gave me a return date.

It was time to **Q.U.I.T.** talking and start listening. **Q.U.I.T.** letting people speak words over me that cut and hurt me, and instead, let the Word wash me clean again, renew my spirit, and return my joy. I didn't know this was the journey I was about to go on, but God did. I thought I knew how it would all go, and some of it did work out how I expected it would, but most of it looked very different. As wonderful as some moments were, others were incredibly painful, unnerving, and confusing to say the least. Childhood triggers of abandonment were firing left and right, and I was spiraling out of control as I tried to maintain my emotional balance surrounded by other people and dogs.

I know, I know, the majority of the world LOVES dogs. I, however, do not. At all. They cause me severe anxiety, not knowing when their ear shattering barking will start or stop, or having their spit be spread all over me that makes me want to vomit.

The sound of the barking causes my adrenaline and cortisol levels to spike, and every day I had to deal with that, but I couldn't express how I really felt because I had nowhere else to go, unless I wanted to drive the 20 hours back home.

So, I stuffed my emotions yet again, and they raged in me and came out in my changes in eating patterns. I was stuffing and stuffing myself to fill this uncomfortable pit inside me, this unmet need for safety and comfort that I was not honoring.

I prayed and prayed every day, but the storm raged on. I tried to spend a lot of time in my room reading about codependency, emotional boundaries (that I was failing miserably at protecting each day), about narcissism and the emotional trauma that wrecked my life in ways I was blind to up until the last couple weeks.

I was a fish in a toxic fishbowl most of my childhood, and I couldn't see fully the poison I had been inhaling daily. This shattering of the image of my childhood, and the final acceptance of what I already inherently knew, was and is a lot to absorb psychologically. I found myself deeply and intensely grieving as I read more and more. I cried as I listened to pastors and coaches I trusted and admired talk about the damage that had been done and some of the effects I would have to learn how to manage for the rest of my life.

I watched as those wounds played out right before my eyes over a thousand miles away from the home where it happened. I watched as I felt those same feelings of being unworthy, a burden, unseen, insignificant, and incapable, come flooding back, and it made me want to run again, but I had this sense that God wanted to me to stay for now and go to the mountains, even if I had to go alone. I was used to going places alone anyway. I love my "Jesus and Jen" retreats when we can get away together, so I was thrilled to get back in the car and head to Asheville for a day trip one Thursday.

I love Asheville, North Carolina. I feel there is an odd spirit of perversion over that town, but I still love that artist/gypsy/mountain vibe. It's a writer's delight to watch people and walk around town window shopping and listening to the conversations of the people as they go by. It was a gorgeous day and a welcome relief from the summer heat of Texas that I wasn't missing at all!

I had this feeling when I arrived in Asheville that I had a **D.A.T.E.** here, a **D**ivine **A**ppointment **T**o **E**ngage with someone specific, but I didn't know who or where this appointment was set for.

When I arrived in Asheville, I parked my car in a lot across from MELA, an Indian restaurant in town, and God said, *There! You will go to eat there in one hour.*

I went walking all over town for the next hour and then made my way back to the restaurant and went in. They had an amazing buffet laid out already and this kind server met me at the door with a warm smile and sparkling eyes. He greeted me and said he had the perfect spot for me and my party of one.

He sat me by the window at the front of the restaurant right next to another woman who was also sitting alone. She caught my eye immediately as I noted her journal, pen, and book as her trusted companions for lunch. I had this "Holy Hunch" that I was here to talk to her. I wasn't sure how to start the conversation though, as she seemed to be thoroughly enjoying her lunch and her book, so I went over the buffet to serve myself some food and came back to my table. I folded my hands in prayer and asked God to show me who I needed to talk to or why I was here. Was it this woman? Was it the server? Was this just a great place for me to enjoy a meal? I knew it was her though, I knew it.

I decided to try an "old move" I'd seen in movies to get her attention, one where I would "accidently" drop something on the floor and she would notice and help me pick it up and "voilà"... the conversation would begin!

I pulled out my stack of Pocket-Praise note cards and started reading them, acting deeply interested, which I actually was, but still, I knew where this was going. I set the cards down on the edge of my table and then... Oops, I knocked them all over the floor.

She never looked up or moved at all. I felt like a fumbling freshman picking up my notecards, but then our sweet server came back to check on her and since she was literally an arm's length away from me, I had no problem hearing their conversation. She told him she had just finished a 5-day retreat in the mountains for mothers and it was amazing.

My heart skipped a beat as I thought, "a woman who writes, and is deep in faith out on a retreat with other ladies, how awesome is that?!" I would come to find out I was right, and wrong, at the same time. She was talking about parenting with the server and by some divine pre-planning on God's part,

I had packed my copy of *Parenting with Love and Logic,* an awesome and insightful book on how to parent without punishment or shame.

Full disclosure: I had only read one chapter at that point because of the other five books I had also been focusing on, but I had watched many videos and I had been practicing those techniques with kids I knew and was amazed by the results already. So, whenever I get a chance, I love recommending this book to parents who are open to growing in their parenting practices.

I pulled out the book and took my shot at breaking into their conversation. I held out the book and said, "You gotta check out this book, it's awesome and I'm not even a parent!" She laughed and was more than happy to take the recommendation, and at that, my divine doorway opened into her world. I asked her if she would mind sitting together and she agreed cheerfully.

When I finally brought all my books and food over to her table and settled down, I looked up, smiled, thanked her for letting me join her and asked her what her name was. She smiled and said, "Jen." I tried not to let my mouth drop open a little, but I still couldn't stop the giggle from rising up, as I leaned back in my chair, smiled a knowing smile, and said "Reeeaaally? How about that? It's a great name isn't? I don't think I have ever met a Jen I didn't like." She looked at me and said, "And what is your name?" I paused, smiled, and then said, "It's Jen." I asked her about her "retreat," excited to hear about this amazing time of faith and fellowship, and I did, but not as I had expected.

She told me it was an amazing time, just her and 22 other "witchy women. I sat stumped. I love words too much to let that turn of phrase slide by without further explanation. I asked her what "witchy women" meant to her. She explained how they had spent the last five days in the woods doing rituals and cleansing ceremonies, calling down spirits of nature and swimming naked together in the river nearby.

I thought to myself, "Holy Crap, am I actually having lunch with a Witch, Lord?" I had a **D.A.T.E.** with a Witch? How did that happen? She was beautiful and kind, well spoken, well-read, and well-mannered for the hour we sat together.

My eyes gazed over the details of her face, her hair, her hands, and then I stopped as I was struck by a tattoo she had on her forearm. I wasn't sure if it was a moth or a Monarch butterfly, since it was a black traced tattoo. I shuddered a little inside when I saw it as I flashed back to sermon I remembered that Jerry Flowers had given about discernment and noting the difference between "moth life" versus "butterfly living."

One was a creature of the night and one flew by the light of day. They do not co-exist. I didn't know what to make of it, so asked. She told me it symbolized "transformation" for her, to which I replied, "to be able to fly in the DARK?" She didn't respond but continued to smile kindly and shrug it off. We talked about working with different spirits and how everyone who is alive is indeed working with a spirit of some sort to pulse energy through their lives and if you do not actively choose which spirit you are working with, a spirit will choose you!

She looked at me and asked, "And what spirit do you work with?" My face lit up, I beamed at the question, and said, "Oh I work with the Holy Spirit, best boss this side of Heaven!"

Her eyes dimmed slightly as she said, "I used to be all into that, but I learned the Holy Spirit, Jesus, and God aren't who they seem to be." She told me that she used to be involved in teaching the Word, grew up in church, and was all about the purity movement, but now she was at a point of deconstructing her faith. She had decided to QUIT believing.

I just sat there; I didn't know what to say. I was waiting for an amazing sermon or testimony to come flooding out of my mouth. Words of such light and power that would call her back home. My mouth stayed shut (the insight came later, of course, but she was long gone). I sat and listened, and I told her more about the lessons I had learned from *Parenting with Love and Logic,* and I told her I was working on my own book. She seemed very interested in it, and even asked me to write down my name and the title so she could get it when it was released.

I was overjoyed at her interest and thought, "YES LORD! You can speak to her way better through the book than I am doing right now because I am at a loss for words here in this moment."

Somewhere out there is another "Jen," who is flying in the dark, embracing the night, but still somehow in her soul, she reaches for the light. She left sooner than she probably needed to, but her soul was stirred, and I could see she wanted to leave. We said goodbye and hugged each other. I prayed blessing over her and her kids. Then, with my name, number, and the title of my book tucked into her purse, she walked out the door.

I sat there struggling with my thoughts of how I wish I had said more, asked more, did more. How can someone who has met Jesus, been held by Him, comforted by His words, worked with Him all over the world, seen the sick healed, the depressed want to live again, the unlovable be loved...How can you just **Q.U.I.T.** ? What happened? How can you see His mighty hand save people over and over and say, "Nope, this crap is overrated. I call Bullshit." I just couldn't wrap my brain around it.

Did she really know Him? Had she ever really held His hand and been kissed by His grace? Who had she met? What spirit deceived her? Because once you've met Him, once He has melted down the door to your heart and walked in, you are simply never the same again, EVER. Once you fall in love with True Love, you will be wrecked for the better! He's too beautiful, too kind, too gentle, too powerful, too loving for you to be indifferent to Him. He's too good and too gracious for you to even want to quit. Once you know, you know and there is no turning back.

I hope one day she meets My "Love," My Jesus, out there on the road of life. I hope His words will find her once more through the pages of this book. Don't quit. I pray for her and all the lost who had the "head" knowledge" but not the heart revelation for who He is…. NOW… for each person who calls out to Him.

After watching her walk out the door, I wrote a few more thoughts down, packed my bag, and left as well.

I never would have thought the story I would recant as I drove back to my cousin's house would start with, "So I had lunch with a witch today…"

The next few days went by with ups and downs, worries and wonders. I went on another road trip to the highest mountain I could find, Mt. Mitchell. It is the tallest mountain east of the Mississippi, but after spending ample time in the Rockies of Colorado, these mountains looked like foothills. It was the highest I could get in the state I was in, literally and metaphorically, so I climbed… and it was beautiful. I sat surrounded by beauty and reflected on all the things that had happened during this trip, as well as in the last year, and over the course of my entire life.

The veil was being lifted and the hurt being revealed. I could now see all too clearly how codependent I really am, and the severe damage that was done to me as a child that caused me to lack ever learning how to have my own sacred, set point anchored in me.

How to have a place where I would not get rocked so easily or blown around like a feather destined to go wherever someone else's "winds of emotion" took me. I was in tears. I was scared. I wanted to run. I wanted to hide. I wanted to be anywhere else, but I had no place to go so that I wouldn't bring my own pain with me.

I didn't want to feel like I was a burden to someone, or a thing they wished would leave them alone. All the books and videos I watched were letting me know that I was chest deep in an emotional flashback and I desperately needed to learn how to **Q.U.I.T.**! I needed to **Q**uiet **U**nderlying **I**nner **T**urmoil so I prayed, and then I got practical, and went out for a run to try to move the emotional energy and corresponding toxic neurochemicals out of my body!

I knew I had to pray for healing from this sad programming, and I won't quit till I learn how to take care of myself and protect myself from ever letting anyone run over my emotional or physical boundaries again. I am running toward my healing because I can't live like this anymore. I can't be at the mercy of other people's moods.

It's a recipe for disaster, and my time away was making it glaringly obvious that I was not healed at all, and in very real danger of emotional chaos in every relationship if I didn't figure out how to set my center and stay in my love's arms, stay in My Lord's holy land of promised freedom, peace, and joy. But how?? I was trying. I was reading. I was praying, but nothing seemed to be changing.

None of this revelation came while I was away, only the hurt and realization that something was desperately out of alignment. I had spent three weeks up in North Carolina, and then I packed my car and headed home. I was desperately trying to understand what the hell had just happened. I had completely trashed my body with excessive eating and drinking. I felt like I had been in a bizarre hypnotic state and needed to snap out of it. Chaos swirled in my soul and as much as I prayed, I couldn't seem to quiet the underlying inner turmoil. I didn't know how to **Q.U.I.T.** being affected so dramatically by other people's moods and words.

When I returned home, I felt peace. I felt the quiet wash over me. I was so thankful for the silence of my house, with not one dog hair to be found in it. I felt my entire being settled again and I was grateful. I knew I still had to get my heart and healing on track and in the silence of my home, I could hear from the Holy Spirit clearly again. I hadn't written a word while I was gone.

I couldn't hear myself think in the presence of the constant barking. I couldn't discern in the dark. I cried as I said to the Holy Spirit, "There you are, there you are," over and over, clutching my chest as I knelt on my prayer pillow, bathing in the warm pinkish glow of my salt rock lamp. The Holy Spirit immediately led me into a fast that next day to let my poor body quiet itself again, and I was grateful. I rested, and I read. I rehydrated my parched body and spirit and washed out all the crap I had put in me. I felt the inflammation and the swelling inside me subside, and I was looking forward to hearing more about this chapter on how to **Q.U.I.T.**

I woke up the next day and as I prayed in my office, with my face in the floor, I heard the Holy Spirit whisper, *"Go see Judy..."*

I thought I wasn't going to see Judy this month because I had already blown through my budget for July, but God had other plans, and He knew what was coming down the road for me, and how much I would need this time with her. I did what I was told and I texted Judy. Not to my surprise, even with her slammed schedule, somehow there was a slot at our regular time still open. I jumped off my prayer pillow, changed clothes, got cash, and drove the hundred miles to see Judy once again.

I love Judy. If I haven't mentioned that enough, let me just say again, Judy is a J.O.Y. and I adore and appreciate that God brought us together. I had no idea how much I needed to sit with her and let her love, peace, and grace pour over me.

Being codependent and an empath makes me extremely porous to other people's energy which can be incredibly painful for me when I'm surrounded by hurt filled people, but around loving people, that ability can raise me up and settle my soul almost immediately. Judy does this for me as she also teaches me to do this for myself. The feeling doesn't last since I am attached to her set point, but it definitely is felt and can lift me and help me climb out of a moment of hurt and into a moment of healing. When I hug Judy, I melt. When she places her hands on me, I feel the healing running through her. When she prays over me, she shows me how and who can recenter and reset my heart. Over and over, she points back to God. Over and over, she guides my hand back into His hand. She is a gift and I am honored to have her as a guide of grace.

We sat together in our usual spot and I poured out my confusion over the past three weeks, the revelations, and ramifications I was now dealing with, and she listened as only Judy does. She pointed out the importance of letting my expectations die or else the pain in my heart never would.

I had to regain my power and acknowledge my worth, remembering I am enough, more than enough, and I had to take my value and worth off the sacrificing altar. My value and worth could not continually be up for debate.

I could no longer allow or need my worth to be validated by another person for me to truly own it and accept it. That validation was already given by the One who paid the price for me, God Almighty. The One who tells me I am worth everything to Him. Everything. She asked me again; how much did I think I was worth to God? She didn't even wait for the answer.

She continued saying: "Jen, you are precious, you are priceless, you are why He came! So please don't cheapen what God paid for. What does Jesus think you are worth? You are to die for, to rise for, and to live for, that's how much you are worth. Quit saying you aren't worthy."

We are all able to receive God's life, his Spirit, in and with us by believing— just the way Abraham received it
(Galatians 3:14, MSG)

Doesn't that privilege of intimate conversation with God make it plain that you are not a slave, but a child? And if you are a child, you're also an heir, with complete access to the inheritance
(Galatians 4:7, MSG)

She went on to say, "**Q.U.I.T.** denying you have full access, Jen, and humble yourself to the fact that He calls you worthy. You think you know yourself so well, can judge yourself so accurately, that you have decided you know what your best is? You deny that what God said about you is for you. You are letting pride and shame say, "I know better than you do, God, who I really am." You have no clue all that you are. You didn't call you, God did.

You didn't design you, God did. You didn't even love you first, God did. And when you deny the love you were created for, you are deceiving yourself and placing yourself over your divine spirit. Humble yourself enough to accept that while you are an earthly vessel, you are HIS earthly vessel and the method He uses to send miracles into this world.

Now that you know the real God—or rather since *God knows you—how can you possibly subject yourself again to those tin gods?*
(Galatians 4:9, MSG)

Quit looking for validation anywhere else because it can't be found.

Judy guided me through the labyrinth of lies and chaos I had found myself in and showed me how to counter hurt with healing. She helped to lead me to the next step up, she held out her hand and said, "Come on, you've got this!" She reminded me of the simple promises and protection God gives each of us. How He whispers to each of us:

I'm right here, I will never leave you, you can ask me anything, and always remember to only listen to my voice. I will lead you through this, every time, all the time.

Judy gave me the words to use to protect and honor myself while at the same time honoring the person who has hurt me. After I finished sharing with her how I had stood up for myself when a friend had been incredibly insensitive and rude, I told her how I pushed back with anger and combativeness to "check him."

Judy listened....

She gently reminded me that the "combative/protective" energy I put out won't lead to peace but to a pulling apart of the relationship. I didn't know what to do because I was finally not allowing people to bully me anymore, wasn't that a good thing? Wasn't that healthy? Wasn't that better than taking another emotional beating from someone who claimed to be a "friend"? How was I supposed to protect myself and stand up to the hurt, if I couldn't fight back?

I didn't realize, until Judy showed me, that bullying a bully doesn't change their heart, it only poisons my own peace, and that there is another way to move in power while retaining my peace. There was a way to protect myself and the other person without a huge confrontation.

Judy reached out her hand and touched mine as she modeled for me what a "Jesus-kind-of-gentle" looks like in confrontation. She said to the person: "No friend, those kinds of words are hurtful to me, so either they need to go, or I do. You choose." She explained that Jesus was able to maintain his peace and power because he did not react to the attack, but rather He would respond from his bond with Father. She reminded me that I had that same powerful peace living in me.

Judy poured the Holy Spirit over me as she reminded me to

Let your conversations be gracious and effective so that you will have the right answers for everyone
(Col 4:6, NLT)

To Devote myself to prayer with an alert mind and a thankful heart
(Col 4:2, NLT)

Don't act thoughtless, but try to understand what the Lord wants you to do...Let the Holy Spirit fill and control you
(Eph 5: 17-18, NLT)

Christ redeemed us from that self- defeating cursed life....
(Galatians 3:13, MSG)

"So **Q.U.I.T.** going back to it!," she said, "because when you live by the Holy Spirit, you escape erratic compulsions. Now that's freedom!"

I had never heard something so powerful and peaceful in my life. Her touch had disarmed me, her eyes said she truly wanted to stay connected, but her words made it very clear that a change was not only necessary, but would be happening now, one way or another. Those words were priceless, and I was changed and empowered by them.

I no longer needed to panic and react in an emotionally charged way to convey my value or diminish someone else's value.

Her words were a beautiful balm, a sweet salve that could heal two hurting souls who longed to connect but sometimes stumbled in the process.

I left our session lifted and ready for the week to come, or so I thought. When I got home, I made myself some lunch and sat down to check my email as it had been a couple of days. I hated checking my email anyway, but the pile up of junk mail gets overwhelming if I don't check it every now and then. I also had another reason I didn't want to check it; I was scared.

I was scared I would have an email from my parents and even though I asked for some distance between us, I knew that if anything happened, an email would show up, but so far so good. I had needed time to process and heal and I knew I couldn't do that with them at this time. I would check my email with anxiety, and not often, but today, as I sat down peace-filled and basking in the joy of Judy and her grace-filled words, I forgot to be guarded.

I opened my email and there it was, a letter from my mom. She had gone to the hospital the night before after passing out from dehydration and hitting her head on the bathroom floor. All was well now and she was back at home but she was deeply distraught at the rift that had been created between myself and my parents. She wanted to tell me how sorry she truly was and how much they never meant to hurt me as severely as they did. The letter ripped through my soul. I didn't know what to do. Part of me wanted to run to her. How could I not have been there for her, to take care of her? How could I be okay with the hurt my healing seemed to be causing her?

My codependent heart was hooked into my mom's feelings and my deeply held, but inaccurate beliefs, that my mother's pain IS my pain and my problem to fix. I felt her pain and it came flooding over me like a torrential tide that I didn't know how to stop. I slid into bed and sobbed.

I rocked myself, holding my head, repeating "Don't quit, don't quit, don't quit, I know it hurts, but don't quit. Don't quit reaching, don't quit healing, don't quit holding God's hand. Please don't quit." I was wrecked, but this chapter, this little 4- letter word was my key, and I knew it.

I had to learn to **Q**uiet **U**nderlying **I**nner **T**urmoil in my heart, but in that moment, I didn't know how. I was being tossed to and fro, the waves of my emotions, my mom's emotions, and the emotions of the past couple of months were raging and I felt helpless, like I was going under again.

I was right on the cliff-edge, ready to fall when God
grabbed and held me
(Psalm 118:13, MSG)

I felt the Holy Spirit come and wrap His loving arms around me as He said

Remember... Remember the gifts that are yours. I give you joy. Do you remember what that feels like?

Instantly I was back in my garden, My Heart Garden with Jesus. I was laying in the "Field of Joy," which is an endless field of bluebonnets, holding His hand as we both looked up into this beautiful blue sky. His laughter and joy running through me as he began singing, "I've got the joy, joy, joy, joy, joy, down in my heart."

The Holy Spirit kept speaking as he poured the fruits of the spirit over me.

I bring you peace, do you remember?

And just like that, I was back in the "garden of peace" laying on the bench in a gorgeous lavender-filled labyrinth with Jesus walking through it as we smelled the fragrance-filled air.

I could see Him smiling quietly as I laid on the bench with the words "In God We Trust" etched in the stone below me. I remembered peace and that it was mine! It was here the time, all the time. Because I had Him, I had peace. As the Holy Spirit hovered over me in my bed, I could feel Him holding me and singing the most beautiful lullaby to help me remember who I am.

He sang:

May you grow in the love, the joy, and the peace,
May you grow in the patience and kindness you'll need,
May goodness and gentleness carry your soul
And give you power of self- control.
These are your gifts, they are holy and true
These are the gifts that belong to you
These are the gifts, they are part of the deal,
You accepted them when you accepted that
I am real.

I can wipe your heart clean and make all things new
I can restore the years and love back to you
I can make your path straight
Turn your wrongs into right You will no longer fear the darkness My child of Light.

Over and over, I asked Him to sing it again, to tell me again what my gifts were, what my life was destined to experience when He holds me.

Over and over, He said:

*Love.... Joy... Peace... Patience... Kindness...
Goodness... Gentleness... Faithfulness... and Self-
control... Remember... and let them fill your soul.*

My tears stopped. The rocking subsided, and my
brain was now releasing the most "Holy High" I could ever
experience. I realized I had the power to release the
neurochemicals in my brain by thinking about these
things. I had the "Holy Spirit Hook-Up" and I could take a
hit anytime I wanted! **His Inspiration Gives Hope** and I
wanted to stay **H.I.G.H.**

I couldn't believe I had missed it. I had been in the
medical profession, I had studied neurology, I knew about
the brain, and yet, I hadn't been harnessing the power.
Our brains are a drug producing factory, so we have the
option to submit it over to the Holy Spirit, and let the
Holy Spirit get us **H.I.G.H.** today! Joy is a high. Peace is
a chemical flooding of your system. Patience has a
corresponding chemical reaction in you. Kindness
releases a feel-good drug that will keep you walking
around with a goofy smile on your face all day long. It
feels good to do good things from the sheer goodness
overflowing from inside your heart.

That's a **H.I.G.H.**! That's a hit that just won't quit!
And it's free! Gentleness will calm a storming mind. The
neurochemicals that are released with gentleness will
melt your own heart as well as the hearts of others who
are open to receiving from you. Breathe in faithfulness
and pass it on. Feast on love, then pass it on. For the
H.I.G.H. to last, it must be passed.

You have to let it flow out of you. The Holy Spirit showed me that the reason Scripture said to "Think on these things," was because it causes the brain to consistently release these "heavenly hits" I will need to maintain His "Holy **H.I.G.H.!**"

As I basked in these feelings, I went wandering again in my mind through my Heart Garden to each of the magical and holy places Jesus had planted that were now in full bloom. I found my way to the Tree of Faithfulness, which looks incredibly similar to the famous Angel Oak Tree in South Carolina, with its huge trunk and amazing sprawling branches that beg to be climbed on...

As I stood there, with just that thought, I was instantly sitting up on the branch, leaning against my Love, My Jesus. My head was leaned back on his shoulder as I sat between His legs that now straddled the massive branch. His heartbeat calmed mine, one of his hands was interlocked with mine, and the other held me secure against Him. We were quiet and my heart was melting all over again.

This Man, this Holy Godman loves me and He has absolutely no intention of being separated from me. He began to speak into my ear the secret I longed for, how could I finally **Q.U.I.T.** the struggle once and for all... He wiped my tears away and said:

*To **Q.U.I.T.**, to **Q**uiet **U**nderlying **I**nner **T**urmoil..... draw close. Draw close to Me and I will quiet your spirit. People are going to "people," so when they get to be too much for you, draw closer to Me rather than clinging to the thoughts of those that are hurting you. **Q.U.I.T.** the struggle... accept the J.O.Y.*

Humble yourself under the mighty power of God and in His good time he will honor you.
(1 Peter 5:6, NLT)

If you'll hold onto me for dear life,... I'll get you out of any trouble. I'll give you the best care if you'll only get to know and trust me
(Psalm 91: 14-15, MSG)

So, draw close. **Q.U.I.T.** faking the fruit! You can't hand out what you don't have.

People will see the actions but will walk away still feeling empty and now confused because what you were doing looked like "fruit," it looked like it was of substance, but it felt like lack, and it left a strong and sick feeling inside them. Don't fake the fruit! If you don't have it, come back to the Garden.

Draw closer to the Holy Spirit, who can create the fruit in you. Ask to be reminded, refreshed, or replanted, if need be, so that you can accept the fruit that was intended to grow and fill you. Take time to replenish. There is time for everything. You cannot give what you do not have, or what you won't accept. Draw closer to My love when you don't feel loving. Draw closer to My peace when the storms rage in your soul.

Cuddle up to My joy and rest on my chest. If you have Jesus, you have Joy! Lean in and let me fill you! Feast on my faithfulness until it radiates out of every pore in your body. You are what you eat. What do you feast on? Did you know that when you fast, you can still feast! You can't quiet the inner hunger with worldly food, so please **Q.U.I.T.** trying.

Quite **U**nderlying **I**nner **T**urmoil by feasting with the Father, savoring the Son, and by hosting the Holy Spirit who will, lo and behold, come to the "party" bearing fruit for you to be completely filled with!

After you have had your fill, you will look around and see so much left over that you will want to go back out into the world and share it with others. No one will ever complain (except pure evil) about the overwhelming peace of a person. A person filled with self-control is satisfied in her soul and wildly attractive. Self- control says to the world, "I have standards, and not just anything is enough for this holy and living sacrifice called My Life." **Q.U.I.T** *the gossiping and* **Q.U.I.T.** *the judging.*

Those are learned behaviors that were programmed into you, but not by Me! You were never meant to learn to judge others, and I'm sorry you were abused with such harsh judgments so early, and for so long. You were supposed to be taught how to discern actions, not to judge others, but to protect yourself. Do not speak ill of others. Their past pain isn't for your present pleasure. The past is there for a reason, and the reason is not judgment, not for you to judge yourself nor to judge others. The purpose of the past is to learn and to grow from it. It is for you to recognize possible patterns that will keep you safe, and to give you many different ways to relate to another, to help build them up and encourage them.

Q.U.I.T. *that "stinking thinking"! Take every thought captive and let yourself be renewed by my love for you. Accept My Word as Truth. My promises as absolute, and My love and mercy as endless. Accept these as gifts.* **Q.U.I.T.** *trying to make things happen, or make fruit grow in your life, you can't. I'm the vine, you are the branch!*

Draw close to God and He will draw close to you
(James 4:8, NLT).

Embrace My control over your life and that will result in what looks like "self-control," but it should really be called "Holy-Spirit control" because, as you have painfully discovered, it is impossible to do with any other spirit you have tried to let have control over your life. These other spirits are not an advocate for your self- control.

The spirit of greed, lust, revenge, depression, anxiety, or gluttony... they all require you to become out of control for them to do their best work.

But the Holy Spirit... the Holy Spirit loves temperance, and protects your body, the temple of the Holy and Living God. He wants to use you as long as He can, so He is fully invested in taking care of your fragile Earthen Vessel. He knows what He is dealing with and He always handles you with care. If your temple does not look cared for, check the garden of your heart for snakes. There is a spirit, there is a weed of shame, a snake of destruction slithering through your soul.

Keep shining the light, keep searching the corners of your caves, keep asking the Holy Spirit to reveal anything that does not belong in your heart, and kill it. He will root it out, and you will be purified. Keep praying and remember I co-sign all of your honest prayers if they align with the calling The Father has on your life and the character He is building for that calling. There is always "two or more" gathered when I walk with you, so pray those prayers even if you are the only one praying because I am here too, and I am always praying with you.

As Jesus held me in that tree, He told me it was profoundly important to continue to come to Him to let Him heal, restore, and remind me who I am. It was vital that I never forget that this place in me, with Him, IS my emotional "set point." It is the centering source for my life. In the garden of my heart, on a branch, wrapped in His arms, leaning on His love, this is my sanctuary, and nothing else can heal like Him. Nothing else will do. He said I have to remember so I can finally step into the outreach I was called to do.

He said the "in-reach" is vital for my outreach. And His message is centered on outreach. When I asked Him what He wanted me to do, He said, "I want to baptize you again in the River of Love." The River of Love is the beautiful river that flows through my Heart Garden, feeding every field, tree, and flower.

I had never spent much time in the river when I went into the Garden, but I saw it, and I knew it was the lifegiving source to everything, but now I found myself standing in the river with Jesus, and He was baptizing me again, but this time it was into **J.O.Y.** He said:

Be baptized into your true spirit, The Spirit of kindness. Let yourself be released forever from having to soak in the stench of this world and rise up!

Rinse yourself again in the River of Love and embrace your own divine nature to be kind to all you see, and that journey begins in the mirror.

*If you do not **Q.U.I.T.** the temple trash talk, you will take that trash out into the world and trash other souls with it as well. Be baptized into **J.O.Y.**! Joy is that "Jesus On You" glow that everyone will recognize! It will attract the lost and the found, the hurting and the healed.*

Jesus truly is the most joyful person I know, even Judy would back me up on that, and she runs a close second in the **J.O.Y.** department. His smile will knock you over. His laughter is contagious. **J.O.Y.** is the feeling you will receive once you have **Jesus On Y**ou! It is what you are signing up for when you say, "Yes, I want you Lord!"

If you want Jesus, you had better be ready to be flooded with the **J.O.Y.** that follows. He will baptize you just like He did with me. When He laid me back into the river, and then brought me back up again changed.

I was ALIVE! I felt the words of the great CeCe Winans when she said "I've got Jesus, so I've Got **J.O.Y.**"

I came out of the river, looked at Jesus beaming, and said, "So what now?." He said I had to surrender the pity party I had been in most of the month and join Him in a "purpose party."

I needed to stop sulking and start serving now that I had been renewed. He reminded me that it was Love Week at Elevation Church, and at many churches all over the country. He said I needed to take this newfound **J.O.Y.** out to the people.

I got out of bed, found my computer, and began to look up what, if anything, was taking place in town. I found one outreach event that caught my eye, it was in association with a non-profit group called C.U.B., Communities Under the Bridge, and my affinity for acronyms drew me to it.

C.U.B. is a non-profit that feeds and ministers to the homeless, and the local Elevation E-fam were going to serve dinner with them that Friday night, so I signed up.

I had no idea how much my life was going to change, and I still don't think I can comprehend the magnitude of my healing that is being birthed out of my helping. I loved it! I chose to be a "ticket giver" for the evening meal so that I could look at, stand with, talk to, smile at, and simply acknowledge every lost soul who came into the dining hall that night. I laughed with them, encouraged them, prayed with them.

I felt the **J.O.Y.** permeating through me, and everyone around me seemed to feel it too. In my smile, my eyes, my laughter, my openness to love everyone. I just had that "**J**esus **O**n **Y**ou" glow that was calling out to people.

I left that night feeling so **H.I.G.H.** and so happy as I was trying to plan how I could get back down there to volunteer again, as the director said their volunteer slots were filled through September. I didn't care, I still felt a longing to come back, and I knew I would.

The next morning, I woke up still basking in the glow of the day before, and extra grateful for the things I had in my life, like the ability to take a shower any time I wanted, and my own place safe from the elements!

Being around the homeless made me massively appreciate my home! As I got out of bed to pray and plan out my day, I was pretty confident in how it was going to go. Rest, relax, read, and hopefully get some writing for this chapter done – NOPE! God had other plans for me that day. The Holy Spirit said,

I want you to go back downtown to C.U.B. today, there is an event happening and I want you to be there.

I thought to myself, "Awesome! I love that idea! It was so fun yesterday. I'm down, let's go!" Not 30 seconds later, fear came slithering in, hissing in my ear. "Are you sure God wants you down there? Isn't it dangerous for a single woman to be down there alone? What if your car gets broken into?" and on and on as he tried to plant fear in me until I realized what was happening and I snapped back, "If God told me to do it, I'm gonna do it, so go find someone else to mess with!" I had never stopped getting ready anyway, I just felt the fear the devil was trying to stop me with and pressed on through it.

Jesus showed up and said to me:

Really Jen, you still don't believe that I got you? Look at that ring on your finger, the one that says you are mine. It means I go where you go.

I lead you where I need you. I can shut the mouths of lions, part seas, and rain down fire, but you still think I can't safely escort you to where I'm asking you to go? I've got you! No hand will harm you. No weapon formed against you will prosper. The God of Angel Armies holds your hand, so GO! And don't forget to shine because you got that **J.O.Y.** *on you!*

So, I went! And I was right, I couldn't park in the gated lot and I did have to walk a few hundred feet from my car to the center, but as soon as I parked the car, I saw another volunteer get out of his car, and I felt safe walking with him near me. I walked up to the center and there was a non-profit program putting on the event.

I had thought the event was hosted by CBC, a local church, for their Love Week program, and I was going to try to "sneak" in and volunteer with them. God had another idea. The actual host of the event was a non-profit called Mastermind Recovery, and it was for addicts who were homeless and ready to make a change and accept the good news of God as the power they would need to make those changes.

I sat there listening to testimony after testimony with my mouth dropped open. The stories of redemption were so powerful and raw. I went up to introduce myself and ask them if there was anything I could do to help them while I was there.

I had this blue and bright neon yellow shirt on with the words "Love Out Loud" written across the front, and that was exactly what I intended to do that day, Love Out Loud. My shirt caught their pastor's attention, as well as my deep desire to encourage each person who spoke, help clean up after people, love, listen, and be supportive to their mission in any way that I could. After everything I had gone through, I never would have thought to take to the streets to find a family or run to the homeless to feel at home.

I met so many wonderful people that day and they invited me to come to their church the next day for service. I was awestruck by each of them, and I knew I wanted to see them again and hear what the Lord was speaking over them.

I also met some people who were at the event that were still living on the streets, and one special soul in particular. Her name was Asia, and we had actually met the night before while I was volunteering. We had joked with each other about old high school rivalries, and she had told me about her time playing basketball and leading her team to victory as team captain. She was still so proud of that.

Asia showed up at the event the next morning and we instantly started talking. She told me she deeply loved the Lord, and then she disappeared to go find a fan from her tent to help keep us cool. She could only find one fan, but she was sure she could fan us both with it, and she did! Her generosity and thoughtful spirit were so apparent.

When she returned, she had found her fan but was also holding this gorgeous teal leather-bound Bible. I was so drawn to it, and I reached out to touch it and bless it. I asked her if I could look at it and she handed it to me. Without missing a beat, I reached into my back pocket where I had placed three of my Pocket Praise notecards. I grabbed one, not knowing which one I grabbed or what verse was written on it, and I slipped it into her Bible. I still have no idea what verse God planted into her Bible, but I know it was the one she will need one day.

Asia and I listened to the service together and when it was done and time for lunch to be served, the emcee announced that they had an insurance agent on site to help anyone who needed insurance to be able to get it for free!

My eyes got huge and I thought, "I NEED health insurance!" I hadn't had it in years, and I certainly couldn't afford it right now, but if there was a person God had brought right to me, I wasn't going to pass up this opportunity.

I walked away from that place with a plate full of fried chicken, free health insurance, and a heart filled with love and gratitude for the goodness of God! I was also escorted safely back to my car, where I had another amazing and God-centered conversation and was once again invited to come to church in the morning.

I couldn't wait that long to get myself to church, so I went home, took a shower, and went to a Saturday night service at CBC. I love to worship and I love to sit in the front row if at all possible. Tonight was no different. I went to the front row, found my seat, and sat down. I had no idea that this was baptism weekend, but it was, and I found out because the volunteers kept asking me, "Are you getting baptized?" I laughed and said jokingly, "I can. I mean I do love a good baptism, and I do it to myself all the time."

The irony was not lost on me that I had just been rebaptized a few nights prior in my Heart Garden and I was still dripping with **J.O.Y.** because of it. I also knew that I had plans to go the following Tuesday to the San Marcos River to baptize myself in **J.O.Y.** again just to solidify the vision I had seen in my Heart Garden.

I did not get baptized that night at church, but I did get anointed, "on accident," with Holy Oil. I say, "on accident," because I did not mean to or ask to have the anointing. The preacher had done an alter call for people experiencing pain that needed healing, so as people started coming up to the front, I raised my hands to pray over them.

I was in the front row, both hands raised, eyes closed, praying for the sick who were standing before me when, I guess at one point, due to the growing crowd, the Pastor asked that people "raise their hands if they still needed the anointing oil" but I wasn't listening, I was lost in prayer so when I opened my eyes, there in front of me stood a woman holding oil and looking at me.

It caught me off guard and I said " Oh.. uhh, I wasn't...." then she smiled and said, " Well it never hurt anyone" and I laughed and bowed my head to accept the anointing God had brought directly to me.

I kept thinking to myself in awe, He has anointed my head with oil, and He blesses me with **J.O.Y.**, My cup truly runneth over. I was humbled and pleasantly surprised at the gifts God kept pouring over me. I left the service and came home dripping with that "**J**esus **O**n **Y**ou" anointing of **J.O.Y.**!

I went to bed and woke up bright and early on Sunday. I was excited to go see my new church family and see what God had in store for me this day. I went to the church and was met by the pastor and his beautiful family. I was the first person to arrive so we got the chance to talk before the service began. I told him about the night before and the "accidental anointing" with Holy oil.

His eyes lit up and he said, as he went on stage and grabbed a full bottle of oil, that God had put it on his heart to do an oil anointing for pain today too, but he wasn't sure if he was going to do it or not until I said that to him. He said he knew it was his confirmation to do what God had asked.

I also met one of the singers on the worship team, Keno, and we were talking about how I had been stuck on that kid's song, "I've Got The Joy, Joy, Joy, Joy, Down in My Heart" for days now and she laughed and said that all of the songs they were singing today were about **J.O.Y.**!

And man, she wasn't lying. For 20 minutes straight we sang songs about **J.O.Y.** to kick off the service! It didn't even seem real. The message was great, the prayers were powerful, and then came the alter call for the anointing of the sick and pain-inflicted with oil.

Once again, I had sat in the front row, but this time, the pastor knew me, and knew I was not raising my hands in need, but in prayer for the people coming forward.

I watched him go to each person and bless their hands and their heads with oil. He moved through the crowd and ended up standing in front of me. I looked at him and he looked back at me with a huge smile and said "Oh, it's happening!" and he smeared oil onto my hands and made the sign of the cross over my forehead.... I had been anointed again!

A double portion had now been poured over me, my blessings were being pressed down, shaken together, and running over. God was breathing fresh life into me. He had brought new people into my presence to acknowledge and anoint my life with the promises God had already spoken over me. I couldn't have planned it if I tried. I spent the afternoon with another plate full of food, faith-filled friends, and a heart beaming with hope that each saint who sat next to me would feel my **J.O.Y.**, and they did!

Every person I spoke to told me I was beautiful, anointed, and appointed for such a time as this. I kept telling them the secret was that I finally **Q.U.I.T.** wanting the world to accept me, I had decided to accept myself, and that what they were seeing radiating from me was **J.O.Y.** It was a "**Jesus On You**" glow that they could also experience!

As I prayed that night, the Lord spoke over me once more saying:

*You have dedicated all of yourself to Me, so now your life will look different. You **Q.U.I.T.** chasing money, you **Q.U.I.T** chasing the lust of the flesh, you **Q.U.I.T.** chasing fun, you **Q.U.I.T.** chasing alcohol.*

*You **Q.U.I.T.** the world. And when you finally came, sat down in my lap, surrendered everything, and said "Lord, I **Q.U.I.T.**, that was when I could finally say, "Good, now let's begin," for*

Everyone who runs toward him Makes it!
(Psalm 18:30, MSG)

*So, **Q.U.I.T** waiting and start running! Do everything I have shown you to be able to **Q**uiet **U**nderlying **I**nner **T**urmoil!*

You won't be sorry, and you'll be saved
(Matthew 24:13, MSG)

Chapter 15

Hey H.O.M.O!
God Loves You!

(He- Only- Makes- Originals)

The Lord Said "I knew you before I formed you in your Mother's womb. Before you were born I set you apart and appointed you as my spokesman to the world" O Sovereign Lord, I Said, "I can't speak for you! I'm too young!"

Don't Say That The Lord replied, "for you must go wherever I send you and say whatever I tell you. And don't be afraid of the people, for I will be with you and take care of you. I, the Lord, have spoken"
(Jeremiah 1:5 – 8, NLT)

I have been waiting for this message about **H.O.M.O.** since the beginning of this book. It was the last word God spoke to me over the course of three weeks, and I still remember it so clearly when He said, *"I have one more 4-Letter word for you, the last one!"* I was so excited about the previous 14 words that I was open and ready to hear the final one. I gleefully exclaimed, "Awesome, lay it on me Lord!"

When He replied, **"H.O.M.O."**... I froze on my staircase, let out a shocked laugh, looked up and I said, "I'm NOT writing that!" He said, *"OH, YES YOU ARE."* I was stubborn and honestly a little scared, so I continued to say, "No, I'm not." Curiosity eventually got the better of me and I asked, "Fine! Why? What is the message you want me to give with that word? What does **H.O.M.O.** mean?"

He replied: *Tell them it means **He Only Makes Originals**.*

My mouth dropped open at the beautiful and profound meaning behind a word that made me cringe most of my life, and I thought: "Oh my God, I guess I AM going to be writing this." As apprehensive as I was, I was also excited because this is a message the world and the church needed to hear, and even as I protested and asked that He use someone else for that message, He responded with the same words He spoke over His prophet, Jeremiah, thousands of years ago when they had the same back and forth discussion.

Just like Jeremiah, I tried to give God my resume and reasons why He can't use me as a spokesperson to deliver this message, but the Lord responded:

Don't Say that ....

*I knew you before I formed you in your mother's womb.
Before you were born I set you apart and appointed you as
my spokesperson to the world.*
(Jeremiah 1:5, NLT)

*....for you must go wherever I send you and say whatever I
tell you, and don't be afraid of the people, for I will   be
with you and take care of you. I, the Lord, have Spoken!
Then the Lord touched my mouth and said, "See, I have
put my words in your mouth!*
Today I appoint you to stand up...."
(Jeremiah 1:7-9, NLT)

Fast forward through the last 14 months, Through all of the chapters, all of the messages, all of the miracles, all of the changes in my life, to this morning where I found myself waking once more at dawn, on the last day of the month. What I believed was the last day to work on this final chapter.

I woke up anticipating to hear a word from the Lord about everything He had been speaking to me on this topic from that day on the stairs to this quiet morning in my office. The message, while vast, was still not solidified, and I was becoming more and more confused by what was appearing to me as two different messages. I had struggled this month with a major blow to my heart, and my spirit, which had knocked me to my knees, which I guess was exactly where God wanted me, so I could once again be drawn even closer to My Love, My Lord.

God reminded me, **H**e **O**nly **M**ade **O**ne who could save me and love me the way I needed to be loved. He stepped in and saved me once again in the most hilarious and loving way that turned my sobs into laughter.

I was so grateful that by the time the end of the month came, I was no longer the emotional wreck I had been just a week prior, with uncontrollable waves of tears and a darkness that was fighting with me to hold me down, believe hurtful lies about myself, and push the painful triggers of abandonment wounds that I thought were healed.

My morning started with prayer, as it always does, and a dedication of this chapter to God, asking for clarity to only write what He has for me, and not my own opinion or perspective. I was already exhausted for some reason, like a weight was still holding me down and making it hard to move.

I got up off my prayer pillow and stood up. I walked to my desk in, what I like to call, a "Holy Haze" and grabbed a pen and my notebook. I watched as my hand was written in big purple letters; WHAT DID YOU EXPECT? Be honest....

I stared at the notebook, and thought, "What? Does it even matter what I expected?" I don't want to write what I expected or even what I think about this topic. I wanted to be a pure vessel to hear what God was saying to me, and writing through me, on this topic. Never during the writing of this book has the Lord asked me to write my own opinions, but there it was, a writing prompt that I wasn't sure how to answer.

I knelt down again confused and began to pray. He told me to go lay back down and sleep awhile longer while that question marinated in my head and my heart, so I did. When I awoke, I sat down and decided the least I could do was to answer the Lord's question.

If the past was any predictor of the future, then I had faith that as I began to write, He would join me and guide me, and I knew He would also stop, remove, change, or delete anything that is not the message He wants to come through me.

I didn't think I would have much to say about my expectation but as I wrote, He wrote with me, reminding me of all the extensive research on the topic we had done, the research on the Hebrew and Greek words that were mistranslated in the early 1900's that were never previously in the Torah or in the New Testament, as well as the direct and personal revelation He had shared with me over the past years. Long before the book had even begun, He was revealing a deeper understanding that kept blowing my mind and softening my heart about how to love like Jesus and how to see others as Jesus did.

Here are the words I wrote back to God's question, in combination with His beautiful confirmations that all I expected him to share was going to be shared in an even deeper and more profound and personal way then I had imagined. Thank you, Lord, for always knowing how to ask just the right question at the right time to help bring forth deeper insight into who you are and how proud you are of all your Originals!

WHAT DID YOU EXPECT? BE HONEST!

What did I expect? Lord, I expected you to share with everyone all you had revealed to me over the last years. All you had shared with me about the confusion, division, and destruction that the Church had and is still causing to the gay population, or anyone who even had questions about how you created them.

I thought you would reveal that you created each person as an original and designed them perfectly for the purpose and problem you created them to be a solution for.

I anticipated your teachings about how the Bible in its original language and context never mentioned the concept of homosexuality as it is understood and able to be expressed today, and how the scriptures erroneously translated Greek and Hebrew words into a word and construct that did not exist. It could not exist as it does today because of the time and culture. The word and concept of "homosexual" as it is understood today was never discussed in the Bible.

The warnings that were discussed in the Old and New Testament had to do with gang rape, inhospitable practices, idol worship, lust, polygamy, sex trafficking of young boys, pagan practices in temples and on mountain tops, and basically turning people into objects to be used instead of honored. It was about complete disregard of the sanctity of another person body and life.

It was about the inferiority of women in a patriarchal society and seeing feminine traits as beneath any man. They were objects to be bought, used, and discarded as desired by the men in their life. This was not the message of the Gospel, and this belief was condemned and corrected when Jesus came. The word of God spoke through him and said, "No more! No more division, no more deciding who is better!"

That means we will not compare ourselves with
each other as if one of us were better and another worse.
We have far more interesting things to do with our lives.
Each of us is an Original.
(Galatians 5:26, MSG)

*Don't compare yourself with others. Each of you must take responsibility for doing the creative
best you can with your own life.
(Galatians 6:5, MSG)*

We are all His beloved and He has no favorites among His children because once they have the Holy Spirit living in them, He only sees One – Jesus.

I thought you would speak about how the story of creation, i.e., Adam and Eve, was about how humans came to be, and not to be used as a weapon to shame and embarrass others as the ONLY way they can be.

I eagerly waited for you to share your teachings about how the Old Testament and the Old Covenant required conception of a child to pass down your promises, because when a Jewish baby was born, immediately a new "child of the law" existed, so having children was the only way to keep the lineage and promises of God alive.

However, with the coming of Christ and the Holy Spirit, Christians are no longer made by being born into the flesh, they are only made by being reborn into the Spirit. Christians are not born, sinners are born, but saints are made through the Spirit. It no longer requires a genetic transference to keep the promises of God alive, it required the finished work of Christ on the cross and the continual rebirth of the Holy Spirit into anyone, at any age, who comes before the throne and accepts the free gift of salvation by grace through faith.

It no longer requires a man and a woman to produce the fruit that only the Holy Spirit has the power to produce. I thought you would tell your people to stop hurting and excluding others simply because they are originals unto themselves, **H**oly -**O**rdained -**M**arvelous-**O**riginals, who can bear abundant fruit if they abide in you.

Single, married, divorced, widowed, gay or straight, you can use anyone to procreate in the Spirit when You are the one doing the creating. I wanted them to hear how you promised

We are ALL able to receive God's life, His Spirit, in and with us by believing just the way Abraham received it. (Galatians 3:14, MSG)

Isn't it obvious that God deliberately chose men and women that the culture overlooks and exploits and abuses, chose these "nobodies" to expose the hollow pretentions of the "somebodies" (1 Corinthians 1:28, MSG)

It is God own truth; nothing could be plainer: God plays no favorites! It makes no difference who you are, or where you are from – If you want God and are ready to do as he says, the door is open. The message he *sent to the children of Israel- that through Jesus Christ everything is being put together again – well,* He's doing it, everywhere, among Everyone. *(Acts 10:34, MSG)*

Outsiders and insiders, Rejoice together. (Romans 15:10, MSG)

So, reach out and welcome one another to God's Glory. Jesus did it, Now you do it! (Romans 15:7, MSG)

I thought you were going to teach about marriage and how it is still your most beloved and sacred gift you have to give to anyone who you've called to it. How you still see marriage to be the union of One God, Two Hearts, One Promise, One Vision, created to produce abundant fruit of the Spirit everywhere they step and to magnify the Lord in how they love and serve each other and the world you've given them to steward.

One God in two people who have chosen to make One commitment to seek first the kingdom, to follow your God-given vision, to protect each other, to love each other, to submit to each other, and to

Go out into the world to preach the Good News to everyone, everywhere
(Mark 16:15, MSG)

From your holy and high perspective, when you look at one of your children who believes in you, you do not see rich or poor, male, or female, black or white, gay, or straight... You see JESUS standing in front of them. You don't see what is different, you see what is glorious, you see the Holy Spirit shining back at you. When you look upon married male and female believers together, you see Jesus and Jesus!

When you look upon married men who dedicated their lives to you, you see Jesus and Jesus, Holy Spirit + Holy Spirit. Both of which are male, so that in itself is pretty gay, but those jokes are for another setting. And when two women are joined in wedded matrimony and have pledged their lives to serve you together, you only see Jesus and Jesus kneeling before you, asking for your blessing! So basically, you are telling us, we are all **H.O.M.O.s** !!

And since

God is not a man that he should lie. He is not a human that He should change his mind
(Num 23:19, NLT)

If He says we are covered by the blood and that Jesus Himself represents us to the Father, what kind of God would then go back on his Word and for "certain people" He chooses to ignore His own promise and "look around Jesus" to ask, "Is that two men who love and worship me?" "Is that two women who have dedicated their hearts and lives to serving me together?"

If we are all One, how is the division back into worldly "identity boxes" even Biblical? Male or female, white or black, gay, or straight, old, or young? If God knows everything about you and said before time began, "That one is Mine," then why would He see two of his precious children come together to live and love Him, and turn from them and say, "Not that ONE! Don't love that One they aren't worthy to be loved fully and completely by you"?

Those words are not the words of a proud and loving father, nor do they sound like anything I have ever heard from the mouth of God, no matter how much I did want Him to judge something I didn't understand.

If two mature loving adults long to live in the covenant of marriage with God and one another, to practice loving the way we are each charged to do, who then has the right to shun such a sacred and selfless commitment? Scripture says

Love is patient and kind. Love is not jealous or boastful or proud or rude. Love does not demand its own way. Love is not irritable, and it keeps no records of when it has been wronged. It does not delight in evil but rejoices with the truth. Love never gives up, never loses faith, is always hopeful, and endures through every circumstance.
(1 Corinthians 13: 4-7, NLT)

Nowhere in this definition of the practice of how to love, does it say, "as long as the person is of the opposite sex." This declaration of love is for every image bearer to strive for as they interact with any, different but equally precious, image bearer of God they have been blessed to meet.

I thought you would speak on the type of "fruit" the Church has been handing out when they wrongly condemn and shame the committed love and marriage of any couple from the pulpit.

A healthy tree produces good fruit, and an unhealthy tree produces bad fruit. A good tree can't produce bad fruit, and a bad tree can't produce good fruit. So, every tree that does not produce good fruit is chopped down and thrown into the fire. Yes, the way to identify a tree or a person, (or a church) is by the kind of fruit that is produced
(Matt 7:20, NLT)

But the "fruit" that comes from the hateful actions and words of some churches tastes like shame, judgment, exclusion, isolation, self-hate, and confusion! What are the fruits of those ugly words and smug stances that are being spewed out over innocent people who have come to worship God?

Does the gay Christian, who is now poisoned after eating such "fake Fruit," have any joy filling his soul? Did their words bring him love, or bring her a sense of peace that passes all understanding? Did those words fill their heart with goodness and kindness? Were they excited to hold onto patience for all their own heavenly promises? No! These souls don't feel fed or edified. These people and places are judging what they do not understand, and they are not authorized to question the fact that **He O**nly **M**akes **O**riginals, and their contempt, disgust and demands that another should cut their original design to "fit in" is mocking God and His original masterpieces.

With their actions and words, they are arrogantly stating to the Almighty, "I know how they were really meant to be created and you have made a mistake with this one, but don't worry with enough shame, judgment, and a lost sense of belonging, I'm sure they will see the error of their ways and be fixed."

What an arrogant and ignorant thought to ever hold about another. Our words are gifts meant to edify and encourage each other. So why do we have "Christians" tearing other people down? Which "fruit" is that one, because I am not familiar with it?

If you are standing in a place of influence and judging people sitting before you; You will not have that place of honor and responsibility for long. Your condemnation and criticism of other people's genuine walk with the Lord will not help you one bit when you come before the Lord to be judged yourself.

You will answer for each and every "child of God" you caused to run away from the Church and from God because of your hurtful and unauthorized judgement and condemnation of another. Scripture doubles down on this by saying it would be better for you if you were to be cast into the ocean with a millstone around your neck then to face the wrath that will be coming because of a religious and pride filled heart.

Yes, each of us will have to give a personal account to God. So don't condemn each other anymore. Decide instead to live in such a way that you will not put an obstacle in another Christian's path.
(Romans 14:12–13, NLT)

Accept each other as Christ has accepted you! Then God will be glorified.
(Romans 15:7, NLT)

Forget about deciding what is right for each other. Here's what you need to be concerned about: that you don't get in the way of someone else, making life more difficult than it already is
(Romans 14:13, MSG)

Then the Lord cut in, as I was hoping He would, and began to speak, He said

*You do not know the plans I have for each of my children, but I do. You do not know the desires, gifts, and trials I have prepared for them, but I do. I set every **H.O.M.O.** apart at the beginning of time, not for your judgment but for My glory and divine purpose on this earth. I called each **H.O.M.O** by name for such a time as this. I looked across all eternity and carefully selected a time I would send each of you out into the world. Make no mistake about it, My children, you are all on assignment.*

Each is different and each divine. Difference makers, by very definition, must be DIFFERENT! Why is the Church so obsessed with turning everyone into clones of their own preferences, and even that is different depending on denomination and individual churches. Instead of being a part of a "Christ making community," you are contributing to a "Crazymaking community" that is planting seeds of division in the very place that was created for unity. Only those who will conform to your man-made church culture are welcome, and anyone else will be made quite aware as they look around that they are not welcome nor wanted there.

Sadly, but not surprisingly, a large percentage of the Church body today would be a part of the crowd yelling, "CRUCIFY HIM!", if Jesus came walking through their doors with all his fellow H.O.M.O.'s by His side. Jesus loved and hung out with anyone who was open to Him, called to Him, and followed Him.

He allowed both men and women to come intimately close to Him and never pushed them away. He was deeply affectionate and even has this recorded by his disciple John who, at a dinner with Jesus, felt compelled to record and profess to the world how close he was to Jesus by describing a time where he was snuggling into Jesus.

He wrote:

Laying back on Jesus' chest was one of his disciples, whom Jesus Loved.
(John 13:23, NASB)

Jesus deeply loved everyone. He welcomed those outcasts and abused, exploited, and shunned. These were His people. They are who He came for.

Personally, every time I hear about Jesus and John all hugged up together at dinner, all I can hear in my head is Margaret Cho imitating her mom's thick accent saying, "THAT GAY!".

I seriously do not know one straight man who will hold and snuggle another man at dinner with guests all around them and no crisis occurring. Maybe some of you do, but as for me and all my travels, I have never seen that. Jesus just loved and I totally get it because I know from my personal and deeply intimate relationship with the Lord that He is in fact a huge snuggler and I adore this trait about him. No one holds me stronger and closer than Jesus does.

I thought you would tell the world, Lord, that ALL are Welcome at your table. You formed each person before they were born, you charted their path, every day was recorded, you saw each of us and hand crafted us with passion and purpose. You designed each person to stand out, not "fit in". An "Original" is not to understood as much as to be experienced to the fullest.

God loves all his **H.O.M.O.'s** – Because **H**e **O**nly **M**akes **O**riginals. And to all you who have been cut off, insulted, belittled, shamed, judged, condemned, and cast out,... The Heavens cry out, "COME HOME"! Letting them know unequivocally that you love them and want them and that no one is excluded from your love.

Everyone is special, everyone is a God's treasured **H.O.M.O.**! I had hoped that you would express what you have shared with me to anyone else who needs to hear it. I wish they could hear your calm and compassionate voice speaking clearly to them as you tell them You are so, so sorry for the hurt that is being caused by the Church, and that this is not as you intended it. That which breaks your children's heart, breaks your heart, and it in no way goes unnoticed.

Jesus hung on the cross and said the word that every dejected **H.O.M.O.** (gay or straight) needs to practice saying,

...Father, Forgive them for them:
for they know not what they do....
(Luke 23: 34, KJV)

The people of Jesus' day thought they were doing the "Good and Godly Thing" by keeping God's laws and putting to death this man, Jesus, who they saw as an abomination and a heretic, as well as a threat to their rigid belief systems. Casting Him out, "in the name of God," to rid the Church of the "false teachings" Jesus was sharing, and to put an end to His unacceptable and unapologetic behavior and relationships with the outcasts of society. Why is the Church still obsessed with hanging people on crosses? Why are they still obsessed with ridding the church of "those people," not seeing the lies they themselves are spreading, nor aware or even care, about the souls they are crushing with the constant lashings they feel justified in handing out.

The pharisees who handed Jesus over felt 100% justified in what they were doing. They were deceived by their own desires to believe they were better than another. They were 100% certain they held the whole truth, and they were 100% WRONG ---- Let that sink in.

These were the most well-spoken, well-read, leaders of the church of the day, and what they were preaching was WRONG, and when Jesus stepped in to call out the error of their ways of thinking, instead of being willing to consider maybe they did not understand everything, they betrayed him and killed Him.

Jesus said,

Love one another as I have Loved you
(John 13: 34, NLT)

Not, love your neighbor if they look like you, or are gifted in the same area you are, or are called like you, or even who's marriage looks like yours. No, the statement was quite plain and simple, no real room to misinterpret; Love God, and Love one another as I have loved you. Opinions and judgements that people become obsessed with about others are often an indication of something they are wrestling with internally.

When the Holy Spirit has taken over, one no longer obsesses over whether God is going to "change" or "fix" another person, you will simply be overjoyed that this brother or sister loves the Lord as you do and is operating under the same Holy Spirit who is now their faithful guide in life.

You have received the Holy Spirit and he lives within you,
so you don't need anyone to teach you what is true. For
the Spirit teaches you all things, and what he teaches is
true – it is not a lie
(1 John 2:27, NLT)

I hoped you would also teach about the perversion that is within a hyper- sexualized community verses your sacred community.

Do people understand how much hurt is done to a precious innocent Soul when one is brainwashed from an early age to believe they are not wanted by their Creator because the words from of an unknowing, misinformed, and misdirected pastor with a mic and a pulpit?

This is fertile ground for Satan to step in and press the issue even further into the hurt and now confused person's mind, whispering to them that they must be worthless and a mistake, having no divine value or use to God. He encourages them to use the flesh to seek the belonging that was stripped from them. Seeing the body no longer as a sacred and holy place of the Lord, but as the one way they could feel something close to a sense of belonging that was beaten out of them by their church community and elders.

This soul is now lost and since they have been made to believe they can't run to God. They run to the only other option left – The World and Themselves. I thought you would tell them this is not the word of the Lord, and it is exiling your children to take refuge under a "Twisted Rainbow" instead of staying safe under your sovereign promises and protection. Under the one true Rainbow Promise. They are forced to seek refuge out in the World. A broken world only too eager to snatch them up.

When someone is led to believe, especially by someone in "perceived authority," that something is wrong with them, that God does not want them and even hates them, the only thing left to do is either adopt that hate and turn it into self- annihilation or refuse to abandon the self and begin to seek out a new and false identity.

Being forced to ask questions that are based on the assumption that you have no place to call home. Turning inward in despair to ask themselves:

Who will love me for everything I am, if even God does not?

Why am I here, if not for God?

Where do I belong, if not with God?

How will I be understood if not even by God?

And the worst and most painful question to be forced to ask, "Who must I become, and what must I change or destroy about myself to be loved and accepted by another or myself, if even God doesn't love the creation He made?".

It's no wonder that with these kinds of gut-wrenching and soul crushing questions, these spirits would run to an organization that promises to "save" them if they will simply place their sexuality on the alter as an offering in exchange for a false sense of community that encourages them to be used and abused by others. They promote pride-filled and perverse ways of living that have nothing to do with loving and serving others as Holy and living vessels. They will take every sacred hurt one has and stomp on it, light a fire to it, and even celebrate the destruction of the sanctity of your God-given sexuality.

If you have been stripped of your divine dignity by people who say they "know God," then you will not be equipped to maintain it when Satan waltzes in and offers you a way to "feel better" even if he never truly delivers on his promises.

A life of going from sexual partner to sexual partner, regardless of gender, looking for what was ripped from you, belonging and a sense of community, will be a journey filled with pain. One can spend an entire lifetime aimlessly seeking a sexual high to numb the pain and suppress the thoughts that torment you. The Father of Lies encouraging you to "Try again. You still don't feel good enough, do you? You still don't feel like you belong even after using one person after another"? He screams into your ear; "What is wrong with you? Why don't you feel complete? Look at everyone else, they seem to be enjoying themselves." It's a tormented life to say the least.

Gay or straight, using sexuality to try to fulfill your spirituality will never work. Sexuality was meant to be a gift from God given for the covenant of marriage to protect and strengthen your spirit. Outside of that sacred promise with your chosen love, it will destroy you. It is too potent and powerful to have no effect on the soul, no matter how much one tries to minimize it.

It has a power like no other to burn your soul down to the ground and when that is all a person has to hold onto; a life of tormented loneliness is all the life led by sexuality will be able to offer. It will be a never-ending roller coaster of an addict who is looking for their next high, and then struggling with the withdrawals when the act alone no longer can sustain them.

People will no longer be seen as treasured gifts from God to be loved, protected, and honored, but instead they will be turned into objects to be used to stop the persisting pain of believing that God is not with them or for them, that the One who made them, and is reported to be "all loving", somehow does not love nor want them.

Let me state as clearly as I can, **THAT IS A LIE FROM THE PIT OF HELL!**

We are one body, one Church, one creation. We have one Savior who is madly in love with every one of us. There is one God and He does not mince words or shy away from telling His children this fact. He boldly proclaims

....I am God, The One and Only
(Isaiah 45:18, MSG)

I am God, the only God you've had or ever will have – Incomparable, irreplaceable. From the very beginning telling you what the ending will be
(Isaiah 46: 9-10, MSG)

*I would no more reject my people than I would change my laws of night and day, of earth and sky
(Jeremiah 33:25, NLT)*

I pray that these promises will comfort anyone out there who is still struggling to believe that they are truly and completely wanted, accepted, and deeply loved by God. There is no other "body" that can heal you, hold you, satisfy you, and save you, then the body of Jesus Christ and the Holy Spirit living and working through you.

You were made with a longing to belong. The world knows that preys on that and works sinisterly inside the church to keep betraying the original message and condemning sacred souls to a spiritual wasteland where they can be deceived and destroyed, their light cast out, and their desire to belong to become so strong that they will believe anything even it if kills them in the process.

The original message from God is still the only message they desperately need to hear...

*....Do not be afraid, for I have ransomed you. I have called
you by name; YOU ARE MINE.
(Isaiah 43:1, NLT emphasis added)*

*You are precious to Me. You are honored, and I love you.
(Isaiah 43:4, NLT).*

With or without other's approval, He approved you, and **H**e **O**nly **M**ade **O**ne who is created to take every step with you down this road called Life – Jesus.

Every step, every breath, every battle, every joy, He is there. He is the only one who truly knows you. I take such comfort in David's words:

You have examined my heart and know everything about me. You know when I sit down and when I stand up. You know my every thought when far away.... Every moment you know where I am.
(Psalm 139:1-3, NLT)

Oh, weary warrior, do not lose hope, for only that from which you came can ever understand your intricate nature, your every need, and who and what you are designed for. Do not look left or right as you walk your marked path, but keep your eyes fixed on the Lord, and not the people in your life. They do not see the world the way you do, and they were not even created to be able to see the world the way you do.

If anyone tries to "fix" you or seems confused or even disappointed in how you follow the call of the Lord, try to forgive them, and let it roll off of you before any harm can be done.

They are not your Divine Designer. They have no idea what He is doing in and through you. They are not your Compass Holder, your Way Maker, or your Wave-Walker.

They are simply trying to give you their best and limited advice on what seemed to work for them, but what works for the world will not work for you, and what works for you will not work for the world, and that is awesome! I know it can seem frustrating because you so want to be understood and have the people you love be inspired by you and your work with God, but sometimes the people who are closest to you, in your family, in your church, in your town, will not be the people who most understand you.

You didn't come into this world, dear one, as an "incomplete set," but as an original even in your family of origin. So don't be surprised if those closest to you do not have the ears to hear and the eyes to see all that God is doing in and through you. They will miss the miracle right before their eyes. If it happened to Jesus, why would it not happen to you? His own siblings didn't believe He was the Son of God until after He was resurrected from the grave. His hometown shunned Him so He was unable to perform any healings or miracles in their midst.

Your life has an anointing on it too, and it will not look like other people's path. It will not look like other people's priorities. For you to make a difference in this world, you cannot be the SAME as the people that surround you. Often this will rub people the wrong way, make them want to warn you about your path, talk you out of it, shun you, shame you, or just be downright confused about the steps you are taking. Just ask Jesus: even his closest friends didn't understand what He was called to do and tried to talk him out of it! Why would you expect anything less on your journey?

The cross wasn't about a life of comfort, but a life of conviction, so even if the world doesn't understand your path, follow it anyway. You are not leaving a legacy; you are living one.

With the Holy Spirit at work in you, you are a new creation, more powerful than you can even comprehend, and you will have more of an impact for Christ than you ever imagined if you do not deviate from the path marked out before you. Keep listening to His voice and no one else's. Keep walking toward Jesus when you are out in the deep.

When everyone else surrounding you is screaming at you about the height of the waves, the depth of the water, the strength of the storm, or the temporary comfort to be had by getting back in the damn boat.

Don't go back! Keep walking. You are walking toward something so special and unique that it will often be a walk you will have to do alone, but with faith and your feet, take the next step. Do not let the waves scare you because you are out there on the water with the one and only Wave Walker! His awesome power reaches out to you as you reach out to him.

Keep walking! You Got this!

As I paused and read the words I had written, I heard the Lord begin to speak again. He said:

I made your hand fit into mine. There is no "match" to you. Everything about you is hand crafted and an original. Your fingerprints are originals, your footprints are originals, and your soul print, too, is an original. There is no one but I who knows how each part of you came into being. You are made with an original soul print so you would leave an original imprint on this world. You are a completed work. From beginning to end. I saw you before you were born. Every day of your life was recorded in my book. Every moment was laid out before a single day had passed. You were made complete, well, whole, and holy. Chosen and dearly loved.

There is no "other" but Me who can satisfy your soul and lead you to all I have called you to be. There is a perfect unity in our shared Divinity. My creation can only be perfectly and completely loved by its Creator. I know you better than you know yourself. I made all the delicate inner parts of your body and knit you together in your mother's womb. You were fearfully and wonderfully made. You are an original, my love, so

...don't be wishing you were someplace else, or with someone else. Where you are right now is God's place for you. Live and obey and love and believe right there....
(1 Corinthians 7:17, MSG)

You don't have to always feel it, to know this is the truth. You don't have to "feel it" to take the next right step. You don't have to "feel it" to accept that all My promises are yours for all eternity. As you understand it, live it out, and accept My love, you will feel My power rise in you and you will begin to step towards the light, first the right foot then the left. We are going somewhere, My child! Come Follow Me! Stay away from people who are going "nowhere."

If I am in you, then we are going somewhere, to help someone, do something. I did not send My only Son to die for "Nothing, No one, or No where." I saved you for such a time as this. Each of you, All of you! I will not forget you. I have held you in the palm of my hand

Bring me your broken hearts and broken dreams, for even those you thought were taken from you, were not destroyed, My Beloved, but held in My hands safely until the time was right. I restore, redeem, and resurrect even the most broken parts of you. It is not with a contentious or punishing heart that I say to you "Wait for it," but one of eager anticipation of a Father who knows how good and perfect My gift will be. I am absolutely certain that the timing will be one of the best parts about it.

I know you will not always understand My ways, but trust Me, I have always loved you, I will always love you, and because of my unending dedication and devotion to your wellbeing, you too will feel like the lucky one if you would simply wait for the gifts I have planned for your life.

Meditate on your wonderful miracles
(Psalm 119:27, NLT)

Ponder the direction of your life. Bask in My presence in this moment, and rest in My tender love for you.

As my daughter, Jennisue Jessen reminds all of you in her profound book; The Lucky One, I will restate it here:

"You were made for more, Dear one. You were made for Glory and to do good works: which He prepared in advance for you. Take a deep breath and jump with both feet into the life he has for you" (Jessen, 2016, p.95)

Jennisue along with her husband K.J., have helped to save the physical lives and the sacred souls of hundreds of thousands of outcasted and exploited people all over the world by bringing them to safety and to Christ through their ministries.

Her book, *The Lucky One*, demonstrates how deep and intimate a relationship with Jesus one can truly experience in this lifetime. That this gift is possible to all who seek His face.

She is not just a miracle story of grace, a profound presence to be experienced, and a friend of God, but she is my friend, and she spoke the following words over me when I was experiencing a dark "cave" moment in my life. Her words helped call me out of the darkness and back to my assignment as the inspirational instrument of God I was designed to be.

She told me later, after I expressed to her how much those words had meant to me, that they were not her own, but were from the book, *Jesus Feminist*, by Sarah Bessey. I feel God urging me to continue to pass along this charge to all the Originals, gay or straight, male or female, young or old. All those who out there who feel lonely, frustrated on your path, questioning if you really matter or are making a difference.

This is for all of you who wonder if God really sees you and wants to use you. All who wonder if the gifts you have been given are enough.

These words are for you:

The Kingdom of God is better because of your Voice
Your Hands
Your Experiences
Your Stories
Your Truth
You can Go where I cannot go
And Someone needs to hear you sing your song.
You are someone's Invitation.
Rest in your God-Breathed worth.
Stop Holding your breath,
Hiding your gifts,
Ducking your head
Dulling your Roar
Distracting your soul
Stilling your hands
Quieting your voice
And satiating your hunger with the lesser things of this
world.
You are Chosen
You are Loved
You are created for Glory
(Bessey, 2013)

I hope when the Lord calls your name and asks,

Whom shall I send as a messenger to my people?
Who will go for us?
(Isaiah 6:8, NLT)

You will shoot your hand high in the air and say:

Lord, I'll Go! Send Me.
(Isaiah 6:8, NLT)

Take this charge to heart. Revel in your road! Rejoice in your uniqueness, because - **H**e **O**nly **M**akes **O**riginals!

Final Thoughts

Be completely humble and gentle;
be patient, bearing with one
another in love
(Ephesians 4:2-3, NIV)

Thank you, thank you, thank you.... Those words poured out of me over and over this morning, to God, to Jesus, to the Holy Spirit. To my friends, my mentors, to the pastors that have encouraged me, related to me, spoken over me, and confirmed for me the words I was hearing even though none of them, except one, had met me yet. I cried out thanks to the people who left me, the ones who hurt me and in turn helped me to correct my vision and fix my eyes once again on My Love, My Lord, alone.

I cried thanks to the new friends in my life who only God could have orchestrated our meeting, and the words God spoke through them to help lift me and push me toward my purpose to finish what God was calling me to do. I thanked God for the songwriters who let me weep to their songs, be filled with strength by their songs, dance to their songs, pray with their songs, and through their songs find an intimacy with Jesus that I never would have without them.

I thanked God for the hurt He healed, the confusion He brought clarity to, the visions He allowed me to see and some that He has allowed me to share in this book. I thanked God for breaking me, crushing me, refining me, and then molding me once again into a new creation with a new family, new friends, a new purpose, and even a new body. The transformation has been nothing less than a miracle.

Thank you to my coach, **Judy**. I could not have walked this out with as much humility, gentleness, and grace if it had not been for your love, kindness, patience, and willingness to be used by the Holy Spirit to speak to me over this past year. Thank you for the comfort, the hugs, the phone calls, the texts, the gifts, the voice of reason when I wanted to open my mouth and you taught me how to keep it shut.

Thank you, more than anything, for the prayers you prayed over me with your arms wrapped tightly around my broken and beaten down soul. Thank you for reminding me of my worth, who gave it to me, and how it should never be put up on the sacrificial altar again. It has been bought and paid for by God, and it is not mine to give away. I am worthy, I am called, I am anointed, and I am now ready to go out into the world and live it. Thank you for giving me the best gift anyone ever has you gave me back to me!

I have been washed in the water, bathed in the blood, christened as **J.O.Y.**, loved by God and deeply in love with Jesus. May every step you take be covered by 10,000 angels. I love you and I know you are always there cheering for me as I take the training wheels off and ride on! May Jesus, Judy and Jen meet again one day, because that team was miraculous!!

To my "other- side -of- the- world" coach, **Wenzes**. You somehow seem to know how my brain works better than I do! Thank you for the beautiful way you have of articulating all of the natural gifts that I have and how to best use them to help me rise up and live out the "Epic Life" I was created for! Thank you for all your YouTube videos and for your Bootcamps where I was able to work with you to address all of the different areas of my life that desperately needed my attention. Thank you for all of the practical and hands on baby steps that you encouraged me to take. But most of all, thank you for cheering for me when I thought all hope was lost at the final chapter and I didn't know how this was all going to come together. It flipped a switch in my soul when you said, with complete confidence, "Jen, IT WILL HAPPEN!" And you were right! I appreciate all of the work you do and the personal time you have taken to encourage all of us who have come to you for understanding and direction. Shine on, Wenzes! You are changing lives daily!

To my friend, **Danielle Rocco**, I love you so much. Thank you for listening to parts of the book as it was being created and speaking the most life-giving and encouraging words over me that anyone could hope for! Thank you for the long-distance hugs that I could always feel. Thank you for believing that "God is definitely up to something" as I walked out the living of this book. Thank you for being in the trenches with me as we pray for the souls of our friends who are hurting and lost. Thank you for never shying away from my tears whenever and however they needed to be expressed.

You embody understanding, love, gentleness, kindness, deep inner strength, faithfulness, joy in the pain, peace in the trials, longsuffering with a smile (prayers up), goodness that should have vanished long ago, empathy like every person should hope to aspire to, so they can inspire others with it as you do, and the ability to LISTEN like few people ever could hope to do, but every person prays they get a friend that can.

Thank you for always answering—or at least calling me back—over the past 19 years! Thank you for all of your herbal remedies. You are amazing! I hope the world feels about the words on these pages the way that you do! Thank you, my friend. May we continue to sing out our sweet Melody, and always believe in God's Grace.

To my friends and business partners, **Keith and Shalamar Outlaw**. Making dreams come true is what you were born to do! Thank you for choosing to help make mine come true here in this book!! The Lord's "Outlaws" are on the loose and powering up to be a force to change the world. I bless your ministry and all that God is calling you both to become to help and heal the most tender and broken of this world. Thank you for the divine timing that brought us together. We both know there was no way we would have come together, if not for the grace of God. Thank you for all the love and hope-filled words you poured over me, and the money was super helpful too!

Thank you for reminding me to constantly "give it to God" and know that He has got me covered. Thank you for not letting me give up when I was on the last lap of this book and had a curve ball thrown at me that knocked me to my knees and made me question if I should continue. You listened and supported me; you answered my calls when you didn't have it in you to even turn on the lights or get out of bed.

I love you my friends, and I am beyond grateful that you two are part of the team of anointed and chosen partners that God has brought to lift The ProdigalWon ministry and strengthen it. We were brought together on purpose, for purpose, and I am grateful.

When God's favorite "Outlaws" are ready to step out and ride again, nothing will stop you two! Shalamar, may your platform be raised so high as you point back to the One who made it all possible. A "Girl Named Outlaw" shared with me her tender soul and offered me the best gift: a friendship to walk beside me in my wilderness. My prayers cover you, Keith, and your angel in heaven, Olivia. My friendship is here for you always! You guys are, and always will be, my favorite Outlaws!

Jennisue Jessen, thank you! You are a miracle walking, a presence of grace and beauty that most will never attain. Thank you for opening your home to me after just meeting me. Thank you for teaching me a new way to pray. Thank you for sharing your stories and your scars with me. Thank you for creating Compass 31 and saving every soul you can around the world from sex-trafficking and the horrific abuses that happen every day.

I pray that your ministry will be blessed beyond understanding and you can see your vision of creating beautiful hotels to house and to train the girls you have saved in the most life-giving of ways. Giving them the opportunities to learn skills and principles they can be proud of, while also counseling their souls, and introducing them to your Jesus.

Thank you for being the only other person I have ever met who has seen Jesus the way I have, in that white shirt and jeans, humble, strong, and beautiful. Thank you for your beautiful paintings, and for letting me use one for the back cover of this book. It takes my breath away every time I look at it.

Thank you for your book, *The Lucky One*, and the power of the testimony you hold because of it. I love you and bless you and cannot wait to hug you again. I pray for your complete healing so that you may live to tell your story for another 50 years. You are a masterpiece. I am humbled to call you a friend and hope to bless you in any way I can in the years to come. My prayers also cover you daily, and my friendship is here for you always. Well done, weary warrior! With 10,000 Angels, I applaud you for your dedication and devotion to be a servant of the Most High God.

To the pastors out there who have walked with me without ever knowing it, I want to send out my love, honor, and recognition. Each one of you that I have been drawn to and have been watching from afar seems to be hearing the exact same thing I have been hearing from the Lord. My mouth has dropped open after hearing each of you say a verse, or a lesson, an insight, or a vision that God was also speaking to me, or one I had just written about in a chapter before listening to the sermon!

I have said out loud to each one of you, "Hey! That's what I just wrote!" or "That's the verse I was just studying, and that's what God said to me too!"

I have been confirmed over and over by the following pastors who seem to hear the Holy Spirit the same way as I do. I do not call anyone "my pastor" but Jesus himself. He is my pastor, my shepherd, my love, my Lord. These amazing men and woman of God I hope to call friends one day, and I definitely call them anointed and appointed. I send my highest praises to them and thank God that they have created churches for people to gather together in one accord and light up a room with the Holy Spirit!

To all of you out there looking for a pastor, or a church to get involved in, all the people and churches that I am about to mention would be honored to serve and worship with you. They love the Lord. No, they aren't perfect. No, you may not agree with every little decision or thing they say or the way they say it, but each one seems to be doing the best they can to hear from God, and serve Him alone with a humble heart recognizing it is not them, but God, who will change your life, lift you up, light you up and reveal to you what He is calling you towards, which is, of course, your own personal, deep, intimate relationship with Him and a full engagement of your own super natural abilities and gifts from the Holy Spirit.

I am excited to meet so many more pastors who are living out this message of love as I prepare for my journey ahead, but these are the ones who got me through dark night, lonely days, broken dreams, muddled understanding, or simply made me crack up laughing with their way of relating to the Word of God and how it is moving in their lives. Here are some of them:

Robert and Taylor Madu at Social Dallas, here in Texas with me, thank you! I love you guys! I have spent countless hours over the last two years watching and tithing to your church. I believe in you! I believe in your future building and what God is going to do with it. I pray I get to be a part of helping make that dream come true. I can't wait to serve you one day! Thank you for the way you bring the Word alive to people in such a cool, expressive, and understandable way. Robert, your sermon messages are so powerful and potent, as well as hilarious and holy. They are said in a way that introduces Jesus to people in the way that I know Him as well! Thank you for bringing the house down with your worship team and never being ashamed to dance before the Lord! Thank you, Taylor, for lifting up the ladies in the house and being a friend to anyone who needs one. Your heart is so beautiful and I look to you as a model of humbled beauty and grace.

Thank you for continuing to reach into the darkness and be a light to anyone who comes to Social Dallas looking for a family. You Guys Rock! America is lucky and blessed to have you both, thank you for your service to God and Country.

Steven and Holly Furtick of Elevation Church in North Carolina, and all over the world, Thank you! If you haven't heard of Steven Furtick, you have to check him out. This man is creating a legacy like nothing I have ever seen. I'm beyond grateful to have been able to see him and his worship team who are so talented they have not only been nominated for but have taken home a Grammy for their amazing songs! Steven Furtick is a gifted preacher, author, song writer, and visionary. Thank you for Elevation Nights! I have been so blessed by his and Holly's ministry in so many ways. Because of their Love Week initiatives, I have met wonderful people I would have never met and had experiences I would have never had if they had not created that vision and sent it across the globe into every city. Thank you, Holly, for your amazing book club and shining a light on so many amazing authors out there. Thank you both and your worship team for all Your songs, your sermons, you heart, and mostly your faithful obedience has changed my life and millions of others across this country and the world! America is lucky and blessed to have you both here. Thank you for your service to God and Country.

Levi and Jennie Lusko, with Fresh Life Church, in Montana, Thank you! This dynamic duo is unstoppable! I love them so much. Their gentle, funny, fun nature and their honesty, whether preaching, podcasting, or writing books, is humbling, and refreshing. Their message is, "Come home, you are welcome and wanted here!" If you feel like an outcast, like you don't fit in, or are unwanted elsewhere, this couple has boldly shouted, "WE WANT YOU!" They are "a church like that," and I cannot wait to serve with them.

I applaud your memorization of scripture and you have challenged me to step up my game and do the same. Thank you for the conferences you put on, the books you have written, and the time you have dedicated to building your church locally and globally.

Thank you for walking through the valley of the shadow of death, and sharing your grief over the loss of your little girl on your platform to be an example of how there is purpose in your pain, and God will use everything to bring Him glory and restore your soul. America is lucky and blessed to have you both. Thank you for your service to God and Country.

Rich and DawnCherè Wilkerson, of VOUS Church in Florida, Thank you! Thank you for your dedication to each other, your local church campuses, and the global church. Thank you for VousCon and your ability to rock a house!! Thank you for your "Single and Secure" series that reminded me of who I am and what defines me: God alone, and not a marital status. Thank you for your humor and your real and raw way of relating. Thank you for creating more and more spaces so that all are welcome. Thank you for raising up and giving as many talented speakers as possible a platform to speak about what the Lord is doing in their life. Shout out to Manouchka, I see you girl, you are rocking it! I am grateful for your gifts and the miracle that you are! Thank you Rich and DawnCherè for your generous nature and your unapologetic joy for what God is doing through your ministry. I cannot wait to come serve with you some day! America is lucky to have you both. Thank you for your service to God and Country.

Craig and Amy Groeschel, of Life Church in Oklahoma and around the country, as well as the inventor of the You Version Bible App, Thank You! This man has raised up more pastors and dedicated his life to taking the message of the Word of God to the farthest ends of the earth with the app he created.

He is one of the most disciplined and devoted mentors and pastors that I have ever seen, down to the number of blueberries he has for breakfast. The verse; " let everything you do be done for the glory of God", this man is passionate about living that conviction out. As well as leading a multisite megachurch, he is an author, a host of a leadership podcast, and mentor to many pastors around the country. He is above all else a devoted husband and father. He has helped shape the "Jesus Revolution" I believe we are once again experiencing in this country and around the world. Thank you for your unending devotion to live, love and serve the people God brings to you. You always handle with care, and it shows. I can't wait to serve you one day. America is lucky to have you both. Thank you for your service to God and Country.

Michael and Natalie Todd, of Transformation Church in Oklahoma, Thank you! I can't talk about this church and their pastors without mentioning how **H.O.T.** they are! **H**umble -**O**pen -**T**ransparent is how this church lives out life, and Micheal and Natalie, fearlessly blaze the trail!! If most churches just feel too "churchy" for you, try this one! This man is amazing! His way of keeping "Hood" and "Holy" in a beautiful balance is awe-inspiring. He welcomes both into his church, and he will pull no punches when telling you what the Lord is telling him to say. I have said over and over, "Yup, Yup, AMEN! He said that to me too!!" as Micheal has been preaching. I hear the Lord the same way Mike seems to, and I resonate with his messages and love his smile. Some people may think, "it doesn't take all that," but I would say YES IT DOES TAKE ALL THAT.

This man has been given an amazing gift for creating sermons, worship music, clothing, productions, and books that bring "All that" out in a bad ass way.

He will not shy away from controversy and understands that Haters are gonna Hate, so Hate on Haters because God is on his side and he will not be shaken or overtaken by the words of men when the Word of God marks this man's steps and has allowed him to introduce the world to what Crazy Faith can look like! This man loves the Word, loves his wife and kids, loves his church, and the global church! If you are looking for an over-the-top, in-your-face, fun, and faithful word from God, check out Transformation Church . If the thought of joining a church makes you jerk back from past pain, consider taking a look at joining the Transformation Nation, all are welcome! Preach on, Michael! America is lucky to have you! Thank you for your service to God and Country.

Bianca and Matt Olthoff, of The Father's House OC in Southern California, Thank you!! I love this couple and this church! Bianca has a gift for speaking and explaining the word of God through her eyes that is so honest, expressive, accurate, and refreshing. She takes "Gangsta and Grace" and wraps them up into a perfect package!

She was raised in the church and her love for God and others shows how deeply ingrained the Word, and her relationship with the Lord, is in her Life. Bianca is spicy and raw. She has no fear of her own emotions and will allow her tears to come forth and let people see her heart. She in no way claims to have it all together, nor does she expect that of anyone else. She sees herself as a servant whose job it is to help direct people to the only one who can truly help a lost and broken soul be renewed, refreshed and reborn, Jesus!

I am so thankful to her for her passion for the prison ministry, and began to cry with thanksgiving when I learned she is seen as the main pastor for all the Women's prisons in California because I have a dear friend who is so lost that she has now found herself in prison, and every time I saw Bianca,

I thought of Melody Grace, and hoped that she could somehow see Bianca from the prison. I still pray this prayer and am so grateful because I don't believe any other preacher but Bianca could tear down the walls that Melody has built around her to be willing to listen to someone who looks beautifully similar to her.

I pray Melody will find her way to The Father's House OC when her time is completed. I know I will definitely find my way there in the future and I look forward to serving the Lord with you when that day comes! Thank you Bianca and Matt for selling everything and believing in the vision that is changing lives and saving souls. You are amazing. America is lucky to have you! Thank you for your service to God and Country!

Jabin and Shanen Chavez, of City Light Church in Las Vegas, Thank you! This church is growing and moving with the Spirit of God! Jabin is a man of vision and the church is dedicated to bringing the Light of God to the City of Lights/Sin City itself! He, and his church, have taken on a huge charge in a town known more for its prostitution than its preaching. But God has raised up this man, Jabin, and he will not back down from the call.

I personally tithe to this church as well, because they are in need of a bigger building to be able to bring forth the vision God has shown to Jabin. I believe in you, and I am praying for you. I hope to be able to continue to help bring your dream of the building to fruition. Jabin is a very calm, stable, gentle, and dedicated soul, but he is a soldier in God's Army, battle ready! His passion for the Word of God comes forth in wildly wonderful ways!

He is funny and real; he is humble and devoted to refining himself constantly. His relationship with Jesus is refreshing and honest, faith-filled and fun. Jabin is one of those pastors that you feel really "gets you," with no shade, no flare, no showy examples, just an honest man with an honest word, a generous nature, and huge heart. I have repeatedly heard the exact same message from God that Jabin has then preached the following Sunday.

My mouth has dropped open so many times when he has shared what verse or book of the Bible the Lord has been directing him towards because it was the same verse or book that God had been speaking with me about that same week!

Thank you for the confirmation you have spoken over me without even knowing that it was for me. I will be honored to come visit your church one day and be a part of what God is doing out there in Vegas! America is lucky to have you! Thank you for your service to God and Country.

Stephanie Ike Okafor, of ONE/A Potter's House Church in southern California, Thank you! Stephanie is one of the most anointed prophetesses and vision seers of this modern day that I have ever heard. She is on staff under the incredibly talented lead pastors Torre and Sarah Jakes Roberts, and her beauty, grace, and voice come second only to her tangible light of love that radiates from this woman every time she speaks of her Jesus. Even if she did not use words, her presence carries power, peace, and love that is a prayer walking.

Stephanie has been given the gift of visions, prophesying, speaking in tongues, healing, preaching, teaching, miracles, joy, and faith. Her voice can calm a soul even if you do not speak the same language. Her insight into the spirit world is breathtaking and the clarity in which she can hear the voice of God is awe-inspiring.

I have heard many of the same messages spoken to me that Stephanie has preached, and I have looked up and thought, "Me too! I heard that too!"

Thank you, Stephanie, for the nights that I listened to your voice when I felt anxious or under attack. Thank you for confirming and reaffirming that I am not "going crazy," but that God always has been, and always will be, a God who SPEAKS to us if we allow ourselves to listen. You are a gift from God.

May your children be blessed, and may you continue to be used as a living answer to prayer. If someone is lost in L.A. and looking for a church that is on fire and also really attractive, check out ONE/A Potter's House Church, you will find the Glory of the Lord there and you might just find a beautiful spouse there as well! There must be something in the water in that place!

I look forward to serving alongside you and your church in the future. America is lucky to have you. Thank you for your service to the Lord and to this Country.

Lisa Harper, thank you! I love you and pray for you all the time! I cannot leave Lisa Harper out from this list even though she does not lead any specific church, she speaks at all of them! Okay, not ALL, but a lot of churches!

Lisa Harper is such a hoot, a holler, and a Hallelujah all wrapped into one!! She is a whirlwind of grace and grit. She is hilarious and doing her best to be Holy! Whether you read her books, see her in person, or watch her on YouTube, her way of explaining the Bible will have you laughing at loud.

She has taken her gift of humor and her dedication to the Holy One and transformed it into an amazing global ministry. She has no qualms about sharing how "jacked up" some parts of her life have been, but also how filled with grace her Jesus is.

Her relationship with Jesus demonstrates all the intricate and infinite ways He wants to be involved in every moment, even the most mundane or pain filled.

Lisa has a heart to teach, preach, love, and laugh. She wants healing and help to come to every broken and lost soul she speaks with. Even though she is highly educated and takes her dedication and study of the Word seriously, she does not speak in a way that elevates her over anyone else. Her straightforward, relaxed, hilarious southern charm comes through when she speaks and writes, and there is zero pretension or air of superiority that would make someone hesitate to come up and say "Hey"!

Single ladies out there, I hope you will look to Lisa Harper as a model of what being "married" to the call of Christ can look like and the adventure He will take you on when you trust him to lead you. You do not need any other man in your life to do what God is calling you to do right now. Lisa Harper demonstrates that we are enough and that we are all holy and whole when we have Jesus as the head of our home.

Thank you, Lisa, I adore you! I hope our paths cross one day, and I can serve alongside you in some capacity! America is lucky to have you! Thank you for your service to God and Country.

Alex and Henry Seeley, of The Belonging Co. in Nashville, Tennessee; Thank you for everything you do! This powerhouse couple left Australia on a word from God to come to America and start a church and launch a music business to lift the name of Jesus to the ends of the earth. They created The Belonging Co for artists and had services during the week so that all the musicians who had gigs on the weekend could still come and gather together to be a part of a community of prayer and worship.

Their church has exploded, and they are deeply connected to lifting Nashville and the nation to the next level of living, loving, giving, serving, singing, and praying as Jesus did.

They both take their cues directly from the Man upstairs and it shows in not just the success of their ministry but in their love and affection for each other and every soul that God places in their care. The Belonging Co gives a platform for singers to come together and blow the roof off the place in praise.

If anyone lives in or near Nashville and can get to this church, they would be honored to serve next to you in the trenches. They are not satisfied with a church that comes, listens, and leaves. This church is a church of action. There are no sidelines in the battle for souls, and Alex and Henry lead the charge as they run toward the lost and broken with, not just prayers, but with the practical tangible resources to help the needs of those they serve too! This church gives, and gives, and then gives some more. I will be honored to one day serve and give side by side with you! America is so lucky you came here to fulfill your divine charge to love and serve the Lord. Thank you for your service to God and to this Country.

Dr. Femi and Mary Popoola, of NTCM here in Texas, Thank you for anointing me with **J.O.Y.**!

You anoint my head with oil, My cup overflows with blessings Surely goodness and mercy will follow me all the days of my life and I will dwell in the house of the Lord forever.
(Psalm 23: 5-6, modified)

A double portion you poured over me that weekend and I am so grateful. It was an anointing of Joy and Healing. I hope I can pour those gifts out as abundantly as you poured them on me. Thank you for listening to my story, encouraging me, and comforting me as a friend! Thank you for opening your heart and your church to me, feeding me, and showering me with all the love and hugs I was able to accept. Thank you for your joy of worship, and your love of the Lord.

Thank you for reminding me that there is opportunity in my pain, and to look for that instead of focusing on the hurt. When I was broken, you hugged me and told me where to look. You helped me to adjust my eyes and remember He only made one who can walk through this life as my Lord and lead, and that is Christ alone.

Thank you for your smile and your laughter that can light up any room. Thank you for encouraging the values of family and community and for always walking the talk in every conversation you both have.

Thank you for investing in me as I struggled to support myself during the publishing of this book. When I reached out for help, you reached back and that meant the world to me. Thank you for your dedication to the Word, to your family, to your patients, to your church, and to new friends who appear out of nowhere! Thank you for leaving Africa to come to the United States and spread the Good News! America is lucky and blessed to have you both. Thank you for your service to God and to Country!

These are just some of preachers and teachers who have directly impacted my life. I hope each of you will find a perfect fit in one or all of them, whether it is in person or online.

The reason I have watched them so closely is because while this book is drawing to a close, the next one is about to begin. *Love Letters to America...A Journey of Faith...* will be the next book the Lord is calling me to write, and it will take me on a journey over the next five years to complete.

I don't understand how it will all come together, but God has spoken it over me and shown me the completed book already. It will involve at least 50 pastors in all 50 states, and I will be traveling and serving each of their churches as I write what the Lord wants to share with His Country, America The Beautiful. His Beloved. His light on a hill...

I know God will lead me to the right churches, the right leaders, and will fill me with the right words to write awe-inspiring and breathtaking love letters to each state I travel too. I thank you in advance to every artist, writer, pastor, teacher, mentor, and friend who God uses to speak to me as I embark on this journey alone with Goodness and Mercy in tow (My RV and Jeep)! I am humbled and honored to step into this vision that baffles me and takes my breath away at the same time. I know there is no way I can do it alone, but I also know I am never alone, because my Love, My Jesus, is taking the wheel on this one and I am simply following His lead.

To all the singers who came through the air waves and kept me going, I pray over you! Especially **Lauren Daigle**, whose song *Rescue* was the first time I saw the vision of what God had in mind for me, and I wept in wonder at how amazing and beautiful being a part of the vision for the "Prodigal Won Tour" will be. I have belted out with arms open wide and tears streaming down my face so many of your songs! Thank you Lauren for being brave enough to step out and be determined to singlehandedly battle for the souls of the "lonely" and to run to the prodigals of the world and say, "I love you, and if you need a friend in this moment, you've got one!"

Shout out to **Cody Carnes** and specifically your song *Nothing Else.* Jesus used this song to reveal himself in the most beautiful, intimate way when He asked me to dance as I wrote about in the chapter **F.O.R.K.** It! Your song has become "our song," and I am able to slow dance with my Lead of Love any time I turn it on. It has created one of my most beautiful and favorite moments that I get to share with Jesus. One where His presence is so intimately close that I can breathe Him in and melt into His shoulder as we slow dance. Thank you for the gift of your song that changed my life, my heart, and my faith forever.

Eminem, thank you!! I know, I know... I can't mean **Marshall Mathers**, not that Eminem, but yes, THAT Eminem, and especially his songs: *Lose Yourself, Not Afraid,* and *Airplanes* with B.O.B.... Thank you for your fighting energy, your strength and power to believe in oneself and to never give up on any dream that is placed in one's heart. You reminded me to fight for it with my last breath.

To leave nothing on the table, to put blood, sweat, and tears into the vision that God put on my heart. Thank you for letting me have a safe outlet for my frustration and words that I could use to express what I was fighting for. I don't know if you know Jesus, but Man, I would love to see what He and you could do together if you ever reached out and asked God to take your miraculous talent, as possibly the greatest word wizard of all time, and work with God Almighty who created your ability to do it! I know you love a great collaboration, and I couldn't think of a better one than Marshall Mathers and the Messiah! Eminem and El Shaddai... Just think about it!

CeCe Winans! Thank you for the "fire" and the "joy" you sang over my life. Your songs have lifted me up and literally had me jumping for joy! Thank God no one lives below me, and I am free to jump as high, as long, and as loud, as I want! I have seen you in concert and it was such a wonderful and grace-filled experience. You are a masterpiece and a vision of grace. Thank you for sharing your voice with the world to remind us of who we are, who God is, what He wants for us. Reminding us, His power still moves! You have helped me to "believe for it" even when I thought there was no way. I honor you and bless you that you will continue to sing all the days of your life! Thank you for your service to God and Country.

Camila Cabello, Thank you! I have no clue if you know Jesus, and I am almost positive the song, *Never Be the Same*, was not created as a worship song, but let me just thank you, because it took my worship to an entirely new level when I sang your song to Jesus. The only one who I am completely and utterly addicted to and have never been the same since the day His blood ran through my veins!

This song, when sang in worship, brought an intimacy with Jesus I had not previously thought was even appropriate. It allowed me to bring my sexuality and sensuality to Him as a sacrifice of praise and worship.

Letting Him touch me in every way, be that lover to me, and in turn changed everything about our relationship and deepened it to one of a true Bridegroom and Bride. Dancing with the Lord to this song is one of my favorite ways to express my physical love and ache for Him and Him alone.

Thank you for this beautiful song and how amazing it is that God can take something not intended for Him and make it all about Him!

I hope you do know Jesus and can feel His deep devotion for you, and you to Him, through the words you wrote years ago, because I promise, YOU too, will Never Be The Same!

Micheal W. Smith, Thank you! The Lord has been speaking to me through you for decades, ever since *Secret Ambition, Friends*, and *Pray for Me* were blasting on the radio. Even when I wandered away, your songs would still find me and bring me to my knees. Recently, the song that changed my life again was *Surrounded.* I have heard this song many times, but in writing this last chapter of Final Thoughts, I was given another vision through your song, and it blew my mind and heart away!

Early one morning on the third day of my prayer fast, as I was preparing myself to write this chapter, I was in my office having my prayer and worship time and I was led back to your song, *Surrounded*, which I have listened to hundreds of times. I was standing and swaying, singing with my eyes closed, in what felt like a holy haze, where the veil between this world and the next is lifted. I felt my head turn to the left and then to the right. I was no longer standing in my office alone, but I could see Angel Armies standing with me. Their wings up, in full armor, massive, and ready for battle. I thought to myself, "Oh my God, we are going to fight in the Spirit," but as the song continued to play and sing over and over, "this is how I fight my battles," they all knelt down together on one knee and put their arms around each other's shoulders and over mine as I was pulled into the kneeling position as well. Their wings stretched out to cover each other and as the Angels on each side of me laid their arms on my shoulders it gave me the appearance and feeling like I had wings now too.

I was pulled way up into space and had a view of the earth and could see thousands of angels that made a complete circle around the earth... all singing "this is how I fight my battles" and praying over the entire planet.

I was blown away. I realized I was allowed to lead the prayer and they would be in accordance, so I just started praying out loud over the entire earth. I could see the light shining out from me and from all of the Angels and I saw that they are at all times surrounding us while praying.

They let me fly with them with locked arms. I had wings because of their arms around me and we completely circled the earth, praying and singing and fighting for every lost soul out there. The invitation went out to everyone everywhere: COME FLY WITH US AND FIGHT WITH US FOR THIS WORLD!

I have played it and prayed with it every morning since then, because honestly, it's one of the most powerful visions I have ever experienced, and I understand now the power we all hold when we have legions of battle-ready Angels waiting for us to rise up and ask them to fight and pray with us!

I realized my prayers were not big enough. I needed to make my prayers global as well as local. So, I have. I have prayed over every single one of YOU. I have prayed for every person who loves to hear from God. Every person who WANTS to hear from God and every person who NEEDS to hear from God!

Every hurting person, every child lost in the world who is abused and tortured, every prisoner who has no one, every parent at the end of their rope, every servant of God who feels like they are only a thimble in the ocean of despair that they are trying to heal.

I have prayed for every hardened heart, every tortured soul, every new baby on the way, every dying person who wonders if there is more to come. I have prayed for every pastor I have yet to meet, every song writer out there who is using their song to change the word.

I have prayed for the teenagers who think suicide would be better than having to live another day in this disturbed, cruel, broken and beaten down world.

I have prayed for those who hurt me so deeply that my wounds might be something I have to bring to Jesus daily as I go through the process of mending. I have prayed for countries I have never stepped foot in and probably never will. I have sent light into every dark place with ten thousand Angels sending their light with me. I have prayed over the outcast, the ostracized, and misunderstood who feel that they don't have a prayer. I send my love to you. You are loved, seen, appreciated, and valued!

There is not a living soul on this planet that can say that they have never had anyone care enough to pray for them. I DID, I DO, and I WILL.

I will continue to cover YOU in prayer and invite YOU to step up and ask for your Angel Armies to wrap their wings around you and empower you with the ability to do the same.

Let us take back this planet, and bring every soul Home again, welcomed, healed, and made holy and whole in the loving arms of Jesus the Christ. He's the only one who can save us now. The time has come to **R.I.S.E.** up, put on the full armor of God, and fight the battles knowing that God is on our side.

RUB SOME D.I.R.T. ON IT.....

As Michael sang out.... "It may look like I'm
surrounded but I'm surround by You!"

*Don't be Afraid for there are more on our side than on
theirs! Oh Lord, open their eyes and let them see!
(2 Kings 6:16, NLT modified)*

*For He is the living God, and he will endure forever. His
kingdom will never be destroyed, and his rule* will never
end. He rescues and saves his people; he performs
miraculous signs and wonders
in the heavens and on earth
(Daniel 6:26-27, NLT)

My final thoughts are this:

Embrace my prayers of Peace over YOU.
Pursue purpose prayerfully, patiently, and
passionately. Love the process, it IS the purpose. Pray
with your 10,000 angels! Keep an enduring and
encouraging heart and mind as you
venture out into this broken world.

Remain "Battle Ready" with eyes fixed and focused
on Jesus and the mission at hand. This is a battle for
souls. This is a battle for life over death.

Sing Loudly, Dance Wildly, Pray Fervently and
without Ceasing. Live a life with Jesus leading the way.

Weep with those who weep and rejoice with those
who rejoice.
Never forsake the gathering of saints.

Refuse to surrender your peace and joy that are
your royal inheritance.

Find a sacred place to slow dance with the Divine. Show the comfort and grace that God has shown to you.

So, reach out and welcome one another to God's glory.
Jesus did it; now you do it!
(Romans 15:7, MSG)

We are all a "Healing In Progress," so handle with care, and feed the deepest needs of your soul. As Eminem once sang, "If you had one shot, or one opportunity, to seize everything you ever wanted, in one moment, would you capture it, or let it slip"?

Here is that moment, that shot, that opportunity. God is inviting you on a **D.A.T.E.**, a **D**ivine **A**ppointment **T**o **E**ngage with Him. I pray you will have the courage to say, "YES", lose yourself, and watch how your life will be forever changed. He loves you; He has always loved you, and He will always love you! Praise God!

I look forward to loving and serving with each and every one of you that will meet me out on the road. Thank you for your prayers of protection as I prepare myself for this Journey of Faith and the writing of *Love Letters to America*. With that, I pray this prayer over you

The LORD bless you and keep you;
the LORD make His face shine on you
and be gracious to you;
the LORD turn His face toward you
and give you peace
(Num 6:24-26 NIV)

Your Friend,

Jen